LE JOURNAL DE JACK L'ÉVENTREUR

Publié pour la première fois en Angleterre en 1993
par SMITH GRYPHON LIMITED
Swallow House - 11/21 Northdown Street
LONDRES N1 9BN

LE JOURNAL DE JACK L'ÉVENTREUR

suivi du Dossier
de
Shirley HARRISON

Traduit de l'anglais par Jérôme Jacobs

JCLattès

INTRODUCTION

De l'éditeur anglais

En juin 1992, une agence littéraire établie de longue date et jouissant d'une réputation sans faille, Rupert Crew Ltd, nous a invités, moi-même et d'autres éditeurs, à examiner un journal manuscrit. Il était signé Jack l'Éventreur et paraissait être l'œuvre d'un marchand de coton de Liverpool, James Maybrick. J'étais intrigué, mais le souvenir des « Carnets d'Hitler », ce canular perpétré neuf ans plus tôt, m'invitait à observer la plus extrême prudence. Rupert Murdoch avait été jusqu'à offrir 3 750 000 dollars à *Stern* pour les droits de publication en langue anglaise dans le monde entier. Son journal londonien, *The Sunday Times*, avait ensuite fait paraître à deux reprises des extraits de ces carnets avant de découvrir que « Hitler » les avait rédigés sur du papier contenant un agent blanchissant jamais utilisé avant 1955. (Rappelons qu'en 1968, *The Sunday Times* avait offert 250 000 livres pour le journal de Benito Mussolini, déjà un faux.)

J'ai essayé de ne pas répéter les erreurs commises par *Stern* et par *The Sunday Times.* Je ne voulais pas que des considérations financières entachent mon jugement et je me suis donc gardé de faire monter les enchères au-delà du réaliste, comme *Stern* l'avait fait aux dépens de Rupert Murdoch à Londres et de *Newsweek* à New York.

Smith Gryphon Ltd est une petite maison d'édition

récente. Nous étions en concurrence avec d'autres éditeurs, mais nous avons réussi à acquérir les droits au prix d'une avance raisonnable. Ainsi, si durant nos recherches ultérieures, nous avions découvert que le journal était un faux, nous aurions été en mesure de nous retirer sans pour autant essuyer de perte significative. A ce jour, nous-mêmes, les maisons d'éditions étrangères et les diverses publications qui s'apprêtent à faire paraître le journal en feuilleton n'avons pas versé de sommes excessives.

Une fois le manuscrit acquis, j'ai commencé par rechercher les signes d'une supercherie. Par exemple, existait-il, comme dans le cas des Carnets d'Hitler et du journal de Mussolini, un intermédiaire entre l'éditeur et le fournisseur, qui aurait été chargé des transactions financières ? Mais il s'est avéré que le propriétaire du journal de Jack l'Éventreur était un certain Michael Barrett, ouvrier de Liverpool. Ce dernier mène une vie modeste, avec pour tous revenus sa pension d'invalidité et le salaire de sa femme, secrétaire. Le journal ne lui a, jusqu'à présent, rapporté qu'une somme minime. Certes, il réalisera un profit beaucoup plus substantiel si le présent ouvrage a du succès; mais Barrett est un fervent catholique, et ce qui compte le plus pour lui, outre sa famille, c'est son rôle de porte-étendard dans la section locale de la *British Legion*, qui réunit les anciens de l'armée. Il n'a rien d'un intermédiaire, et il ne sert pas de paravent à quelque mystérieux conspirateur. Lorsqu'il a entrepris de vendre le journal, c'est lui qui a pris toutes ses décisions, sans en référer à personne.

Quant à l'auteur du commentaire, Shirley Harrison, elle a été contactée par l'agence littéraire Rupert Crew Ltd. Ni Barrett ni moi-même ne l'avions rencontrée auparavant, mais elle compte plusieurs publications à son actif.

La provenance du journal était, et demeure, une énigme. Michael Barrett nous a confié qu'un de ses amis,

Tony Devereux, le lui avait remis en mai 1991. Mais Devereux est mort quelques mois plus tard, sans avoir révélé comment le Journal était tombé entre ses mains, et ce malgré les questions persistantes de Michael Barrett. J'ai appris pour ma part que des travaux d'électricité avaient été effectués à diverses reprises, entre décembre 1989 et mars 1992, dans la maison de Liverpool où James Maybrick avait vécu et où il était mort. Pour la première fois depuis 1888, des lattes du plancher ont été soulevées, et il est tentant d'imaginer que l'un des électriciens aurait alors découvert le journal. Mais aucun des ouvriers qui ont travaillé à Battlecrease House n'a donné foi à cette hypothèse. La vérité, c'est que nous ne savons toujours pas d'où provient le journal.

Durant les recherches que j'ai entreprises en vue d'en établir l'authenticité, j'ai pris conscience de l'éventail et du niveau des compétences qu'un faussaire aurait dû maîtriser pour fabriquer un document si complexe. Il lui aurait fallu parvenir à une compréhension détaillée des motivations et du comportement imprévisible des auteurs de crimes en série, de façon à n'éveiller aucun soupçon chez les experts. L'un d'entre eux, le Dr David Forshaw, de l'hôpital psychiatrique Mauldsley de Londres, a examiné le journal. Or, ce spécialiste de psychopathologie a estimé en conclusion de son rapport qu'il était tout à fait possible que le journal ait été rédigé par un auteur de crimes en série.

Notre « faussaire » aurait également dû acquérir une connaissance précise des effets physiques et psychologiques de l'arsenic et de la strychnine, dont l'abus était courant à l'époque victorienne, mais que seuls des spécialistes tels que le Dr Forshaw sont aujourd'hui en mesure de décrire avec la précision requise.

Il lui aurait fallu tout savoir de la composition de l'encre et du papier. Sinon, comment aurait-il pu être sûr qu'aucun ingrédient postérieur à 1888 ne s'y était glissé?

Pour analyser l'encre, le Dr Nicholas Eastaugh, dont la spécialité consiste à établir l'authenticité de tableaux et de documents rédigés à l'encre, a utilisé un microscope électronique et une microsonde à protons. Notre faussaire aurait-il pu avoir accès à cet équipement ultramoderne ? Bien sûr, nous nous sommes également demandé s'il lui aurait été possible de se procurer une bouteille d'encre datant de l'époque victorienne. Mais quand bien même il aurait été en mesure de confirmer qu'elle était âgée de plus de cent ans, l'encre se serait évaporée depuis longtemps. Par contre, il ne lui aurait pas été difficile de dénicher un album victorien partiellement utilisé.

Notre homme serait également un spécialiste de l'histoire du crime, et il aurait consulté des documents inaccessibles aujourd'hui pour parfaire ses connaissances au sujet de deux affaires qui ont défrayé la chronique à l'époque victorienne : les meurtres commis par Jack l'Éventreur à Whitechapel et l'empoisonnement de James Maybrick par son épouse. En décrétant alors que l'Éventreur et James Maybrick ne faisaient qu'un, le faussaire aurait couru le risque de voir les faits ou les dates le contredire. La probabilité de découvrir une incompatibilité entre les mouvements de l'Éventreur et ceux de Maybrick aurait été d'autant plus grande que ce dernier résidait à Liverpool, c'est-à-dire à quelque quatre cents kilomètres de Londres. Mais rien n'est apparu qui mette sérieusement en doute l'identification de Maybrick avec l'Éventreur. De fait, lorsque Shirley Harrison et son équipe ont retracé les activités de Maybrick avant et pendant 1888 et 1889, il s'est avéré que ce dernier disposait d'un mobile (sa femme était infidèle), d'un alibi (ses visites à Londres pour affaires ou chez son frère), et qu'il avait eu l'opportunité d'agir sans éveiller les soupçons de ses collègues (tous les meurtres ont été commis durant le weekend). En outre, dans sa jeunesse, Maybrick avait vécu à Whitechapel en compagnie de sa maîtresse, Sarah Robertson. Ce territoire lui était donc familier.

A cause du secret qui entourait les Carnets d'Hitler, ces derniers n'avaient été lus par aucun historien ni par aucun expert jusqu'au jour où ils ont été soumis à Hugh Trevor-Roger afin qu'il produise une authentification éclair pour *The Sunday Times*. Pour notre part, nous avons commencé par demander à trois spécialistes de Jack l'Éventreur, Martin Fido, Paul Begg et Keith Skinner, de lire le journal et de nous faire parvenir leurs commentaires. Ensuite, d'autres experts ont été invités à l'examiner, au nombre desquels Martin Howells, Melvin Fairclough, Colin Wilson, Donald Rumbelow et Bill Waddell, l'ancien conservateur du *Black Museum* à New Scotland Yard. Tous, à l'exeption de Donald Rumbelow et de Bill Waddell, ont avancé le nom de « leur » suspect dans des publications diverses : nous nous attendions donc qu'ils considèrent le Journal d'un œil très critique. Mais tous, qu'ils soient ou non convaincus, se sont déclarés fascinés. Les doutes exprimés par certains d'entre eux reposaient sur une opinion personnelle, non sur des faits historiques. L'un estimait improbable que l'Éventreur ait trouvé refuge dans Middlesex Street, un autre s'inquiétait d'apparents anachronismes dans le vocabulaire employé par l'auteur du Journal, un troisième doutait que l'Éventreur ait pu manger un utérus. En lisant ce livre, vous découvrirez qu'aucune de ces objections ne résiste à l'épreuve des faits.

De même, lorsque nous avons comparé l'écriture du Journal et celle du testament attribué à James Maybrick – dont la première page est reproduite dans le cahier hors-texte – nous avons d'abord réagi avec suspicion : en effet, elles étaient différentes. Pourtant ce testament conservé dans Somerset House, à Londres, est accessible à tout le monde, y compris donc à un faussaire potentiel. Et comme il n'existe aucun autre échantillon connu de l'écriture de James Maybrick, à l'exception de sa signature sur son certificat de mariage, on aurait pu s'attendre qu'un faussaire digne de ce nom s'efforce de l'imiter. Mais si, comme le suggère le présent ouvrage, le testament en question est un faux, il est normal que l'écriture du Journal, c'est-à-dire l'écriture authentique de Maybrick, soit différente.

Nous ne sommes pas les premiers à contester la légalité de ce testament. L'avocat Alexander MacDougall a émis cette hypothèse dès 1891, dans l'ouvrage qu'il a consacré au procès de Florence Maybrick. Elle reposait sur deux interrogations. Comment un homme réputé pour l'affection qu'il portait à ses deux enfants aurait-il pu mal orthographier le prénom de sa fille (Eveleyn au lieu d'Evelyn) ? Et surtout, comment aurait-il pu déshériter sa femme et ses deux enfants, pour léguer de fait la totalité de ses biens à ses frères ? Les pressions exercées par ces derniers sur James Maybrick durant ses derniers jours, ainsi que leur rôle probable dans la fabrication du testament en question, sont décrits en détail dans le commentaire de Shirley Harrison.

La question de l'écriture s'est également posée lorsque nous avons comparé le journal et une lettre signée Jack l'Éventreur, adressée au « Cher Patron » le 25 septembre 1888. Il ne fait aucun doute qu'à l'époque la police a pensé que cette lettre provenait du meurtrier, à telle enseigne qu'elle en a placardé une reproduction dans toute l'Angleterre.

La lettre en question offre quelques similitudes linguistiques avec le journal, comme l'utilisation des expressions « substance rouge » (pour le sang), « drôles de petits jeux » et le « ha ha » provocateur. L'écriture en est moulée, et, de l'avis des graphologues consultés, ne correspond pas à celle du journal. Mais on imagine sans peine que le meurtrier ait fait tout son possible pour déguiser son écriture dans une lettre destinée à la police ou à la publication. Il se peut même que Maybrick ait demandé à un ami digne de confiance de la rédiger pour lui. On pense à George Davidson, dont le nom revient à plusieurs reprises dans le journal : il devait mourir trois ans après le décès de Maybrick, dans des circonstances qui laissent envisager un suicide. Son sentiment de culpabilité était-il devenu insupportable ?

Voilà pour les doutes. Venons-en maintenant aux nombreuses indications qui, de l'avis des mêmes experts, prouvent l'authenticité du journal. Le texte de Shirley Harrison les examine toutes dans le détail. Qu'il me suffise donc d'en citer trois parmi les plus convaincantes.

Jusqu'en 1987, date à laquelle les conclusions de l'enquête sur le meurtre de Mary Jane Kelly ont été publiées, personne ne savait que l'Éventreur avait ôté le cœur de sa victime, car cette information n'avait pas été divulguée à l'époque. Mais lorsque l'auteur du Journal mentionne ce crime, il fait le commentaire suivant : « pas de cœur, pas de cœur ».

Le journal fait également plusieurs fois référence à une boîte d'allumettes en fer-blanc vide, retrouvée par la police à l'endroit où Catharine Eddowes avait été assassinée. Or, la présence de cet objet sur le lieu du crime n'a été mentionnée que sur la liste officielle établie par la police, liste restée secrète jusqu'en 1984. Aucun journal de l'époque n'avait mentionné cette boîte, ni aucune publication antérieure à 1987.

Certes, on peut imaginer que notre faussaire imaginaire ait pu vivre à l'époque victorienne. Mais il faut savoir que jusque dans les années 1950 les spécialistes étaient unanimes à attribuer deux autres meurtres à l'Éventreur : celui d'Emma Smith et celui de Martha Tabram. Nous savons aujourd'hui qu'il s'agit là d'une erreur, mais un faussaire de l'époque les aurait sans aucun doute inclus dans le Journal. Rappelons qu'il n'aurait pas su non plus que le cœur de Mary Jane Kelly avait disparu, ni qu'une boîte d'allumettes en fer-blanc avait été retrouvée dans la poche de Catharine Eddowes.

Le parcours de Jack l'Éventreur s'inscrit parfaitement dans la vie de James Maybrick, au sujet de laquelle on dispose d'une multitude d'informations. En outre, en trois occasions, on a retrouvé un « M », l'initiale de Maybrick, sur le lieu des crimes commis par l'Éventreur. Or, deux d'entre eux n'avaient jamais été remarqués, bein qu'ils soient visibles sur une photoghraphie et sur un dessin en possession de la Metropolitan Police. Cette information est publiée pour la première fois dans le présent ouvrage.

En guise de conclusion, j'aimerais mentionner un autre détail, tout aussi fascinant. Le 10 octobre 1888, c'est-à-dire dix jours après les meurtres d'Elizabeth Stride et de Catharine Eddowes à Whitechapel, un article paru dans le *Daily Post* a rapporté qu'un homme originaire de Liverpool avait été interrogé par le *Criminal Investigation Department* dans le cadre de l'enquête sur les meurtres de l'Éventreur. Or, d'après l'article, l'homme en question fréquentait les bas quartiers de l'East End de Londres, et il avait de surcroît oublié un sac de cuir noir dans un hôtel de première catégorie du West End, le Charing Cross. La police avait pris possession du sac et avait trouvé à l'intérieur « certains documents, articles d'habillement, carnets de chèques, gravures à caractère obscène, lettres, etc. ».

Le 14 juin 1888, le Charing Cross Hotel avait passé une annonce dans *The Times* pour retrouver les propriétaires des multiples objets oubliés dans ses murs l'année précédente par des clients distraits. Or, l'un des noms figurant sur cette liste n'était autre que Mibrac. Maybrick aurait-il signé le registre de l'hôtel sous ce nom à peine maquillé ? La coïncidence est frappante, d'autant plus que le *Daily Post* du 10 octobre suggérait en outre que le propriétaire du sac s'était souvent rendu en Amérique, tout comme James Maybrick.

Si Mibrac était bel et bien Maybrick, il avait donc été soupçonné par la police. Mais les documents qui auraient prouvé sa culpabilité ont disparu, comme tant d'autres dans cette affaire.

Nous publions aujourd'hui son Journal pour que chacun puisse se forger une opinion et déterminer si oui ou non, la plus grande énigme criminelle de tous les temps est maintenant résolue.

LE JOURNAL

what they have in store for them they would stop this instant. But do I desire that? my answer is no. They will suffer just as I. I will see to that. Received a letter from Michael perhaps I will visit him. Will have to come to some sort of decision regarding the decision. I long for peace of mind but I sincerely believe that that will not come until I have sought my revenge on the whore and the whore master.

Foolish bitch, I know for certain she has arranged a rendezvous with him in Whitechapel. So be it, my mind is firmly made. I took refreshment at the Poste House it was there I finally decided London it shall be. And why not, is it not an ideal location? Indeed do I not frequently visit the Capitol and indeed do I not have legitimate reason for doing so. All who sell their dirty wares shall pay, of that I have no doubt. But shall I pay? I think not I am too clever for that

As usual my hands are cold, my heart I do believe is colder still. My dearest Gladys is unwell yet again, she worries me so. I am convinced a dark shadow lays over the house, it is evil. I am becoming increasingly weary of people who constantly enquire regards the state of my health. True my head and arms pain me at times but I am not duly worried, although I am quite certain Hopper believes to the contrary. I have him down as a bumbling buffoon. Thomas has requested that we meet as soon as possible. Business is flourishing so I have no inclination to neglect the matter he describes as most urgent. Nevertheless I shall endeavour to meet his request.

Time is passing much too slowly, I still have to work up the courage to begin my campaign. I have thought long and hard over the matter and still I cannot come to a decision to when I should begin. Opportunity is there, of that fact I am certain. The bitch has no inclination.

The thought of her taking her is beginning to thrill me, perhaps I will allow her to continue, some of my thoughts are indeed beginning to give me pleasure. Yes I will visit Michael for a few weeks, and allow her to take all she can from the whoring master. Tonight I shall see sissie. I may return to Battlecrease and take the unfaithfull bitch. Two in a night, indeed pleasure. My medicine is doing me good, in fact I am sure I can take more than any other person alive. My mind is clear I will put where through pen tonight.

---

am begining to believe it is unwise to continue writing, If I am to
... a whore then nothing shall lead the police back to me,
nd yet there are times when I feel an overwhelming compulsion
place my thoughts to paper. It is dangerous, that I
now. If Smith should find this then I am done
fore my campaign begins. However, the pleasure of writing
f all that lays ahead of me, and indeed the pleasure of
oughts.. of deeds that lay ahead of me, thrills me so. And
h what deeds I shall commit. For how could one suspect
t I could be capable of such things, for am I not,
s all believe, a mild man, who it has been said would
ever hurt a fly. Indeed only the other day did
ot Edwin say of me, I was the most gentlest of men he had
ncountered. A compliment from my dear brother which
I find exceedingly flattering.

Have decided my patience is wearing thin. The bitch has made a fool of me. Tomorrow I travel to Manchester. Will take some of my medicine and think hard on the matter. I believe I could do so, though I shake with fear of capture. A fear I will have to overcome. I believe I have the strength. I will force myself not to think of the children. The whore, that is all that shall be on my mind. My head aches.

My dear God my mind is in a fog. The whore is now with her maker and he is welcome to her. There was no pleasure as I squeezed. I felt nothing. Do not know if I have the courage to go back to my original idea. Manchester was cold and damp very much like this hell hole. Next time I will throw acid over ~~them~~, the thought of them riddled and screaming while the acid burns ... deep thrills me, ha, what a joke it would be if I could gorge an eye out and leave it by the whores body for all to see, to see, <u>ha, ha</u>.

I believe I have caught a chill I cannot stop shaking, my body aches. There are times when I pray to God that the pain and ~~torment~~ will stop. Summer is near the warm weather will do me good. I long for peace but my work is only beginning. I will have a long wait for peace. All whores must suffer first and my God how I will make ~~them~~ suffer as she has made me. Edwin asked [illegible] Thomas and business, I informed him that Thomas was well and business was flourishing, bother time. I have it in my mind that I should write to Michael, perhaps not, my hands are far too cold, another day. I will take the bitch tonight. I need to take my mind off the nights events. The children are well.

Strolled by the drive, encountered Mrs Hammersmith; she enquired of Bobo and Gladys. and much to my astonishment about my health. What has that whore said ? Mrs Hammersmith is a bitch The fresh air and stroll did me good. For a while I succeeded in forgetting the bitch and her whoring master. Felt completely refreshed when I returned to my office. I will visit Michael this coming June.

June is such a pleasant month, the flowers are in full bl the air is sweeter and life is almost certainly much easier I look forward to its coming with pleasure. A great deal of pleasure. I feel compelled to write to Michael if not obliged. My mind is clear, my hands are not cold.

I am vexed. I am trying to quell my anger. The whore has suggested she accompany me on my ~~trip~~ to Michael. I need time to put my mind in order. Under no circumstances can I let the bitch accompany me, all my hard work and plans will be destroyed if she were to do so. The pain was bad today. I believe the bitch has found one of my bottles, it had been moved. I am tired and need sleep the pain kept me awake for most of last night. Will return early avoid the bitch al~~together~~.

Frequented my club. George stated that he had never seen me in better health. I believe the bitch has changed her mind. My thoughts are becoming increasingly more daring. I have imagined doing all manner of things. Could I eat part of one? Perhaps it would taste of fresh fried bacon. ha ha My dear God it thrills me so.

Michael is expecting me ~~towards~~ the end of June, hence~~forth~~ from July my campaign will gather momentum. I will take each and everyone before I return ~~them~~ to their maker, damaged of course, severely damaged

I try to repel all thoughts of the children from my mind. I feel strong, stronger than I have ever felt. My thoughts keep returning to Manchester, next time it will thrill me. I know in my heart it will. I cannot understand why William will not accept my offer to dine. He is not unlike me, he hates the bitch. I believe if chance prevails I will burn St. James's to the ground. Tomorrow I will make a substantial wager. I feel lucky.

If I could have killed the bastard Lowry with my bare hands there and then I would have done so. How dare he question me on any matter, it is I that should question him. Damn him damn him damn him should I replace the missing items? No that would be too much of a risk. Should I destroy this? My God I will kill him. Give him no reason and order him politely to drop the matter, that I believe is the only course of action I can take. I will force myself to think of something more pleasant. The whore will suffer more than she has ever done so tonight, that thought revitalises me. June is drawing to a close I shake with anticipation.

I have taken too much my thoughts are not what they should be. I recall little of the events of yesterday. Thank God I stopped myself in time. I will show my wrath towards the bastard in such a manner that he will wish he had never brought up the subject. No one, not even God himself will deny the pleasure of writing my thoughts. I will take the first whore I encounter and show her what hell is really like. I think I will ram a cane into the whoring bitches wound and leave it there for them to see how much she could take. My head aches, God has no right to do this to me the devil take him.

How I succeeded in controlling myself I do not know. I have not allowed for the red stuff, gallons of it in my estimation. Some of it is bound to spill onto me. I cannot allow my clothes to be blood drenched, this I could not explain to anyone least of all Michael. Why did I not think of this before? I curse myself. The struggle to stop myself was overwhelming, and if I had not asked Michael to lock me in my bedroom for fear of sleepwalking, to which I had said I had been prone to do recently, was that not clever? I would have done my dirty deeds that very night.

I have taken a small room in Middlesex Street that in itself is a joke. I have paid well and I believe no questions will be asked. It is indeed an ideal location. I have walked the streets and have become more than familiar with them. I said Whitechapel it will be and Whitechapel it shall. The bitch and her whoring master will rue the day I first saw them together. I said I am clever, very clever. Whitechapel Liverpool, Whitechapel London, ha ha. No one could possibly place it together. And indeed for there is no reason for anyone to do so.

The next time I travel to London I shall begin. I have no doubts, my confidence is most high. I am thrilled writing this, life is sweet, and my disappointment has vanished. Next time for sure. I have no doubts, not any longer, no doubts. No one will ever suspect. Tomorrow

I will purchase the finest knife money can buy, nothing shall be too good for my whores, I will treat them to the finest, the very finest, they deserve that at least from I.

I have shown all that I mean business, the pleasure was better than I imagined. The whore was only too willing do her business. I recall all and it thrills me. There s no scream when I cut. I was more than vexed when e head would not come off. I believe I will need e strength next time. I struck deep into her. et I never had the cane, it would have been a light to have rammed it hard into her. The bitch ened like a ripe peach. I have decided next time I will rip all out. My medicine will give me trength and the thought of the whore and her honey matter will spur me on no end

ie wait to hear about my triumph seemed long, though it was not. I am not disappointed, they ave all written well. The next time they will have a great deal more to write, of that fact I have no doubt ha ha. I will remain calm and show no interest in my deed, if anyone should mention it so, but I will laugh inside, oh! how I will laugh.

I will not allow too much time to pass before my next. Indeed I need to repeat my pleasure as soon as possible. The whoring Master can have her with pleasure and I shall have my pleasure with my thoughts and deeds. I will be clever. I will not call on Michael on my next visit. My brothers would be horrified if they knew, particularly Edwin after all did he not say I was one of the most gentlest of men he had ever encountered. I hope he is enjoying the fruits of America. Unlike I. For do I not have a sour fruit.

I could not resist mentioning my deed to George. I was
clever and brought up the subject by way of how
fortunate we were not having murders of that kind in this
city. He agreed with me completely. Indeed he went on
to say, that he believed we had the finest police
force in the world, and although we have our fair share
of troubles the women folk can walk the streets in
safety. And indeed they can for I will not play
my funny little games on my own doorstep <u>ha ha</u>.

The gentle man with gentle thoughts will strike again soon
have never felt better, in fact, I am taking more than
ver and I can feel the strength building up within
e. The head will come off next time, also the whores
ands. Shall I leave them in various places around
hitechapel? Hunt the head and hands instead of
e thimble <u>ha ha</u>. Maybe I will take some part
way with me to see if it does taste of like
esh fried bacon. The whore seen her master
oday it did not bother me. I imagined I was with
hem, the very thought thrills me. I wonder if
he whore has ever had such thoughts? I believe
he has, has she not cried out when I demand
he takes another. The bitch. She will suffer but
ot as yet. Tomorrow I travel to London. I have
ecided I cannot wait any longer. I look forward

to tomorrow nights work. it will do me good,
a great deal of good.

One dirty whore was looking for some gin.
Another dirty whore was looking for the same

Am I not clever? I thought of my funny little rhyme on my travel to the City of Whores. I was vexed with myself when I realised I had forgotten the chalk. So vexed infact, that I returned to the bitch and cut out more. I took some of it away with me. It is in front of me. I intend to fry it and eat it later ha ha. The very thought works up my appetite I cannot stop the thrill of writing. I ripped open my God I will have to stop writing of the children they distract me so I ripped open

it has taken me three days to recover, I will not feel guilty. it is the whoring bitch to blame not I.
I ate all off it, it did not taste like fresh fried bacon but I enjoyed it never the less. She was so sweet and pleasurable. I have left the stupid fools a clue which I am sure they will not solve. Once again I have been clever, very clever

~~A ray or two will leave~~ this clue

~~One pill thats true~~

M ~~will catch Sir Jim with~~ no pills
~~each two~~

two partners,
two pills
the whores M
rings?

Thirty

It shall come, if Michael can succeed in rhyming verse then I can do better, a great deal better he shall not outdo me. Think you fool, think. I curse Michael for being so clever, I shall outwit him, I will see to that. A funny little rhyme shall come forth. Patience is needed patience. The night is long, time is on my hands

the pills are the answer
and with pills. Indeed do I always not oh what a joke.

Begin with the rings,

One ring, two rings

bitch, it took me a while before I could wrench them off. Should have stuffed them down the whores throat I wish to God I could have taken the head. Detest her for wearing them, reminds me too much of the whore. Next time I will select a whore who has one. The bitch was not worth the farthings

Return, return, essential to return. Prove you are no fool.

One ring, two rings,
a farthing one and two
~~Gin [illegible] will do true~~
~~lottery M its true~~
Along with M ha ha
Will catch clever Jim,
its true.
~~left two~~
No pill, left but two

One ring, two rings.
a farthing, one and two,
Along with M ha ha
Will catch clever Jim
its true.
No pill, left but two

Am I not indeed a clever fellow? It makes me laugh they will never understand why I did so. Next time I will remember the chalk and write my funny little rhyme. The eyes will come out of the ext. I will stuff them in the whores mouth. That ll certainly give me pleasure, it does so as I rite. Tonight I will see Mine, she will be leased as I will be gentle with her as ndeed I always am.

am still thinking of burning St. James's to the ground may do so on my next visit. That will give the fools omething more to think on I am beginning to think ins of the children, part of me hates me for doing so. e day God will answer to me, so help me hake would be proud of my funny little rhyme r he knows only too well the art of verse. Have not proven I can write better than he. eel like celebrating, the night has been long d I shall award myself with the pleasures the flesh, but I shall not be cutting ~~her her~~

will save ~~that thrill~~ for another day.

The whore is in debt. Very well I shall honour the latter's notes but the whores are going to pay more than ever. I have read all of my deeds they have done me proud, I had to laugh, they have me down as left handed, a Doctor, a slaughterman and a Jew. Very well, if they are to insist that I am a Jew ~~then~~ a Jew I shall be. Why not let the Jews suffer? I have never taken to them, far too many of them on the Exchange for my liking. I could not stop laughing when I read Punch there for all to see was the first three letters of my surname. They are blind as they say.

" Turn round three times, And catch whom you

MAY"

ha ha ha ha ha ha

I cannot stop laughing it amuses me so shall I write them a clue?

May comes and goes.
~~this May pleases~~ with a ~~knife in his hand~~
In the dark of the night
~~He does please~~
When he comes and goes

with a ring on my finger
and a knife in my hand
~~This May comes and goes~~

May comes and goes
In the dark of the night
~~he does pierce the whores~~ he kisses
~~and~~ gives ~~them a fright~~
he kisses the whores
then gives them a fright

May comes and goes
in the dark of the night
he kisses the whores
then gives them a fright

With a ring on my finger
and a knife in my hand
This May spreads May-hem
~~all through the land~~
throughout this fair land

~~The Jews and slaughtermen~~

~~The Jews and Doctors.~~

The Doctors and Jews.

~~way~~

will get all the blame – blame – tame
same – game

his dirty game.

May playing

~~The Doctors ...~~

The Jews and the Doctors

Will get all the blame

but its only May

playing his dirty game

~~He will not shed a tear~~

He will kill all the whores

and not shed a tear

~~He will give them a clue~~

I will give them a clue

but nothing too clear

I will kill all the whores

and not shed a tear.

May comes and goes
in the dark of the night
He kisses the whores
and gives them a fright

The Jews and the Doctors
will get all the blame
but its only May playing
his dirty game

I will give them a clue
but nothing too clear
I will kill all the whores
and not shed a tear

With a ring on my finger
and a knife in my hand.
This May spreads Mayhem
throughout this fair land.

They remind me of chickens with their heads cut off running
fools with no heads, ha ha. It is nice to laugh at bastards
and fools and indeed they are fools. I need much more
pleasure than I have had. Strange my hands feel
colder than they have ever done so.

I am fighting a battle within me. My desire for revenge
is overwhelming. The whore has destroyed my life. I
try whenever possible to keep all sense of respectability
I worry so over Bobo and Gladys, no others matter.
Tonight I will take more than ever. I miss the
thrill of cutting them up. I do believe I have
lost my mind. All the bitches will pay for the pain.
Before I am finished all of England will know the
name I have given myself. It is indeed a name
to remember. It shall be, before long, on every
persons lips within the land. Perhaps her gracious
Majesty will become acquainted with it. I
wonder if she will honour me with a
knighthood ha ha.

Abberline says he was never amazed,
I did my work with such honour.
For his decree

he had to agree,
I deserve at least an honour
so all for a whim,
I can now rise Sir Jim — I cannot
think of another word to accompany Jim I like
my words to rhyme damn it. It is late, mine is
waiting, I will enjoy this evening. I will be
gentle and not give anything away.

I miss Edwin. I have received but one letter from
him since his arrival in the whores country. The
bitch is raising me worse as each day passes. If I
could I would have it over and done with
I united my mother and fathers grave. I long to be
reunited with them. I believe they know the torture
the whore is putting me through. I enjoy the
thrill of thinking of all I have done. But there
has been, but once, regret for my deeds. I dispelled
my remorse instantly. The whore still believes I
have no knowledge of her whoring master. I have
considered killing him, but If I was to do so. I
would surely be caught. I have no desire for that,
curse him and the whore their time will come.

---

to my astonishment I cannot believe I have not been caught. My heart felt as if it had left my body. Within my fright I imagined my heart bounding along the street with I in desperation following it. I would have dearly loved to have cut the head of the damned horse off and stuff it as far as it would go down the whores throat. I had no time to rip the bitch wide, I curse my bad luck I believe the thrill of being caught thrilled me more than cutting the whore herself. As I write I find it impossible to believe he did not see me, in my estimation I was less than a few feet from him. The fool panicked, it is what saved me. My satisfaction was far from complete, damn the bastard, I cursed him and cursed him, but I was clever, they could not outdo me. No one ever will. Within the quarter of the hour I found another dirty bitch willing to sell her wares. The whore like all the rest was only too willing. The thrill she gave me was unlike the others, I cut deep deep deep. Her nose annoyed me so I cut it off, had a go at her eyes, left my mark, could not get the bitches head off. I believe now it is impossible to do so. The whore never screamed. I took all I could away with me. I am saving it for a rainy day, ha ha.

Perhaps I will send Abberline and Warren a sample or two, it goes down well with an after dinner Port. I wonder how long it will keep? Perhaps next time I will keep some of the red stuff and send it courtesy of yours truly. I wonder if they enjoyed my funny Jewish Joke? Curse my bad luck had no time to write a funny little rhyme. Before my next will send Central another to remember me by. My God life is sweet. Will give them something to know its is me.

Red-head
horse,
cryed
smelt breath

A rose snatched the red
I did cut the head
down it I cried, hence forth I did hide,
The horse went and shied

With a rose to match the red
I tried to cut off the head.
Damn it I cried,
The horse went and shied
But I could still smell her sweet scented breath

I

Sir Jim,
tin match box empty
~~cigarette case~~
~~make haste~~
~~my shiny knife~~
~~the whores knife~~
first whore no good

One whore no good,
decided Sir Jim strike another.
I showed no fright and indeed no light,
damn it, the tin box was empty

II

tea and sugar
~~sugar, pay, did say~~
me, flea, be
~~tea and sugar paid my fee~~

Sweet sugar and tea. could have paid my small
fee he he.
~~then I did flee~~

Showed ~~my~~ glee
a kidneys for supper.

Sweet sugar and tea,
could have paid my small fee.
But instead I did flee
and by way showed my glee
By eating cold kidney for supper

III

bastard
Abberline
bonnett
hides all
clue
clever
will tell you more

~~Mr Abberline is a funny little man~~

Oh Mr Abberline, he is a clever little man
he keeps back all that he can
~~But I know better~~
For do I know better, indeed I do
did I not leave him a very good clue
Nothing is mentioned, of this I know sure
ask clever Abberline, ~~he does know more~~

Oh Mr Abberline, he is a clever little man
he keeps back all that he can.
For do I not know better, Indeed I do.
did I not leave him a very good clue
Nothing is mentioned; of this I am sure;
ask clever Abberline. could tell you more

IV

Gin [illegible] trips over
fear
have it near
redeem it near
[illegible]
poste [illegible]

He believes I will trip over
but I have no fear
~~I cannot redeem it here~~
For I could not possibly redeem it here
of this certain fact, I could send him ~~forte~~ ~~taste~~
of he requests that be the case.

Am I not a clever fellow

That should give the fools a laugh, it has done so
for me, wonder if they have enjoyed the name I have
given? I said it would be on the lips of all, and indeed
it is. Believe I will send another. Include my funny
little rhyme. That will convince them that it is the
truth I tell. Tonight I will celebrate by
wining and dining George. I am in a good mood,
believe I will allow the whore the pleasure
of her whore master, will remark an evening in the
city will do her good, will suggest a concert. I have
no doubt the carriage will take the bitch straight
to him. ~~I will go ...~~ I will go to sleep
thinking about all they are doing. I cannot wait for
the thrill.

With a rose to match the red
I tried to cut off the head.
Damn it I cried,
the horse went and shied
hence forth I did hide,
but I could still smell
her sweet scented breath.

One whore no good, decided Sir Jim strike another.
I showed no fright, and indeed no light.
Damn it, the tin box was empty

Sweet sugar and tea
could have paid my small fee
But instead I did flee and by way showed my glee
by eating cold kidney for supper.

Oh, Mr Abberline he is a clever little man,
he keeps back all that he can.
For do I not know better, Indeed I do,
did I not leave him a very good clue
Nothing is mentioned of this I know sure,
ask clever Abberline, could tell you more.

He believes I will trip over,
but I have no fear.
For I could not possibly
redeem it here.
Of this certain fact I could send them postehaste
If he requested that be the case.

---

t has been far too long since my last, I have been
well. The whole of my body has pained. Hopper did not
lieve me. One day I will take revenge on him. The whore
s informed the bumbling buffoon. I am in the habit
taking strong medicine. I was furious when the
ch told me. So furious I hit her hard. The
ore begged me not to do so again. It was a pleasure,
great deal of pleasure. If it was not for my work,
would have cut the bitch up there and then. But
m clever. Although the gentle man has turned, I did
show my hand true. I apologised, a one off
ance, I said, which I regretted and I assured the whore
would never happen again. The stupid bitch believed
e.

I have received several letters from Michael. In all he enquires about my health and asked in one if my sleepwalking has reoccurred. Poor Michael he is so easily fooled. I have informed him it has not. My hands still remain cold. I shall be dining tonight. I hope kidneys are on the menu, ha ha. Will set me in the mood for another little escapade. Will visit the city of whores soon, very soon. I wonder if I could do three?

If it were not for Michael insisting that we take dinner I would have tried my hand that very night. I cursed my brother as I have never cursed him before. I cursed my own stupidity, had I not informed Michael that I no longer sleepwalked I was forced to stop myself from indulging in my pleasure by taking the largest dose I have ever done. The pain that night has burnt into my mind. I vaguely recall putting a handkerchief in my mouth to stop my cries. I believe I vomited several times. The pain was intolerable, as I think I shudder. No more.

I am convinced God placed me here to kill all whores, for he must have done so, am I still not here. Nothing will stop me now. The more I take the [illegible] stronger I become.

[M]ichael was under the impression that once I had [f]inished my business I was to return to Liverpool that very day. And indeed I did one day later he-he. I fear not for the fact will not [c]ome to his attention as he addresses all letters to me

. .

[I] have read about my latest, my God the thoughts, [th]e very best. I left nothing of the bitch, nothing. I [spr]ead it all over the room, time was on my hands, [unlik]e the other whore I cut off the bitches nose, all [of] it this time. I left nothing of her face to remember [he]r by. She reminded me of the whore. So young [un]like I. I thought it a joke when I cut her [br]easts off, kissed them for a while. The taste of blood [wa]s sweet, the pleasure was overwhelming, will have [to] do it again, it thrilled me so. Left them on [th]e table with some of the other stuff. Thought [the]y belonged there. They wanted a slaughterman so [I] stripped what I could, laughed while I was doing so. [Like] the other bitches she ripped like a ripe peach. [One] of these days I will take the head away [wi]th me. I will boil it and serve it up for supper. The key and burnt clothes puzzle them he he

rings	rip
pills	initial
hat	whore master
handkerchief	back to the whore
whore	light
Mother	fire
father	

~~with the key I did flee~~

I had the key,
and with it I did flee
~~the clothes I burnt~~
~~along with the hat~~
The hat I did burn
for light I did yearn
~~For the sake of the whore mother~~
And I thought of the whoring mother

I had the key,
And with it I did flee
The hat I did burn
for light I did yearn.
And I thought of the
whoring mother.

I

A handkerchief red,
tied to the bed
and I thought of the whoring mother

II

~~For Sir Jim with his whim~~

A whores whim,
caused Sir Jim
to cut deeper, deeper and deeper.
~~away with it I did go~~
~~back to the whoring mother~~
All did go.
As I did so
back to the whoring mother.

A whores whim,
caused Sir Jim
to cut deeper deeper and deeper
All did go,
As I did so
back to the whoring mother

III

~~for mitial there~~

An initial here and a initial there
would tell of the whoring mother

I had a key,
and with it I did flee
The hat I did burn,
for light I did yearn.
And I ~~thought~~ of the whoring mother

A handkerchief red,
led to the bed
And I ~~thought~~ of ~~the~~ whoring mother

A whores whim
caused Sir Jim,
to cut deeper, deeper and deeper
All did go,
As I did so,
back to ~~the~~ whoring mother

An initial here and an initial there
will tell of the whoring mother.

I left it there for the fools but they will never find
it I was too clever. Left it in front for all eyes
to see. Shall I write and tell them? That amuses me.
I wonder if next time I can carve my funny little
rhyme on the whores flesh? I believe I will give it a
try. It amuses me if nothing else. Life is sweet, very
sweet. Regret I did not take any of it away with
me. It is supper time, I could do with a kidney
or two ha ha.

I cannot live without my medicine. I am afraid
to go to sleep for fear of my nightmares reoccurring.
I see thousands of people chasing me, with Abberline
in front dangling a rope. I will not be hanged
of that fact I am certain. It has been far too long
since my last, I still desire revenge on the whore
and the whore master, but less than the desire

to repeat my last performance The thought, still thrill me so. I am tired and I fear the city of whores has become too dangerous for I to return Christmas is approaching and Thomas has invited me to visit him. I know him well. I have decided to accept his offer, although I know the motive behind it will strictly be business. Thomas thinks of nothing else except money unlike me, ha ha.

My first was in Manchester so why not my next. If I was to do the same as the last, that would throw the fools into a panick, especially that fool Abberline. The children constantly ask what I shall be buying them for Christmas, they shy away when I tell them a shiny knife not unlike Jack the Rippers in order that I cut their tongues out for peace and quiet. I do believe I am completely mad. I have never harmed the children in the years since they have been born But now I take great delight in scaring them so. May God forgive me. I have lost my battle and shall go on until I am caught. Perhaps I should stop myself and save the hangman a job. At this moment I have no feeling in my body, none at all. I keep asking

self I have done no wrong. It is the whore
ho has done so, not I. Will peace of mind ever
me? I have visited Hopper too often this month
ill have to stop; for I fear he may begin
suspect. I talk to him like no other.

~~Sir Jim shall,~~
Am I insane?
Come, gain
Sir Jim ~~with~~ his fancy cane
will soon strike again

One whore in heaven,
two whores side by side,
three whores all have died.
four

Sir Jim he cuts them first

damn it

Abberline says he is now amazed,
Sir Jim has not struck another.
He waits patiently
to see hastily

Christmas soon the whore mole bonnett
damn the bitches damn Michael
Give Sir Jim his dues
He detests all the Jews
For he has no favourite men
As he runs away to his den.

He likes to work with but you

Give Sir Jim his dues
He detests all the Jews
and indeed was it not in tribe

~~I kissed them;~~
~~I kissed them~~
~~They tasted so sweet~~
~~I thought of leaving them by the whores feet~~
~~but the fable it was bear~~
~~so I went and left them there~~

damn it damn it damn it

so help me God my next will be far the worst,
my head aches, but I will go on. damn abberline
for being so clever the art of verse is far from
simple. I curse him so. Abberline Abberline
I shall destroy that fool yet, So help me God
Banish him from my thoughts, he will not
catch Sir Jim yet

Abberline Abberline Abberline Abberline
The devil take the bastard

I am cold curse the bastard Lowry for making
me rip I keep seeing blood pouring from
the bitches. The nightmares are hideous.
I cannot stop myself from wanting to eat more.
God help me, damn you [illegible] noone will stop me
God be damned.

think think think write ~~tell~~ all prove to them
you are who you say you are make them believe
it is the truth I tell. Damn him for creating
them, damn him damn him damn him. I wish
to boil boil boil. See if there eyes pop.
I need more ~~thrills~~, cannot live without
my ~~thrills~~. I will go on, I will go on, nothing
will stop me nothing cut Sir Jim ~~cut~~. Cut deep
deep deep.

~~Sir Jim will cut them all~~

Oh costly intercourse
of death

Banish the ~~thoughts~~ banish them banish them
he he he, looks towards the sensible brother
chickens running around with
their heads cut off

ha ha ha ha. ha ha ha ha ha

Am I not a clever fellow
out foxed them all, they will never know

—

~~Sir Jim will cut them all,~~
~~Sir Jim he does so well~~

Sir Jim ~~makes his~~ call
he ~~cuts them~~ all.
with his ~~knife~~ in ~~his~~ bag.

will have to take up lodgings on my return. Middlesex Street that was a joke. The fools, several times they could have caught me if they had looked good and proper. My God am I not clever? Gods I am. My head spins will someone have to find the ~~strength~~ for my journey home. The devil ~~take~~ this city, it is too cold for me. Tomorrow I will make Bunny suffer. The ~~thought~~ will ~~thrill~~ me on my journey home.

I cannot bring myself to look back, all I have written scares me so. George visited me today. I believe he knows what I am going through, although he says nothing I can see it in his eyes. Poor George, he is such a good friend. Michael is well, he writes a rarely. In my heart I cannot blame him for doing so. I regret I shall not see him this Christmas.

Encountered an old friend on the Exchange floor. I felt regret for was he not Jewish. I had forgot how many Jewish friends I have. My revenge is on whores not Jews. I do believe I am truly sorry for the scare I have thrown amongst them. I believe this is the reason I am unable to write my funny little rhymes. I thank God I have had the courage to stop sending them. I am convinced they will be my undoing.

I am tired, very tired. I yearn for peace, but I know in my heart I will go on. I will be in Manchester within a few days. I believe I will feel a great deal better when I have repeated on my last performance. I wonder if I can improve on my fiendish deeds. Will wait and see, no doubt I will think of something. The day is drawing to a close, bunny was in fine spirits. I am pleased. I regret, as with my Jewish friends I have shown my wrath. This coming Christmas I will make amends.

e bitch, the whore is not satisfied with one whore
ster, she now has eyes on another. I could not
t like my first, visions of her flooded back as I struck
tried to put all thoughts of love. I left her for dead,
at I know. It did not amuse me. There was thrill.
have showered my fury on the bitch. I struck and
ruck. I do not know how I stopped. I have left
penniless, I have no regrets. The whore will suffer
like she has ever suffered. May God have mercy
on her. for I shall not, so help me.

omas was in fine health. The children enjoyed Christmas.
did not. My mood is no longer black, although my
d aches. I shall never become accustomed
the pain. I curse winter. I yearn for my
ourite month, to see flowers in full bloom would
ase me so. Warmth is what I need, I think.
. Curse this weather and the whoring bitch
heart has been soft. All whores will feel the
of Sir Jim's shining knife. I regret I
not give myself that name, curse it, I prefer
much much more than the one I have given.

Sir Jim with his shining knife,
cuts through the night,
and by God,
does he not show his might ha ha

It shall not be long before I strike again. I am taking f
more than ever. The bitch can take two. Sir Jim
shall take four, a double double event ha ha.
If I was in the city of whores, I would do my
fiendish deeds this very moment. By God I would

I curse myself for the fool I have been, I shall
have no more regrets, damn them all. Beware you
Abberline I will return with a vengeance. Once m
I will be the talk of England. What pleasure my
thoughts do give me. I wonder if the whore will
take the bastard? The bitch is welcome to hi
I shall think about them deeds, what pleasure. Tonig
I shall reward myself, I will visit mine, but I w
not be gentle. I will show my whore what I
am capable of. Sir Jim needs to wet his appetite,

all whores be damned. A friend has turned, so be it, Sir Jim will turn once more. When I have finished my fiendish deeds, the devil himself will praise me but he will have a long wait before I shake hands with him. I have worko to do a great deal of worko to do. Kidney for supper

---

I am tired of keeping up this pretence of respectability. I am finding it increasingly difficult to do so I believe I am a lucky fellow. Have I not found a new source for my medicine. I relish the thoughts that will bring me I enjoy thinking of the whores waiting for my nice shiny knife. Tonight I write to Michael. Soon I shall be visiting the city of whores soon. Very soon. I cannot wait. The whore may take as many whore masters as she wishes. I no longer cry. I have my thoughts and pleasure of deeds to come, and of what deeds I shall commit. Much. Much finer than my last. Life is indeed sweet, very very sweet.

Dear Mr Abberline,
I am a lucky man
Next time I will do all that ~~I can~~
~~rip, cut, [illegible], down~~
~~out and throat~~
with a little cut here,
and a little cut there
I will go laughing
away to my lair

Dear Mr Abberline,
I am a lucky man
Next time I will do
all that I can.
With a little cut here
and a little cut ~~there~~
I will go laughing
away to my lair.

Damn it damn it damn it the bastard
almost caught me, curse him to hell, I will
cut him up next time, so help me. A few
minutes and I would have done, bastard. I will seek
him out, teach him a lesson. No one will stop
me. Curse his black soul. I curse myself for
striking too soon, I should have waited until it
was ~~trinity~~ quiet so hope me if any t[illegible]
ll next time and eat it will leave
nothing not ~~even the~~ head. I will boil
it and eat it with freshly picked
carrots. I shall think about Abberline
as I am doing so, that will give me a
laugh ~~ha ha~~ the whore will suffer tonight for
the deed she has done.

The bitch has written all,
tonight she will fall.

So help me God I will cut the bitch up and
serve her up to the children. How dare the whore
write to Michael. The damn bitch had no right
to inform him of my medicine. If I have my
my little way the whore will be saved
this very night. I stood my ground and

informed Michael it was a damn lie.

The bitch visits the city of whores soon, I have decided I will wait until the time is ripe then I will strike with all my might. I shall buy the whore something for her visit. Will give the bitch the impression I consider it her duty to visit her aunt. She can nurse the sick bi and see her whoring master ha ha.

Ha, what a joke, let the bitch believe I have no knowledge of her whoring affairs. When she returns the whore will pay. I relish the thought of striking the bitch once more. Am I not a cle fellow. I pride myself no one knows how clever I am. I do believe if George was to rea this, he would say I am the cleverest man alive. I yearn to tell him how clever I have been, but I shall not, my campaign is far from over yet. Sir Jim will give nothing away, not How can they stop me now. Sir Jim may live fo ever. I feel strong, very strong, strong enough to strike on this damn old city. believe I wil

why not, nobody does suspect the gentle
man born. Will see how I will feel on my
journey home, if the whim takes me then
so be it. Will have to be careful not to
get too much of the red stuff on me.
Perhaps I will just cut the once, fool the fools,
what a joke, more chickens running around with
their heads cut off. ha ha I feel clever.

Sir Jimmy

live

forever

ha ha ha ha ha

His dear Sir Jim,
he loves his whims,
tonight he will call
and take away all. ha he he ha

Am I not a clever fellow, the bitch gave me the greatest pleasure of all. Did not the whore see her whore master in front of all. True the race was the finest I have seen, but ~~the thrill~~ of seeing the whore with the bastard ~~thrilled~~ me none so than knowing his Royal Highness was but a few feet away from yours truly ha ha what a laugh, if the greedy bastard would have known he was less than a few feet away from the name all England was talking about he would have died there and then. Regret I could not tell the foolish fool. To hell with sovereignty, to hell with all whores, to hell with the bitch who rules.

~~Victoria the bitch~~
~~Queen fool Sir Jack knows all~~
~~The queen she knows all~~

Victoria, Victoria
The queen of them all
When it comes to Sir Jack
She knows nothing at all

I

~~She knows one day~~

who knows,
perhaps one day,
I will give her a call

II

~~Shiny knife~~
~~my life~~
~~honour my knife~~
Show her my knife
and she will honour me for life

III

~~Come Sir Jim she will say~~
Arise Sir Jack she will say,
and now you can go,
as you may ha ha ha

ha ha ha ha ha

Victoria, Victoria
the queen of them all.
When it comes to Sir Jack
she knows ~~nothing~~ at all.

Who knows,
Perhaps one day,
I will give her a call.

Show her my knife
and she will honour me for life

Arise Sir Jack she will say
and now you can go
as you may

Jim, Jack Jack Jim ha. ha ha

I was clever. George would be proud of me, told the bitch in my position I could not afford a scandal. I struck her several times an eye for an eye, ha ha. Too many interfering servants, damn the bitches. Hopper will soon feel the edge of my shiny knife, damn the meddling buffoon, damn all. Once more the bitch is in debt, my God I will cut her. Oh how I will cut her. I will visit the city of whores. I will pay her dues and I shall take mine, by God I will. I will rip rip rip. May see the bastard out who stopped my funny little game and rip him to. I said he would pay. I will make sure he damn will. I feel a numbness in my body, the whore will pay for that. I wonder if Edwin is well. I long for him to return. I have decided that next time I will take the whores eyes out and send them to that fool Abberline.

bastard

bastard

take the eyes,
take the head,
leave them well for dead

It does not amuse me. Curse that bastard Abberline, curse him to hell. I will not dangle from any rope of his. I have thought often about the whore and her loving master. The thoughts still thrill me. Perhaps one day the bitch will allow me to participate. Why not? All have taken her. Have I no right to the whore. wish to do so.

The bitch

the bitch

the bitch

Fuller believes there is very little the matter with me. Strange, th
thoughts he placed into my mind. I could not strike, I belie
I am mad, completely mad. I try to fight my thoughts I walk
the streets until dawn. I could not find it in my heart to
strike, visions of my dear Bunny overwhelm me. I still l
her, but how I hate her. She has destroyed all and yet my he
aches for her, oh how it aches. I do not know which pain
is the worse my body or my mind

My God I am tired, I do not know if I can go on. Bunny
and the children are all that matter. No regrets, no regrets
I shall not allow such thoughts to enter my head. Tom
I will take my shining knife and be rid of it. Throw
it deep within the river I shall return to Battlecrease with
the knowledge that I can no longer continue my campaign. Tis l
that spurned me so, tis love that shall put an end to it

I am afraid to look back on all I have written. Perhaps
t would be wiser to destroy this, but in my heart I
annot bring myself to do so. I have tried once before,
ut like the coward I am, I could not. Perhaps in my
ormented mind I wish for someone to read this and understand
hat the man I have become was not the man I was born.

My dear brother Edwin has returned. I wish I could tell
im all. No more funny little rhymes. Tonight I write of love

tis love that spurred me so,

tis love that does destroy

tis love that I yearn for

tis love that she spurned

tis love that will finish me

tis love that I regret.

May God help me. I pray each night he will take me,
the disappointment when I awake is difficult to describe
I no longer take the dreaded stuff for fear I will harm
my dear Bunny, worse still the children

I do not have the courage to take my life. I pray each night I will find the strength to do so, but the courage alludes me. I pray constantly all will forgive. I deeply regret striking her, I have found it in my heart to forgive her for her lusts.

I believe I will tell her all, ask her to forgive me as I have forgiven her. I pray to God she will understand what she has done to me. Tonight I will pray for the women I have slaughtered. May God forgive me for the deeds I committed on Kelly, no heart no heart

The pain is unbearable... My dear Bunny knows all. I do not
now if she has the strength to kill me. I pray to God
she finds it. It would be simple, she knows of my
nedicine, and for an extra dose or two it would be all over.
No one will know I have seen to that. George knows of my
habit and I trust soon it will come to the attention of Michael.
e truth I believe he is aware of the fact. Michael will
ow how to act, he is the most sensible amongst us all
do not believe I will see this June, my favourite of all months.
e begged Bunny to act soon, I curse myself for the coward
am. I have redressed the balance of my previous will. Bunny
d the children are well cared for and I trust Michael
d Thomas will carry out my wishes.

on, I trust I shall be laid beside my dear mother and father. I shall
k their forgiveness when we are reunited. God I pray will allow me
least that privilege, although I know only too well I do not
rve it. My thoughts will remain in tact, for a reminder to all how love
s destroy. I place this now in a place were it shall be found.
pray whoever should read this will find it in their heart
forgive me. Remind all, whoever you may be, that I was
ce a gentle man. May the good lord have mercy on my soul, and
give me for all I have done.

give my name that all know of me, so history do tell, what love
do to a gentle man born.

Yours truly

Jack the Ripper

Dated this third day of May 1889.

La traduction française qui suit ce fac-similé du *Journal* reproduit scrupuleusement la ponctuation et le style tels qu'ils sont dans l'original.

Les premières pages du *Journal* ayant été arrachées (voir le Dossier), le texte débute donc au milieu d'une phrase.

[...] ce qui les attend, ils arrêteraient tout de suite. Mais est-ce vraiment ce que je désire ? Ma réponse est non. Ils souffriront autant que moi. J'en fais mon affaire. Reçu une lettre de Michael peut-être que je lui rendrai visite. Il va falloir que je finisse par prendre une décision quant aux enfants. J'aspire à la tranquillité d'esprit mais sincèrement je ne la trouverai pas tant que je n'aurai pas exercé ma vengeance sur la putain et sur le maquereau.

Garce stupide, je sais pertinemment qu'elle s'est arrangée pour le retrouver à Whitechapel. Eh bien soit, ma décision est prise, et bien prise. J'ai mangé un morceau au Poste House c'est là que je me suis enfin décidé : ce sera Londres. Et pourquoi pas, n'est-ce pas un endroit idéal ? N'est-il pas vrai que je me rends fréquemment dans la capitale et n'est-il pas vrai que j'ai une raison légitime de le faire. Toutes celles qui vendent leurs marchandises sordides paieront, de cela je ne doute pas. Mais moi, faudra-t-il que je paie ? Je ne le pense pas je suis trop malin pour ça.

Comme d'habitude mes mains sont froides, mais mon cœur je le crois vraiment est encore plus froid. Une fois de plus, ma chère petite Gladys est souffrante, elle m'inquiète tant. Je suis convaincu qu'une ombre obscure flotte sur la maison, c'est le mal. Je suis de plus en plus las des gens qui posent constamment des questions quant à mon état de santé. C'est vrai ma tête et mes bras me font mal de temps en temps, mais je ne m'inquiète pas outre mesure, bien que je sois tout à fait sûr que Hopper est de l'avis contraire. Pour moi, ce n'est rien qu'un crétin bavard. Thomas veut que nous nous rencontrions dès que possible. Mais les affaires sont florissantes alors je ne suis guère enclin à me pencher sur cette question qu'il décrit comme des plus urgentes. Néanmoins, je ferai mon possible pour satisfaire sa demande.

Le temps passe bien trop lentement, je dois encore rassembler le courage nécessaire pour entamer ma campagne. J'ai longuement réfléchi à cette question et je ne peux toujours pas décider quand je devrais commencer. L'opportunité est là, de ce fait je suis certain. La garce ne se doute de rien.

L'idée du maquereau en train de la prendre commence à m'exciter, je la laisserai peut-être continuer, certaines de mes pensées commencent vraiment à me donner du plaisir. Oui je vais aller passer quelques semaines chez Michael, et je la laisserai profiter du maquereau autant qu'elle peut. Ce soir je vais voir la mienne. Je rentrerai peut-être à Battlecrease pour prendre la garce infidèle. Deux dans la même soirée, quel plaisir en vérité. Mon médicament me fait du bien, en fait, je suis sûr que je peux en prendre plus que n'importe quelle autre personne vivante. J'ai les idées claires je ferai souffrir de la putain ce soir.

Je commence à croire qu'il n'est pas sage de continuer à écrire. Si je dois buter une pute alors rien ne conduira les autorités jusqu'à moi, mais pourtant il y a des moments où je sens une contrainte irrésistible qui me pousse à jeter mes pensées sur le papier. C'est dangereux, ça je le sais. Que Smith trouve ceci, et je suis fait avant que ma campagne commence. Cependant, le plaisir d'écrire tout ce qui m'attend, et en vérité le plaisir de penser aux actes qui m'attendent, m'excite tant. Et oh quels actes je m'en vais commettre. Car comment pourrait-on soupçonner que je puisse être capable de telles choses, car ne suis-je pas, comme tout le monde le croit, un homme doux, dont on a pu dire qu'il ne ferait jamais de mal à une mouche. En vérité pas plus tard que l'autre jour Edwin n'a-t-il pas dit de moi que j'étais le plus gentil des hommes qu'il avait rencontrés. Un compliment de mon cher frère que j'ai trouvé excessivement flatteur.

Décidé que ma patience avait des limites. La garce s'est payé ma tête. Demain je me rends à Manchester. Prendrai un peu de mon médicament et réfléchirai sérieusement à la question. Je crois que j'y arriverais, bien que je tremble de peur à l'idée d'être capturé. Une peur qu'il va me falloir surmonter. Je crois que j'en ai la force. Je m'obligerai à ne pas penser aux enfants. La putain, c'est tout ce à quoi je penserai. J'ai mal à la tête.

Oh mon Dieu je ne sais plus où j'en suis. La putain est maintenant avec son créateur et il peut se la garder. Je n'ai pas eu de plaisir à serrer, je n'ai rien ressenti. Ne sais pas si j'ai le courage de revenir à mon idée de départ. Il faisait froid et humide à Manchester tout à fait comme ici dans ce bouge. La prochaine fois, je leur balancerai de l'acide dessus. La pensée de les voir se tortiller et hurler pendant que l'acide les ronge m'excite. Ha, quelle farce ce serait si je pouvais arracher un œil et le laisser à côté du corps de la putain pour que tout le monde le voie, le voie, *ha, ha.*

Je crois que j'ai pris un coup de froid. Je ne peux pas m'arrêter de trembler, j'ai mal dans tout le corps. Il y a des moments où je prie Dieu pour que la douleur et le supplice s'arrêtent. L'été approche le temps chaud me fera du bien. J'aspire à la paix mais mon travail ne fait que commencer. Il me faudra attendre longtemps la paix. D'abord toutes les putains doivent souffrir et mon Dieu comme je m'en vais les faire souffrir autant qu'elle m'a fait souffrir. Edwin m'a demandé des nouvelles de Thomas et des affaires, je l'ai informé que Thomas allait bien et que les affaires étaient florissantes, vrai dans les deux cas. Je me dis que je devrais écrire à Michael, peut-être pas, j'ai bien trop froid aux mains, un autre jour. Je prendrai la garce ce soir. J'ai besoin d'oublier un moment les événements de la nuit dernière. Les enfants vont bien.

Me suis promené dans l'allée, rencontré Mme Hammersmith, elle a demandé des nouvelles de Bobo et de Gladys et à mon grand étonnement de ma santé. Qu'est-ce que cette putain a dit ? Mme Hammersmith est une garce. L'air frais et la promenade m'ont fait du bien. Pendant un moment j'ai réussi à oublier la putain et son maquereau. Me sentais complètement revigoré quand je suis retourné à mon bureau. Je rendrai visite à Michael en juin prochain. Juin est un mois si agréable, les fleurs sont tout en bourgeons l'air est plus odorant et la vie est presque certainement plus rose j'attends sa venue avec plaisir. Un très grand plaisir. Je me sens contraint d'écrire à Michael, sinon obligé. J'ai les idées claires, je n'ai pas froid aux mains.

Je suis fâché. J'essaie de réprimer ma colère. La putain a proposé de m'accompagner chez Michael. J'ai besoin de temps pour remettre de l'ordre dans mes idées. Je ne peux en aucun cas laisser la garce m'accompagner, tous mes efforts et mes plans seront détruits si elle le faisait. J'ai eu très mal aujourd'hui. Je crois que la garce a trouvé une de mes bouteilles, elle avait été déplacée. Je suis fatigué et j'ai besoin de dormir la douleur m'a tenu éveillé pendant presque toute la nuit dernière. Rentrerai tôt éviter tout contact avec la garce.

Fréquenté mon club. George a déclaré qu'il ne m'avait jamais vu en meilleure santé. Je crois que la garce a changé d'avis. Mes pensées deviennent de plus en plus audacieuses, j'ai imaginé de faire toutes sortes de choses. Pourrais-je en manger un morceau ? Ça aurait peut-être le goût de bacon frais grillé *ha ha.* (Oh) mon Dieu que ça m'excite.

Michael m'attend vers la fin juin, à partir de juillet ma campagne va s'accélérer. Je les prendrai toutes sans exception avant de les rendre à leur créateur, abîmées bien sûr, très très abîmées.

J'essaie de chasser de mon esprit toutes les pensées qui ont trait aux enfants. Je me sens fort, plus fort que jamais. Je retourne sans arrêt à Manchester en pensée, la prochaine fois ça m'excitera. Je le sais au fond de mon cœur. Je ne peux pas comprendre pourquoi William ne veut pas accepter mon invitation à dîner. Il n'est pas si différent de moi, il déteste la garce. Je crois que si la chance est avec moi je réduirai St. James en cendres. Demain je ferai un pari substantiel. Je me sens en veine.

Si j'avais pu tuer ce salaud de Lowry sur-le-champ de mes propres mains, je l'aurais fait. Comment ose-t-il mettre ma parole en doute sur quelque sujet que ce soit, c'est moi qui devrais mettre sa parole en doute. Qu'il aille au diable au diable au diable devrais-je replacer les objets manquants? Non ce serait un trop grand risque. Devrais-je détruire ceci? Mon Dieu je vais le tuer. Ne pas lui donner de raison et lui ordonner séance tenante de laisser tomber l'affaire, voilà je crois la seule ligne de conduite que je puisse adopter. Je vais me forcer à penser à quelque chose de plus agréable. La putain va souffrir plus que jamais ce soir, cette pensée me revitalise. Ce sont les derniers jours de juin je tremble de plaisir en pensant à ce qui se prépare.

J'en ai pris trop je n'arrive pas à penser aussi clairement que je le devrais. Je ne me rappelle presque rien de ce qui s'est passé hier. Grâce à Dieu je me suis arrêté à temps. Je vais montrer ma colère envers ce salaud d'une telle façon qu'il regrettera d'avoir jamais abordé le sujet. Personne, pas même Dieu lui-même ne me privera du plaisir d'écrire mes pensées. Je prendrai la première putain venue et je lui montrerai ce qu'est vraiment l'enfer. Je crois que j'enfoncerai une canne dans le mont de cette putain de garce et que je la laisserai en place pour qu'ils puissent voir combien elle pouvait en prendre. J'ai mal à la tête, Dieu n'a pas le droit de me faire ça que le diable l'emporte.

Comment suis-je parvenu à me maîtriser, je n'en sais rien. Je n'ai pas tenu compte de la substance rouge, des litres selon mon estimation. A coup sûr, je vais être éclaboussé. Je ne peux pas laisser mes vêtements s'imbiber de sang, ça je ne pourrais l'expliquer à personne, surtout pas à Michael. Pourquoi n'y ai-je pas pensé plus tôt ? Je me maudis. Pour m'arrêter j'ai dû lutter jusqu'à mes dernières forces, et si je n'avais pas demandé à Michael de m'enfermer dans ma chambre par crainte d'une crise de somnambulisme, dont j'ai expliqué qu'elles étaient devenues fréquentes récemment, n'était-ce pas astucieux ? j'aurais commis mes sales actes ce soir-là.

J'ai pris une petite chambre dans Middlesex Street, ce qui est une plaisanterie en soi. J'ai payé largement et je crois qu'on ne posera pas de questions. C'est en vérité un endroit idéal. J'ai marché dans les rues et je me suis plus que familiarisé avec elles. J'ai dit ce sera Whitechapel et ce sera Whitechapel. La garce et son maquereau regretteront amèrement le jour où je les ai vus ensemble pour la première fois. J'ai dit je suis malin, très malin. Whitechapel Liverpool, Whitechapel Londres, *ha ha*. Personne n'aurait jamais l'idée de faire le rapprochement. Et en vérité parce qu'il n'y a aucune raison de le faire.

La prochaine fois que je me rendrai à Londres je commencerai. Je n'ai pas de doutes, ma confiance est au plus haut. Je suis excité d'écrire ces lignes, la vie est douce, et ma déception s'est dissipée. La prochaine fois, c'est sûr. Je n'ai pas de doutes, plus maintenant, pas de doutes. Personne ne soupçonnera jamais. Demain j'achèterai ce qu'il y a de mieux comme couteau, rien ne sera trop bon pour mes putains, je leur offrirai ce qu'il y a de mieux, le summum, je leur dois bien ça.

J'ai montré à tout le monde que je ne plaisante pas, le plaisir était bien supérieur à ce que j'avais imaginé. La putain n'était que trop heureuse de faire son boulot. Je me rappelle tout et ça m'excite. Il n'y a pas eu de cri quand j'ai coupé. J'étais plus que contrarié quand la tête n'a pas voulu se détacher. Je crois qu'il me faudra plus de force la prochaine fois. J'ai frappé profondément en elle. Je regrette de n'avoir pas eu la canne il aurait été délicieux de l'enfoncer en elle bien à fond. La garce s'est ouverte comme une pêche bien mûre. J'ai décidé que la prochaine fois j'éventrerai complètement. Mon médicament me donnera de la force et à la pensée de la putain et de son maquereau, je redoublerai d'énergie.

J'ai eu l'impression de devoir attendre longtemps avant de lire le récit de mon triomphe, mais ce n'était pas le cas. Je ne suis pas déçu, ils ont tous bien écrit. La prochaine fois ils en auront beaucoup plus à écrire, je n'ai aucun doute là-dessus *ha ha*. Je resterai calme et ne manifesterai aucun intérêt pour mon acte, si d'aventure quelqu'un le mentionnait, mais je rirai sous cape, oh comme je rirai.

Je ne laisserai pas passer trop de temps avant ma prochaine. En vérité, j'ai besoin de répéter mon plaisir dès que possible. Le Maquereau peut l'avoir avec plaisir et je prendrai mon plaisir dans mes pensées et mes actions. Je serai malin. Je ne passerai pas chez Michael lors de ma prochaine visite. Mes frères seraient horrifiés s'ils savaient, en particulier Edwin après tout n'a-t-il pas dit que j'étais l'un des hommes les plus gentils qu'il ait jamais rencontrés. J'espère qu'il apprécie les fruits de l'Amérique. Pas comme moi, car mon fruit à moi est bien aigre.

Je n'ai pas pu résister à l'envie de parler de mon action à George. J'ai été malin et j'ai amené le sujet en disant combien nous avions de la chance de ne pas avoir de pareils meurtriers dans cette ville. Il était tout à fait d'accord avec moi. Il a même continué en affirmant que selon lui nous possédons la meilleure police du pays, et que nous avons notre part de problèmes mais que les femmes peuvent marcher dans les rues en sécurité. Et en vérité elles le peuvent car je ne vais pas jouer à mes petits jeux devant ma propre porte *ha ha*.

Le gentleman aux gentilles pensées va bientôt frapper de nouveau. Je ne me suis jamais senti aussi bien, en fait, j'en prends plus que jamais et je sens la force s'accumuler en moi. La tête viendra la prochaine fois, et aussi les mains de la putain. Et si je les laissais dans différents endroits un peu partout dans Whitechapel ? Elles courent elles courent la tête et les mains, comme le furet *ha ha*. Peut-être que j'en emporterai un morceau avec moi pour voir si ça a bien le goût de bacon frais grillé. La putain vu son maquereau aujourd'hui ça ne m'a pas dérangé. J'ai imaginé que j'étais avec eux, cette seule pensée m'excite. Je me demande si la putain a jamais eu de telles pensées ? Je crois que oui, n'a-t-elle pas poussé un grand cri quand j'exige qu'elle en prenne un autre. La garce. Elle va souffrir mais l'heure n'est pas encore venue. Demain je vais à

Londres. J'ai décidé que je pouvais pas attendre plus longtemps. J'attends avec impatience le travail de demain soir, ça me fera du bien, beaucoup de bien.

Une sale putain cherchait à gagner de l'argent.
Une autre sale putain cherchait pareillement.

Ne suis-je pas malin ? Je songeais à mon drôle de petit poème pendant le voyage vers la Cité des Putains. J'étais fâché avec moi-même quand je me suis rendu compte que j'avais oublié la craie. Si fâché en fait que je suis retourné voir la garce et que j'en ai encore découpé. J'en ai emporté avec moi. C'est devant moi. J'ai l'intention de le faire frire et de le manger plus tard *ha ha.* A cette seule pensée, j'en ai l'eau à la bouche je suis trop excité pour m'arrêter d'écrire. J'ai éventré mon Dieu il va falloir que j'arrête de penser aux enfants ils m'empêchent de me concentrer j'ai éventré

Il m'a fallu trois jours pour me remettre. Je ne me sentirai pas coupable c'est la putain de garce à blâmer pas moi. J'ai tout mangé, ça n'avait pas le goût de bacon frais grillé mais c'était bon quand même. Elle était si douce et agréable. J'ai laissé un indice à ces crétins stupides mais je suis sûr qu'ils n'en comprendront jamais le sens. Une fois de plus j'ai été malin, très malin.

* [1] Une bague ou deux indiquent
* Un cachet c'est véridique
* M attrapera Sir Jim sans cachets
* laissé deux

deux farthings [2]
deux cachets
le M de la putain
bagues

Réfléchis

Ça viendra, si Michael peut réussir à faire rimer des vers, alors je peux faire mieux, beaucoup mieux il ne me surpassera pas. Réfléchis imbécile, réfléchis. Je maudis Michael d'être si malin, je le surpasserai, j'en fais mon affaire. Un drôle de petit poème verra le jour, *je le veux.* C'est de la patience qu'il faut de la patience. La nuit est longue, j'ai tout mon temps.

Les cachets sont la réponse
finir avec les cachets. En vérité, n'est-ce toujours pas ce que je fais oh quelle farce.

Commencer par les bagues
Une bague, deux bagues
garce, il m'a fallu un moment pour les arracher. Aurais dû les enfoncer dans la gorge de la putain. Par Dieu, comme j'aurais voulu pouvoir prendre la tête. Lui en ai voulu à mort de les porter, ça me rappelle trop la putain. La prochaine

1. * : Ligne biffée sur le manuscrit original.
2. Le farthing valait un quart de l'ancien penny. *(N.d.T.)*

fois je choisirai une putain qui n'en a pas. La garce ne valait pas les farthings. Retourner, retourner, essentiel de retourner. Prouve que tu n'es pas un imbécile.

Une bague, deux bagues,
Un farthing un et deux
* Sir Jim fera la vérité
* Lettre M c'est vrai
Avec M ha ha
Attrapera Jim le malin,
C'est vrai
* Laissé deux
Pas de cachet, laissé que deux

Une bague, deux bagues,
un farthing, un et deux
Avec M ha ha
Attrapera Jim le malin,
C'est vrai
Pas de cachet, laissé que deux

En vérité, ne suis-je pas un type malin ? Ça me fait rire de penser qu'ils ne comprendront jamais pourquoi j'ai agi ainsi. La prochaine fois je penserai à la craie et j'écrirai mon drôle de petit poème. Les yeux de la prochaine seront arrachés. Je les enfoncerai dans la bouche de la putain. Ça me donnera certainement du plaisir, j'en ai rien qu'à l'écrire. Ce soir je vais voir la mienne, elle sera contente parce que je serai gentil avec elle comme en vérité je le suis toujours.

Je pense toujours à réduire St. James en cendres. Je le ferai peut-être lors de ma prochaine visite. Cela donnera à ces imbéciles quelque chose de plus à réfléchir. Je commence à moins penser aux enfants, mais une partie de moi me le reproche. Un jour Dieu me répondra, qu'Il me juge. Michael serait fier de mon drôle de petit poème car il ne connaît que trop bien l'art de la poésie. N'ai-je pas prouvé que je pouvais écrire mieux que lui. Envie de faire la fête, la nuit a été longue et je vais m'accorder les plaisirs de la chair, mais je ne découperai pas *ha ha*. Je me réserverai ce frisson pour un autre jour.

La putain a des dettes. Très bien j'honorerai les reconnaissances de cette garce mais les putains vont payer plus cher que jamais. J'ai tout lu de mes actions j'ai de quoi être fier, je n'ai pas pu m'empêcher de rire, ils me présentent comme gaucher, médecin, employé d'abattoirs et juif. Très bien, s'ils insistent pour dire que je suis juif, juif je serai. Pourquoi ne pas laisser les juifs souffrir ? Ils ne m'ont jamais été sympathiques, il y en a bien trop à la bourse pour mon goût. Je ne pouvais plus m'arrêter de rire quand j'ai lu Punch tout le monde pouvait voir les trois premières lettres de mon nom. Ils ont raison, ils sont aveugles.

« Faites trois tours sur vous-même les yeux bandés, et voyez si vous m'attrapez ja...

MAY »

ha ha ha ha ha ha

« Faites trois tours sur vous-même et attrapez qui vous

POURREZ [1] »

ha ha ha ha ha ha

1. Jack joue constamment sur le mot MAY, constitué des trois premières lettres de son nom. Ce verbe auxiliaire indique la possibilité, la permission ou la suggestion.

Je ne peux pas m'arrêter de rire ça m'amuse tellement vais-je leur écrire pour leur donner un indice ?

May s'en vient puis s'en va
* Ce May fait plaisir un couteau à la main
Au cœur de la nuit noire
* Il fait vraiment plaisir
Quand il arrive puis s'en va
Avec une bague à mon doigt
Et un couteau dans ma main
* Ce May s'en vient puis s'en va
May s'en vient puis s'en va
Au cœur de la nuit noire
* Il fait vraiment plaisir aux putains qu'il embrasse
* et puis leur fait très peur
il embrasse les putains
et puis leur fait très peur

May s'en vient puis s'en va
au cœur de la nuit noire
il embrasse les putains
et puis leur fait très peur

Avec une bague à mon doigt
et un couteau dans ma main
Ce May répand la mutilation
* partout dans le pays
aux quatre coins de ce beau pays.

* Les Juifs et les tueurs
* Les Juifs et les Docteurs
Les Docteurs et les Juifs
* mon
seront accusés – accusés – apprivoisés
même – jeu
son vilain petit jeu

May joue
* Les Docteurs
Les Juifs et les Docteurs
Seront accusés
mais c'est juste May
qui joue à son vilain petit jeu

* Il ne versera pas une larme
Il tuera toutes les putains
et ne versera pas une larme
* Il leur donnera un indice
Je leur donnerai un indice
mais rien de trop évident
Je tuerai toutes les putains
et ne verserai pas une larme.

May s'en vient puis s'en va
au cœur de la nuit noire
Il embrasse les putains
et puis leur fait très peur

Les Juifs et les Docteurs
seront accusés
mais c'est juste May qui joue
à son vilain petit jeu

Je leur donnerai un indice
mais rien de trop évident
Je tuerai toutes les putains
et ne verserai pas une larme

Avec une bague à mon doigt
et un couteau dans ma main
Ce May répand la destruction
aux quatre coins de ce beau pays.

Ils me font penser à des poulets décapités continuant à courir comme des imbéciles sans tête *ha ha*. C'est agréable de se moquer des salauds et des imbéciles et ce sont vraiment des imbéciles. J'ai besoin de beaucoup plus de plaisir que j'en ai eu. Étrange j'ai la sensation que mes mains sont plus froides qu'elles l'ont jamais été.

Je mène une bataille en moi-même. Mon désir de vengeance est irrésistible. La putain a détruit ma vie. J'essaie autant que possible de conserver toutes les apparences de la respectabilité. Je m'inquiète tant au sujet de Bobo et de Gladys, personne d'autre ne compte. Ce soir j'en prendrai plus que jamais. L'excitation que j'éprouve à les découper me manque. Je crois sincèrement que j'ai perdu la raison. Toutes les garces paieront pour la douleur. Avant que j'en aie terminé, toute l'Angleterre connaîtra le nom que je me suis donné. C'est en vérité un nom à garder en mémoire. Il sera, avant longtemps, sur les lèvres de tout le monde dans le pays. Peut-être que sa gracieuse Majesté fera sa connaissance. Je me demande si elle me fera chevalier *ha ha*.

Abberline le dit, il n'a jamais été stupéfait,
Que j'aie accompli mon œuvre avec tant d'honneur.
Dans sa déclaration
il a dû admettre
Que je mérite au moins un honneur
Alors tout ça pour un caprice

Je peux maintenant élever Sir Jim – je ne peux pas songer à un autre mot pour accompagner Jim. J'aime que mes mots riment bon sang. Il est tard, la mienne m'attend, je vais passer une bonne soirée. Je serai doux et ne me trahirai pas.

Edwin me manque. Je n'ai reçu qu'une lettre de lui depuis son arrivée au pays des putains. La garce me contrarie davantage chaque jour. Si je pouvais, j'en finirais une bonne fois pour toutes. Je me suis rendu sur la tombe de ma mère et de mon père. J'ai hâte que nous soyons réunis. Je crois qu'ils savent quelle torture la putain me fait subir. J'aime l'excitation que je ressens en pensant à tout ce que j'ai fait.

Mais cela est arrivé, une fois seulement, il est vrai que je regrette mes actes. J'ai chassé mes remords instantanément. La putain croit toujours que je ne connais pas l'existence de son maquereau. J'ai songé à le tuer, mais si je le faisais je serais sûrement pris. De cela je n'ai aucun désir, qu'ils soient maudits lui et la putain leur heure viendra.

A mon grand étonnement je ne peux pas croire que je n'aie pas été pris. Mon cœur s'est senti comme s'il avait quitté mon corps glacé de ma peur, j'ai imaginé que mon cœur faisait des bonds dans la rue et que je le suivais au comble du désespoir. J'aurais vraiment adoré couper la tête de ce damné cheval et l'enfoncer aussi loin que possible dans la gorge de la putain. Je n'ai pas eu le temps d'éventrer complètement la garce, je maudis ma déveine. Je crois que l'excitation d'être pris m'a excité encore plus que de découper la putain elle-même. En écrivant ces mots je trouve impossible de croire qu'il ne m'a pas vu, selon mon estimation j'étais à moins de quelques mètres de lui. L'imbécile a paniqué, c'est ce qui m'a sauvé. Ma satisfaction était loin d'être complète, damné salaud, je l'ai maudit encore et encore, mais j'ai été malin, ils n'ont pas pu me surpasser. *Personne* ne le pourra jamais. En un quart d'heure j'ai trouvé une autre sale garce prête à vendre sa marchandise. Cette putain comme toutes les autres en voulait seulement trop. L'excitation qu'elle m'a donnée était différente des autres, j'ai coupé profond profond profond. Son nez m'agaçait alors je l'ai découpé, essayé d'arracher ses yeux, laissé ma marque, pas pu enlever la tête des garces. Je crois maintenant qu'il est impossible d'y arriver. La putain n'a pas poussé un cri. J'ai emporté tout ce que je pouvais avec moi. Je garde une poire pour la soif *ha ha*.

J'enverrai peut-être à Abberline et à Warren un ou deux échantillons, ça descend bien avec un verre de porto après le dîner. Je me demande combien de temps ça se gardera ? La prochaine fois peut-être que je garderai un peu de la substance rouge et que je l'enverrai avec mes compliments sincères. Je me demande s'ils ont apprécié ma drôle de petite blague juive ? Maudite soit ma malchance pas eu le temps d'écrire un drôle de petit poème. Avant ma prochaine en adresserai un autre à Central [1] en souvenir de moi. Mon Dieu la vie est douce. Leur donnerai quelque chose pour qu'ils sachent que c'est moi.

Rouge
Écarlate – tête
cheval
pleuré
respiré haleine

1. Central News Agency : agence de presse. *(N.d.T.)*

* Une rose lutte bien avec le rouge
* J'ai bel et bien coupé la tête
* bon sang ai-je crié, après ça je me suis caché,
* le cheval s'est cabré

Avec une rose pour lutter avec le rouge écarlate
J'ai essayé de détacher la tête
bon sang ai-je crié,
Le cheval s'est cabré
Mais je sentais encore son haleine sucrée

I

Sir Jim,
boîte métallique d'allumettes vide
* étui à cigarettes
* faire vite
* mon couteau étincelant
* le couteau de la putain
première putain pas bien

Une seule putain pas bien,
décidé que Sir Jim en frapperait une autre.
Je n'ai montré aucune peur et en vérité aucune lueur,
bon sang, la boîte métallique était vide.

II

du thé et du sucre
* partir, payer, a dit

moi, appel, être
* du thé et du sucre ont payé mes honoraires
Du sucre et du thé doux, auraient pu servir à payer
mes petits
honoraires ha ha
* puis j'ai dû m'enfuir
Montré mon plaisir
Un rognon pour dîner.

Du sucre et du thé doux,
auraient pu payer mes petits honoraires
Mais à la place j'ai dû m'enfuir
et au fait j'ai montré mon plaisir
En mangeant du rognon froid pour dîner

III

salaud
Abberline
bonnet
cache tout
indice
malin
vous en dirai plus

* M. Abberline est un drôle de petit bonhomme

Oh M. Abberline, c'est un malin petit monsieur
il garde pour lui tout ce qu'il peut
* Mais moi je sais mieux
Car ne sais-je pas mieux, oui c'est indiscutable
ne lui ai-je pas laissé un très bon indice
Rien n'est mentionné, de cela je suis sûr
demandez au malin Abberline.

Oh M. Abberline, c'est un malin petit monsieur
il garde pour lui tout ce qu'il peut.
Car ne sais-je pas mieux, oui c'est indiscutable
ne lui ai-je pas laissé un très bon indice.
Rien n'est mentionné, de cela je suis sûr,
demandez au malin Abberline, pourrait vous en dire
plus

IV

Sir Jim faire un faux pas
peur
l'avoir près
le racheter près
cas
séance tenante

Il croit que je vais faire un faux pas
mais je n'ai pas peur
* Je ne peux pas le racheter ici
Parce qu'il est impossible que je le rachète ici
de ce fait certain, je pourrais lui envoyer très vite
S'il veut que ce soit le cas.

Ne suis-je pas un type malin

Cela devrait faire rire ces imbéciles, c'était le cas pour moi, me demande si le nom que je leur ai donné leur a plu ? J'ai dit qu'il serait sur les lèvres de tous, et en vérité il l'est. Crois que j'en enverrai un autre. Inclurai mon drôle de petit poème. Ça les convaincra que c'est la vérité que je dis. Ce soir, je fêterai ça en invitant George à dîner. Je suis de bonne humeur, crois que je vais autoriser la salope à prendre du plaisir avec son maquereau, remarquerai qu'une soirée en ville lui fera du bien, suggérerai un concert. Je ne doute pas que la voiture conduira la garce tout droit chez lui. J'irai me coucher en pensant à tout ce qu'ils font. A la pensée de cette excitation, je ne tiens pas en place.

Avec une rose pour lutter avec le rouge
J'ai essayé de détacher la tête.
Bon sang ai-je crié,
Le cheval s'est cabré
après ça je me suis caché,
Mais je sentais encore
son haleine sucrée

Une seule putain pas bien, décidé que Sir Jim en frapperait une autre.
Je n'ai montré aucune peur et en vérité aucune lueur.
Bon sang, la boîte métallique était vide

Du sucre et du thé doux
auraient pu servir à payer mes petits honoraires
Mais à la place j'ai dû m'enfuir et j'ai montré mon plaisir
En mangeant du rognon froid pour dîner.

Oh M. Abberline, c'est un malin petit monsieur
il garde pour lui tout ce qu'il peut.
Car ne sais-je pas mieux, oui c'est indiscutable,
ne lui ai-je pas laissé un très bon indice
Rien n'est mentionné, de cela je suis sûr,
demandez au malin Abberline, pourrait vous en dire plus

Il croit que je vais faire un faux pas
mais je n'ai pas peur.

Parce qu'il est impossible
que je le rachète ici
De ce fait certain je pourrais leur envoyer très vite
s'il voulait que ce soit le cas.

Il s'est écoulé trop de temps depuis ma dernière, je n'ai pas été bien. J'ai eu mal dans tout mon corps. Hopper ne m'a pas cru. Un jour je me vengerai sur lui. La putain a informé le crétin bavard. J'ai l'habitude de prendre des médicaments puissants. J'étais furieux quand la garce me l'a dit. Si furieux que je l'ai frappée ha. La putain m'a suppliée de ne pas recommencer. Ça m'a donné du plaisir, un très grand plaisir. Si je n'avais pas mon travail, j'aurais découpé cette garce en morceaux sur-le-champ. Mais je suis malin. Bien que le gentleman se soit rebiffé [1], je n'ai pas exposé mon jeu. Je me suis excusé, un écart exceptionnel, ai-je dit, que je regrettais et j'ai assuré la putain que cela ne se reproduirait jamais. Cette garce stupide m'a cru.

J'ai reçu plusieurs lettres de Michael. Dans toutes il me pose des questions sur ma santé et dans une il m'a demandé si mon somnambulisme avait repris. Pauvre Michael on le berne si facilement. Je l'ai informé que non. J'ai encore froid aux mains. Je vais dîner ce soir. J'espère qu'il y a des rognons au menu, *ha ha.* Histoire de me remettre en forme avant une autre petite escapade. Visiterai bientôt la cité des putains, très bientôt. Je me demande si je pourrais en buter trois ?

---

1. *The gentleman has turned* s'inspire de l'expression *the worm has turned* (« il en a assez de se laisser mener par le bout du nez »). (*N.d.T.*)

Si Michael n'avait pas insisté pour que nous dînions, j'aurais tenté le coup ce soir-là. J'ai maudit mon frère comme jamais auparavant. J'ai maudit ma propre stupidité, si je n'avais pas informé Michael que je n'avais plus de crises de somnambulisme j'ai été forcé de refréner mon plaisir en prenant la dose la plus forte que j'ai jamais prise. La brûlure cette nuit-là a incendié mon esprit. Je me rappelle vaguement avoir placé un mouchoir dans ma bouche pour étouffer mes cris. Je crois que j'ai vomi plusieurs fois. La douleur était intolérable, je tremble rien que d'y penser. Plus jamais.

Je suis convaincu que Dieu m'a placé ici-bas pour tuer toutes les putains, car c'est ce qu'il a dû vouloir, ne suis-je pas toujours là. Rien ne m'arrêtera maintenant. Plus j'en prends plus je me renforce.

Michael avait dans l'idée qu'une fois mon travail terminé je rentrerais à Liverpool le jour même. Et en vérité, c'est ce que j'ai fait un jour plus tard *ha ha*. Je n'ai pas peur, car il ne s'en rendra pas compte puisqu'il adresse toutes ses lettres à moi.

J'ai lu le récit de ma dernière, mon Dieu les pensées, la meilleure de toutes. Je n'ai rien laissé de la garce, rien. J'en ai disposé un peu partout dans la pièce, j'avais du temps devant moi, comme l'autre putain j'ai découpé le nez de la garce, complètement cette fois. Je n'ai rien laissé de son visage, pas le moindre souvenir. Elle m'a rappelé la putain. Si jeune pas comme moi. J'ai trouvé que c'était une bonne farce de découper ses seins, les ai embrassés un moment. Le goût du sang était doux, le plaisir irrésistible, faudra que je recommence, ça m'a tellement excité. Les ai laissés sur la table avec une partie du reste. Pensé qu'ils seraient à leur place là. Il leur fallait un boucher alors j'ai dépiauté tout ce que je pouvais, et ri pendant que je le faisais. Comme les autres garces, elle s'est fendue comme une pêche mûre. Un de ces jours, je réussirai à prendre la tête avec moi. Je la ferai bouillir et la servirai pour mon dîner. La clé et les vêtements brûlés les laissent perplexes *ha ha*.

clé	fendre
fuir	initiale
chapeau	
mouchoir	maquereau
caprice	s'occuper de la putain
Mère	lumière
père	feu

* Avec la clé j'ai pris la clé des champs
J'avais la clé,
Et avec elle j'ai pris la clé des champs
* les vêtements j'ai brûlés
* avec le chapeau
Le chapeau j'ai brûlé
la lumière j'ai cherché
* Pour l'amour de la mère putain
Et j'ai pensé à la mère putain.
J'avais la clé,
Et avec elle j'ai pris la clé des champs.
Le chapeau j'ai brûlé
la lumière j'ai cherché.
Et j'ai pensé à la
mère putain

I

Un mouchoir rougi
conduisait au lit
et j'ai pensé à la mère putain

II

⋆ Car Sir Jim avec son caprice
Un caprice des putains,
A poussé Sir Jim
à couper plus profond, plus profond, plus profond
⋆ avec je suis retourné
⋆ à la mère putain
Tout est retourné,
Comme moi,
à la mère putain.

Un caprice de putain
a poussé Sir Jim
à couper plus profond, plus profond, plus profond.
Tout est retourné,
Comme moi
à la mère putain

III

⋆ Son initiale là
Une initiale ici et une initiale là
désigneraient la mère putain

J'avais une clé,
et avec j'ai pris la clé des champs.
Le chapeau j'ai brûlé,
la lumière j'ai cherché.
Et j'ai pensé à la mère putain

Un mouchoir rougi,
conduisait au lit
Et j'ai pensé à la mère putain.
Un caprice de putain
a poussé Sir Jim,
à couper plus profond, plus profond, plus profond
Tout est retourné,
Comme moi,
à la mère putain.
Une initiale ici et une initiale là
désigneront la mère putain.

Je l'ai laissée sur place pour les imbéciles mais ils ne la trouveront jamais. J'ai été trop malin. L'ai laissée *devant* pour que tous les yeux les voient. Devrais-je leur écrire pour leur dire ? Ça m'amuse. Je me demande si la prochaine fois je pourrai graver mon drôle de petit poème sur la chair de la putain ? Je crois que je tenterai le coup. Au moins, ça m'amuse. La vie est douce, très douce. Regrette de ne pas en avoir emporté avec moi c'est l'heure du dîner, je me taperais bien un ou deux rognons *ha ha.*

Je ne peux pas vivre sans mon médicament. J'ai peur de m'endormir de crainte que mes cauchemars reviennent. Je vois des milliers de gens qui me pourchassent, avec Abberline en tête qui agite une corde. Ils ne me pendront pas de ce fait je suis certain. Il s'est écoulé beaucoup trop de temps depuis ma dernière, je désire encore me venger de la putain et du maquereau mais moins que le désir de répéter ma dernière prestation. Les pensées m'excitent encore tant. Je suis fatigué et j'ai peur que la cité des putains soit devenue trop dangereuse pour que j'y retourne. Noël approche et Thomas m'a invité à lui rendre visite. Je le connais bien. J'ai décidé d'accepter son offre, bien que je sache ce qui se cache derrière, il veut parler affaires un point c'est tout. Thomas ne pense à rien d'autre qu'à l'argent à l'inverse de moi, *ha ha*.

Ma première était à Manchester alors pourquoi pas ma prochaine ? Si je devais faire pareil qu'avec la dernière, ça plongerait les imbéciles dans la panique, surtout cet imbécile d'Abberline. Les enfants me demandent constamment ce que je vais leur acheter pour Noël ils prennent peur quand je leur dis un couteau étincelant pas très différent de celui de Jack l'Éventreur afin que je puisse leur couper la langue pour avoir la paix. Je crois sincèrement que je suis complètement fou. Je n'ai jamais fait de mal aux enfants depuis qu'ils sont nés. Mais maintenant je prends grand plaisir à leur faire peur de cette façon. Que Dieu me pardonne. J'ai perdu mon combat et continuerai jusqu'à ce que je sois pris. Peut-être que je devrais me pendre moi-même pour éviter au bourreau de le faire. A ce moment précis je n'ai aucun sentiment dans mon corps, aucun. Je n'arrête pas de me répéter que je n'ai rien fait de mal. C'est la putain qui l'a fait, pas moi. Trouverai-je jamais la tranquillité d'esprit ? J'ai rendu visite à Hopper trop souvent ce mois-ci. Il va falloir que j'arrête, car j'ai peur qu'il ne commence à soupçonner. Je lui parle à lui comme à personne d'autre.

---

* Sir Jim va,
Suis-je aliéné ?
canne, gain
* Sir Jim avec sa drôle de canne
* Va encore frapper bientôt

* Une putain au paradis
* deux putains côte à côte
* trois putains sont toutes mortes
* quatre

* Sir Jim il les découpe d'abord
bon sang

* Abberline dit qu'il est maintenant stupéfait,
* Sir Jim n'en a pas frappé une autre
* Il attend patiemment
* pour voir rapidement

* Noël sauve le bonnet de taupe des putains
* damnées soient les garces   damné soit Michael
* Donnez son dû à Sir Jim
* Il déteste tous les Juifs
* Car parmi les hommes il n'a pas de favori
* Quand il se hâte vers son abri.

* Il aime écrire avec sa plume
* Donnez son dû à Sir Jim

* Il déteste tous les Juifs
* et en vérité n'était-ce pas d----s

* Je les ai embrassés,
* Je les ai embrassés
* Leur goût était si doux
* J'ai pensé les laisser près des pieds des putains
* mais sur la table il y avait rien
* Alors je suis parti et les ai laissés là

bon sang bon sang bon sang

si Dieu le veut ma prochaine sera de loin la pire, ma tête me fait mal, mais je continuerai maudit soit Michael d'être si malin l'art de la poésie est loin d'être simple. Je le maudis tellement. Abberline Abberline, je finirai par démolir cet imbécile, si Dieu le veut. Bannis-le de mes pensées, il n'est pas près d'attraper Sir Jim

Abberline Abberline Abberline Abberline
Que le diable emporte ce salaud

J'ai froid maudit soit ce salaud de Lowry qui m'a poussé à éventrer. Je n'arrête pas de voir des flots de sang jaillir de ces garces. Les cauchemars sont abominables. Je ne peux pas m'empêcher de vouloir en manger encore. Que Dieu me vienne en aide, va au diable. Non personne ne m'arrêtera. Que Dieu aille au diable.

Réfléchis réfléchis réfléchis écris dis-leur à tous prouve-leur que tu es qui tu dis que tu es fais-les croire que c'est la vérité que je dis. Qu'il aille au diable pour les avoir créées, qu'il aille au diable au diable au diable. Je veux faire bouillir bouillir bouillir. Voir si les yeux leur sortent de la tête. J'ai besoin de plus d'excitation, ne peux pas vivre sans mes frissons. Je continuerai, je continuerai, rien ne m'arrêtera rien. Coupe Sir Jim coupe. Coupe profond profond profond.

* Sir Jim les découpera toutes
Oh coûteux rapports
de mort

Bannis les pensées bannis-les bannis-les ha ha ha,
tourne-toi vers le frère raisonnable
Des poulets qui tournent en rond avec la tête coupée

ha ha ha ha ha ha ha ha ha
Ne suis-je pas un type malin
les ai tous rusés, ils ne sauront jamais

* Sir Jim les découpera toutes
* Sir Jim il marche la tête si haute

* Sir Jim rend une petite visite
* il les découpe toutes,
* avec son couteau dans son sac

devrai trouver à me loger lors de ma prochaine visite. Middlesex Street c'était une sacrée blague. Les imbéciles, plusieurs fois ils auraient pu m'attraper s'ils avaient bien regardé. Mon Dieu ne suis-je pas malin ? En vérité je le suis. La tête me tourne va pourtant me falloir trouver la force de rentrer à la maison. Que le diable emporte cette ville, il y fait trop froid pour moi. Demain je ferai souffrir Lowry. La pensée m'excitera pendant mon voyage de retour.

Je ne peux pas me résoudre à me relire, tout ce que j'ai écrit m'effraie tellement. George m'a rendu visite aujourd'hui. Je crois qu'il sait ce que j'endure, bien qu'il ne dise rien. Je le vois dans ses yeux. Pauvre George, c'est un si bon ami. Michael va bien, il écrit une joyeuse mélodie. Au fond de mon cœur je ne peux pas le lui reprocher. Je regrette de ne pas le voir à Noël cette année.

Rencontré un vieil ami à la Halle. J'ai éprouvé du regret car n'était-il pas juif. J'avais oublié combien j'ai d'amis juifs. Je me venge sur les putains, pas sur les Juifs. Je crois sincèrement que je regrette vraiment la crainte que j'ai semée parmi eux. Je crois que c'est la raison pour laquelle je suis incapable d'écrire mes drôles de petits poèmes. Je remercie Dieu de m'avoir donné le courage d'arrêter de les envoyer. Je suis convaincu qu'ils causeront ma perte.

Je suis fatigué, très fatigué. J'aspire à la paix, mais je sais bien au fond que je continuerai. Je serai à Manchester d'ici quelques jours. Je crois que je me sentirai beaucoup mieux quand j'aurai répété ma dernière prestation. Je me demande si je peux apporter des améliorations à mes actes diaboliques. Je verrai bien, nul doute que je penserai à quelque chose. Le jour tire à sa fin, Lowry était de bonne humeur. Je suis satisfait. Je regrette, car j'ai montré ma colère avec mes amis juifs. A Noël je ferai amende honorable.

Cette garce, cette putain n'est pas satisfaite avec un seul maquereau, maintenant elle lorgne un autre. Je n'ai pas pu découper comme ma dernière, je n'arrêtais pas de la revoir en frappant. J'ai essayé de réprimer toutes pensées d'amour. Je l'ai laissée pour morte, ça je le sais. Ça ne m'a pas amusé. Il y a eu de l'excitation. J'ai déchaîné ma fureur sur la garce.

J'ai frappé encore et encore. Je ne sais pas comment je me suis arrêté. Je l'ai laissée sans un sou, je n'ai pas de regrets. Cette putain va souffrir comme elle n'a jamais souffert. Que Dieu ait pitié d'elle car, moi je n'en aurai pas, je le jure.

Thomas était en bonne santé. Les enfants se sont bien amusés à Noël. Pas moi. Mon humeur n'est plus noire, bien que j'aie mal à la tête. Je ne m'habituerai jamais à la douleur. Je maudis l'hiver. J'attends avec impatience mon mois favori, ça me ferait tant plaisir de voir les fleurs tout épanouies. C'est de chaleur que j'ai besoin, je tremble tant. Maudit soit ce temps et cette putain de garce. J'ai été trop tendre. Toutes les putains sentiront le tranchant du couteau étincelant de Sir Jim. Je regrette de ne pas m'être donné ce nom, quelle malédiction, je le préfère de beaucoup à celui que je leur ai donné.

Sir Jim avec son couteau étincelant,
passe la nuit à découper,
et au nom de Dieu,
ne montre-t-il pas sa puissance *ha ha*

Il ne se passera pas longtemps avant que je frappe de nouveau. J'en prends plus que jamais. La garce peut en prendre deux, Sir Jim en prendra quatre, un double double événement *ha ha.* Si j'étais dans la cité des putains j'accomplirais mes actes diaboliques séance tenante. Au nom de Dieu je le ferais.

Je me maudis d'avoir été si bête, je n'aurai plus de regrets, qu'ils aillent tous au diable. Attention M. Abberline je reviendrai me venger pour de bon. Une fois de plus, on ne parlera que de moi en Angleterre. Mes pensées me donnent tant de plaisir. Je me demande si la putain prendra le salaud ? Il peut se la faire cette garce. Je penserai à leurs actes, quel plaisir. Ce soir je me récompenserai, je rendrai visite à la mienne, mais je ne serai pas doux. Je vais montrer à ma putain ce dont je suis capable. Sir Jim a besoin d'aiguiser son appétit, que toutes les putains aillent au diable. Un ami s'est rebiffé, qu'il en soit ainsi, Sir Jim se rebiffera une fois de plus. Quand j'aurai terminé mes actes diaboliques, le diable lui-même me félicitera. Mais il lui faudra attendre longtemps pour que je lui serre la main. J'ai des travaux à faire beaucoup de travaux *ha ha* du rognon pour le dîner.

Je suis las de feindre la respectabilité. Je trouve ça de plus en plus difficile. Je crois que je suis un chanceux. N'ai-je pas trouvé une nouvelle source d'approvisionnement pour mon médicament. Je savoure à l'avance les pensées qu'il va m'apporter. J'aime penser aux putains qui attendent mon joli couteau étincelant. Ce soir j'écris à Michael. L'informer que je me rendrais bientôt dans la cité des putains, très bientôt. Je meurs d'impatience. La putain peut prendre autant de maquereaux qu'elle le souhaite. Je ne m'inquiète plus. Je pense avec plaisir aux actes à venir, et oh quels actes je vais commettre. Bien, bien plus raffinés que mes derniers. En vérité la vie est douce, très très douce.

Cher M. Abberline
Je suis un chanceux
La prochaine fois je ferai tout ce que je peux
* enfoncer, pouvoir, attiser, damner
* frapper de la pointe et du tranchant
avec une petite coupure ici,

et une petite coupure là
je m'en retournerai en riant
vers mon repaire
Cher M. Abberline,
Je suis un chanceux
La prochaine fois je ferai
tout ce que je peux.
avec une petite coupure ici
et une petite coupure là
je m'en retournerai en riant
vers mon repaire

Bon sang bon sang bon sang ce salaud m'a presque attrapé, qu'il soit maudit qu'il aille au diable, la prochaine fois je le découperai en morceaux, je le jure devant Dieu. Quelques minutes et je l'aurais fait, *salaud*. Je m'en vais le dénicher, lui donner une leçon. Personne ne m'arrêtera. Que son âme noire soit maudite. Je me maudis d'avoir frappé trop tôt, j'aurai dû attendre que tout soit vraiment calme je le jure devant Dieu j'emporterai tout la prochaine fois et je le *mangerai*. Ne laisserai *rien* pas même la tête. Je la ferai bouillir et je la mangerai avec des carottes nouvelles. Je penserai à Abberline en le faisant, ça me fera bien rire *ha ha* la putain va souffrir ce soir pour ce qu'elle a fait.

La garce a tout révélé
ce soir elle va tomber

Je le jure devant Dieu je vais découper cette garce et la servir aux enfants. Comment cette putain ose-t-elle écrire à Michael, cette maudite garce n'avait aucun droit de l'informer de mon médicament. Si j'en fais à ma drôle de petite tête la putain sera servie à table ce soir même. Je ne me suis pas laissé faire et j'ai informé Michael que c'était un maudit mensonge.

La garce se rend bientôt en visite dans la cité des putains, j'ai décidé d'attendre le bon moment alors je frapperai de toute ma puissance. J'achèterai quelque chose à la putain pour sa visite. Donnerai à cette garce l'impression que je considère qu'il est de son devoir d'aller rendre visite à sa tante. Elle peut jouer la garde-malade avec la garce malade et voir son maquereau *ha ha.*

Ha, quelle farce, laisser la garce croire que je n'ai pas connaissance de ses petites affaires de putain. Quand elle reviendra, cette putain paiera. Je me réjouis à la pensée de frapper cette garce une fois de plus. Ne suis-je pas un type malin. Je suis fier que personne ne sache combien je suis malin. Je crois sincèrement que si George devait lire ceci, il dirait que je suis l'homme le plus malin du monde. J'adorerais lui dire combien j'ai été malin, mais je ne le ferai pas, ma campagne est loin d'être terminée. Sir Jim ne révélera rien, rien. Comment peuvent-ils m'arrêter maintenant que ce Sir Jim va peut-être vivre éternellement. Je me sens fort, très fort, assez fort pour frapper dans cette maudite cité si froide, crois que je vais le faire. Pourquoi pas, personne ne soupçonne le gentleman né. Verrai comment je vais me sentir pendant mon voyage de retour vers la maison, si le caprice s'empare de moi alors ainsi soit-il. Devrai faire attention à ne pas mettre trop de substance rouge sur moi. Peut-être que je ne couperai qu'une fois, pour berner les imbéciles, oh quelle farce, encore plus de poulets courant dans tous les sens avec la tête coupée, *ha ha.* Je me sens malin.

Sir Jim [1]
vivra peut-être

---

1. *Sir Jimay* est une contraction de *Sir Jim may* (il est possible que Sir Jim...). (*N.d.T.*)

éternellement
ha ha ha ha ha

Ce malin Sir Jim
il adore ses caprices
ce soir il se présentera
et tout emportera. *ha ha ha ha*

Ne suis-je pas un type malin, la garce m'a donné le plus grand plaisir possible. La putain n'a-t-elle pas vu son maquereau devant tout le monde, certes la course était la plus rapide que j'ai vue, mais l'excitation de voir la putain avec le salaud m'a plus excité que de savoir que son Altesse Royale était à peine à quelques mètres de votre humble serviteur ha ha quelle farce, si ce salaud trop gourmand aurait su qu'il était à moins de quelques mètres du nom dont toute l'Angleterre parlait il serait mort sur le coup. Regrette de n'avoir pas pu le dire à ce stupide imbécile. Au diable la souveraineté, au diable toutes les putains, au diable la garce qui règne.

* Victoria la garce
* Reine idiote Sir Jack sait tout
* La reine elle sait tout

Victoria, Victoria
Qui est leur reine à tous
Au sujet de Sir Jack
Elle ne sait rien du tout

I

* Elle sait qu'un jour
qui sait,
peut-être un jour
Je lui rendrai visite

II

* Couteau étincelant
* ma vie
* honorez mon couteau
Je lui montrerai mon couteau
et elle m'honorera pour la vie

III

* Venez Sir Jim dira-t-elle
Levez-vous Sir Jack [1] dira-t-elle
et maintenant vous pouvez partir,
je vous le perMAY ha ha ha
ha ha ha ha

Victoria, Victoria
Qui est leur reine à tous
Au sujet de Sir Jack
elle ne sait rien du tout

qui sait,
Peut-être qu'un jour,
Je lui rendrai visite
Je lui montrerai mon couteau
et elle m'honorera pour la vie.

---

1. Jack est une variante de Jim. (*N.d.T.*)

Levez-vous Sir Jack dira-t-elle
et maintenant vous pouvez partir
je vous le per*MAY*

Jim, Jack Jack Jim ha ha ha

J'ai été malin. George serait fier de moi, dit à la garce que dans ma position je ne pouvais pas me permettre un scandale. Je l'ai frappée plusieurs fois œil pour œil, *ha ha* trop de serviteurs qui se mêlent de ce qui ne les regarde pas, au diable les garces. Hopper va bientôt sentir le tranchant de mon couteau étincelant, au diable l'intrigant ébahi, qu'ils aillent tous au diable. Une fois de plus la garce a des dettes, mon Dieu je vais la découper. Oh comme je vais bien la découper. Je me rendrai dans la cité des putains je paierai ce qu'elle doit et je réclamerai mon dû, au nom de Dieu je le ferai. Je m'en vais éventrer éventrer éventrer. Je dénicherai peut-être le salaud qui a interrompu mes drôles de petits jeux et je l'éventrerai lui aussi. J'ai dit qu'il paierait. Et bon sang il va payer, je ferai ce qu'il faut pour. Je sens que mon corps est engourdi, les putains paieront pour ça. Je me demande si Edwin va bien ? J'attends avec impatience qu'il revienne. J'ai décidé que la prochaine fois j'arracherai les yeux de la putain et que je les enverrai à cet imbécile d'Abberline,

salaud
salaud

enlever les yeux
enlever la tête
les laisser toutes pour mortes

Ça ne m'amuse pas. Maudit soit ce salaud d'Abberline, qu'il aille en enfer je ne me balancerai pas au bout d'une de ses cordes. J'ai souvent pensé à la putain et à son maquereau.

Ces pensées m'excitent encore. Peut-être qu'un jour la garce m'autorisera à participer. Pourquoi pas ? Ils l'ont tous prise. N'ai-je pas droit à la putain. Je souhaite le faire.

La garce
　　la garce
　　　　la garce

Fuller croit que je n'ai pas vraiment de problème. Étrange, les pensées qu'il a placées dans mon esprit. Je n'ai pas pu frapper, je crois que je suis fou, complètement fou. J'essaie de combattre mes pensées je parcours les rues jusqu'à l'aube. Je n'ai pas eu le cœur de frapper, des visions de ma chère Bunny m'accablent. Je l'aime encore, mais comme je la hais. Elle a tout détruit et pourtant mon cœur souffre pour elle, oh comme mon cœur souffre. Je ne sais pas quelle souffrance est la pire mon corps ou mon esprit.

Dieu que je suis fatigué, je ne sais pas si je peux continuer. Bunny et les enfants sont tout ce qui compte. Pas de regrets, pas de regrets. Je ne permettrai pas que de telles pensées entrent dans ma tête. Ce soir je prendrai mon couteau étincelant et je m'en débarrasserai. Le jetterai au plus profond du fleuve. Quand je rentrerai à Battlecrease, je saurai que je ne peux plus continuer ma campagne. C'est l'amour qui m'a éconduit, et c'est l'amour qui y mettra un terme.

J'ai peur de relire tout ce que j'ai écrit. Il serait peut-être plus sage de détruire ceci, mais je n'ai pas le cœur de m'y résoudre. J'ai déjà essayé une fois, mais lâche comme je suis, je n'ai pas pu. Peut-être que dans mon esprit tourmenté je souhaite que quelqu'un lise ces pages et comprenne que l'homme que je suis devenu n'était pas l'homme que j'étais à ma naissance. Mon cher frère Edwin est revenu. J'aimerais pouvoir tout lui raconter. Plus de drôles de petits poèmes. Ce soir, je parle d'amour.

c'est l'amour qui m'a éconduit
c'est l'amour qui détruit
c'est l'amour auquel j'aspire
c'est l'amour qu'elle a éconduit
c'est l'amour qui causera ma perte
c'est l'amour que je regrette

Que Dieu me vienne en aide. Je prie chaque soir pour qu'il m'emporte, la déception quand je me réveille est difficile à décrire. Je ne prends plus de la substance redoutable de peur de faire du mal à ma chère Bunny, pire encore aux enfants.

Je n'ai pas le courage de me supprimer. Je prie chaque soir pour trouver la force de le faire, mais le courage m'échappe. Je prie constamment pour que tous pardonnent. Je regrette profondément de l'avoir frappée, j'ai trouvé dans mon cœur la force de lui pardonner ses amants.

Je crois que je vais tout lui raconter, lui demander de me pardonner comme je lui ai pardonné. Je prie Dieu pour qu'elle comprenne ce qu'elle m'a fait. Ce soir je prierai pour les femmes que j'ai massacrées. Que Dieu me pardonne pour les actes que j'ai commis sur Kelly   pas de cœur   pas de cœur.

La douleur est insupportable. Ma chère Bunny sait tout. Je ne sais pas si elle a la force de me tuer. Je prie Dieu pour qu'elle la trouve. Ce serait simple, elle connaît mon médicament, et avec une dose ou deux de plus tout serait fini. Personne ne saura que j'y ai moi-même pourvu. George connaît mon habitude et je ne doute pas que Michael en ait bientôt vent. En vérité, je crois qu'il est au courant. Michael saura comment agir c'est lui le plus raisonnable de nous tous. Je ne crois pas que je verrai le mois de juin, de tous les mois mon favori. Ai supplié Bunny d'agir bientôt, je me maudis d'être si lâche. J'ai rétabli l'équilibre dans mon testament. Bunny et les enfants auront ce qu'il leur faut et je fais confiance à Michael et à Thomas pour exécuter mes souhaits.

Bientôt, je ne doute pas qu'on m'étendra à côté de ma chère mère et de mon cher père. Je chercherai à obtenir leur pardon quand nous serons réunis. Je prie pour que Dieu m'accorde au moins ce dernier privilège, même si je ne sais que trop que je ne le mérite pas. Mes pensées demeureront intactes, pour rappeler à tous comment l'amour peut détruire. Je place maintenant ceci dans un endroit où on le trouvera. Je prie pour que quiconque lira ces pages ait le cœur de me pardonner. Rappelez à tous, qui que vous soyez, que j'étais autrefois un gentleman. Que le Seigneur ait pitié de mon âme, et me pardonne tout ce que j'ai fait.

Je donne mon nom que tous me connaissent, que l'histoire dise, ce que l'amour peut faire à un gentleman né.

Votre humble serviteur
Jack l'Éventreur
en ce troisième jour de mai 1889

SHIRLEY HARRISON

LE DOSSIER

Cette deuxième partie, le Dossier, présente l'enquête menée par Shirley Harrison et qui défend la thèse de l'authencité ainsi que l'identification de Jack l'Éventeur comme James Maybrick.

Chapitre 1

Un jour de mai 1889, en fin d'après-midi, trois médecins se retrouvèrent à Aigburth, faubourg cossu de Liverpool, afin d'y procéder à une autopsie peu habituelle. Dans une chambre décorée de panne rouge et d'acajou, étendu sur le lit où la mort l'avait surpris, gisait le corps d'un homme d'affaires entre deux âges. A côté, dans la pièce voisine, sa jeune veuve bouleversée, traumatisée, semblait proche de défaillir. Sous l'œil vigilant d'un commissaire de police, deux des médecins entreprirent de disséquer le cadavre et d'examiner les organes du mort, pendant que le troisième prenait des notes.

Le cerveau, le cœur et les poumons, normaux d'apparence, furent aussitôt réintégrés à leur place. Toutefois, le tube digestif montrait une légère inflammation et on pouvait observer un ulcère de petite taille sur le larynx, ainsi qu'une érosion au sommet de l'épiglotte. Aussi l'estomac, noué à chaque extrémité, les intestins, la rate et certaines parties du foie réservés dans des bocaux furent remis à un inspecteur de police.

Environ deux semaines plus tard, les trois médecins eurent à se rendre au cimetière où le corps du défunt avait été inhumé. Arrivés peu avant minuit, ils attendirent, autour du tumulus fraîchement retourné, sous la lumière jaune de lampes à naphte, que les fossoyeurs aient fini de déterrer le cercueil.

Puis, sans même retirer le corps de la bière, ils en prélevèrent le cerveau, le cœur, les poumons, les reins et la langue et ce, en vue d'analyses approfondies.

Finalement, les services compétents arrivèrent à la conclusion que James Maybrick, cinquante ans, marchand de coton bien connu à Liverpool et qui se rendait souvent à Londres pour ses affaires, avait été victime d'un « empoisonnement irritant » du système nerveux, dans le langage médical du XIXe siècle. S'il était impossible de spécifier la nature de la substance incriminée, il y avait eu indiscutablement assassinat. Quant à l'identité du meurtrier, elle ne faisait guère de doute.

Au mois d'août suivant, à l'issue d'un procès à sensation qui fascina tout autant la Grande-Bretagne que les États-Unis, la veuve de Maybrick, Florie, âgée de vingt-six ans, fut reconnue coupable de meurtre et condamnée à mort. De fait elle avait été la première femme américaine a être jugée par un tribunal britannique.

Londres, le 9 novembre 1888, soit six mois avant le décès de Maybrick. En cette fin de matinée, une foule bruyante se pressait pour admirer sur son passage le carrosse d'or, clou des célébrations traditionnelles qui de nos jours encore saluent l'investiture annuelle d'un nouveau *Lord Mayor*.

Traversant à la hâte les rues de Whitechapel, quartier sordide de l'East End, Thomas Bowyer venait d'arriver chez Mary Jane Kelly, la locataire du 13 Miller's Court, pour percevoir un loyer en retard.

Quand Bowyer frappa à la porte, il n'entendit pas de réponse. Après avoir passé le bras à travers la vitre brisée, il écarta la toile jaunie qui servait de rideau et glissa un œil à l'intérieur du taudis pitoyable qui abritait Mary Jane Kelly.

Sur le lit ensanglanté, reposait ce qui avait été le corps d'une jeune femme.

Une fine chemise en cachait à peine la nudité. D'évidence, on avait tenté de décoller la tête. L'abdomen, béant, avait été éventré; le nez, les seins et les oreilles, découpés; les lambeaux de peau arrachés au visage et aux cuisses reposaient avec les reins, le foie et d'autres organes disposés autour du cadavre écorché. Au centre du visage mutilé, méconnaissable, fixes et emplis de terreur, les yeux étaient demeurés grands ouverts.

Mary Jane Kelly était la dernière victime en date du monstre qui, depuis la fin du mois d'août, massacrait des prostituées. Les meurtres avaient tous eu lieu durant le week-end et dans le même périmètre, à peine 1,5 km^2, de ces rues sordides et surpeuplées qui constituait l'une des zones les plus démunies de Londres. Les femmes avaient été étranglées, tailladées et enfin dépecées au cours d'agressions de plus en plus brutales.

Mary Ann Nichols dite « Polly », la première victime, était fille de serrurier. Agée d'une quarantaine d'années, elle était allée d'hospice en hospice. Avaient suivi Annie Chapman, quarante-sept ans, Elizabeth Stride, quarante-quatre ans, et Catherine Eddowes, quarante-six ans. Il fallait maintenant ajouter à cette liste Mary Jane Kelly. A vingt-cinq ans, c'était la plus jeune de toutes.

Pour atroces que fussent ces crimes, on les aurait peut-être oubliés ou mis au compte des risques inhérents à la prostitution si le meurtrier n'avait pas nargué la police à coups de notes et d'indices, et s'il ne s'était pas, dans une lettre moqueuse et infamante, donné un surnom qui, chaque fois qu'on l'entendait prononcer, faisait tressaillir tout Londres et au-delà : Jack l'Éventreur.

Il aura fallu attendre un siècle pour qu'en 1991, nous parvienne du passé un journal intime qui permet de relier de manière spectaculaire et inattendue James Maybrick aux meurtres de Whitechapel. Certes, de nombreuses interrogations restent entières : où le journal intime attribué à Maybrick est-il resté caché pendant tout ce temps ? Comment a-t-il été découvert ? A défaut de réponses précises, et comme pour ajouter à la complexité de son histoire, c'est de manière tout aussi paradoxale que ce journal est arrivé entre les mains de Mike Barrett, un gaillard de Liverpool.

Si l'on excepte la période durant laquelle il a sillonné les océans pour la marine marchande et un séjour sur une plate-forme pétrolière, Mike a passé toute sa vie à Liverpool, où il a travaillé comme cuisinier, puis comme ferrailleur. Et c'est au Centre culturel irlandais de la ville qu'il a rencontré sa femme Anne, il y a de cela dix-sept ans. Quelques semaines leur ont suffi pour décider de se marier.

Mais la maladie a contraint Mike à cesser de travailler. Il s'est alors consacré à l'éducation de leur fille, Caroline, aujourd'hui âgée de onze ans. Pour sa part, Anne avait un emploi de secrétaire. De temps en temps, Mike aidait Caroline à entretenir le minuscule jardin sur lequel donnait la cuisine. Un jardin qui regorgeait de fleurs, car le rêve de Mike, c'était de posséder une serre.

Lorsqu'il allait chercher Caroline à l'école, il faisait souvent halte au Saddle, ce pub accueillant qui n'a guère changé depuis l'époque de James Maybrick. Il aimait à y déguster une pinte de bière en discutant avec son copain Tony Devereux. Mais Tony a lui aussi été victime d'un coup du sort : en 1990, à Noël, il s'est fracturé la hanche. Solidaire, Mike est alors devenu son bon Samaritain. Il faisait les courses de Tony et se chargeait d'autres menues tâches quotidiennes. Quelques mois plus tard, en arrivant chez Tony, il a vu sur la table un paquet enveloppé dans du papier d'emballage.

« Prends-le. Je veux que ce soit toi qui l'aies. Tâche d'en faire quelque chose. » Tony n'a rien dit de plus.

Mike a rapporté le paquet chez lui et l'a ouvert avec Anne. A l'intérieur se trouvait un mince volume qui allait changer le cours de leur existence. Cela ressemblait à un album victorien, avec une demi-reliure en cuir de veau noir, sans titre, et dont le dos portait sept nerfs en feuilles d'or. De très bonne qualité, la reliure et le papier étaient bien préservés. A en juger par les taches de colle et les traces oblongues qui subsistaient sur la feuille de garde, ce livre avait servi à conserver des cartes postales, des photographies, des autographes et autres petits souvenirs. Les quarante-huit premières pages avaient été découpées à l'aide d'un couteau. Suivaient soixante-trois pages manuscrites, qui contenaient le texte le plus extraordinaire que Mike ait jamais lu. Le ton passait du larmoyant au frénétique, et de nombreuses lignes avaient été furieusement biffées.

Anne et Mike se sont installés sur le sofa de leur salon, et Mike s'est mis à lire, pendant que son épouse l'écoutait. Ils furent, tous deux, profondément impressionnés, par des révélations, dont l'écriture inégale renforçait la violence des mots.

> La prochaine fois j'emporterai tout et je le *mangerai*. Ne laisserai *rien* pas même la tête. Je la ferai bouillir et je la mangerai avec des carottes nouvelles.

> Le goût du sang était doux, le plaisir irrésistible.

A la fin du journal, le ton s'adoucissait :

> Ce soir, je parle d'amour.
> C'est l'amour qui m'a motivé,
> c'est l'amour qui détruit.

A la dernière page, Anne et Mike purent lire ces mots :

Bientôt, je ne doute pas qu'on m'étendra à côté de ma chère mère et de mon cher père. Je chercherai à obtenir leur pardon quand nous serons réunis. Je prie pour que Dieu m'accorde au moins ce dernier privilège, même si je ne sais que trop que je ne le mérite pas. Mes pensées demeureront intactes, pour rappeler à tous comment l'amour peut détruire. Je place maintenant ceci dans un endroit où on le trouvera. Je prie pour que quiconque lira ces pages ait le cœur de me pardonner. Rappelez à tous, qui que vous soyez, que j'étais autrefois un gentleman. Que le Seigneur ait pitié de mon âme, et me pardonne tout ce que j'ai fait.
Je donne mon nom que tous me connaissent, que l'histoire dise, ce que l'amour peut faire à un gentleman né.
Votre humble serviteur
Jack l'Éventreur
en ce troisième jour de mai 1889.

« Je n'oublierai jamais l'expression de Mike », s'est souvenue Anne. « C'était cette signature – comme si un couteau venait de rentrer en moi, avoua Mike. Mais je ne l'ai pas cru. Qui pourrait croire une chose pareille ? »

Il téléphona immédiatement à Tony : « Qu'est-ce que c'est que cette plaisanterie ? » Son ami lui a seulement répondu : « Ne me pose pas de questions. »

Se pouvait-il vraiment que Mike Barrett ait la solution de l'un des plus grands mystères criminels de tous les temps ? Il a relu le journal, encore et encore, essayant de reconstituer l'existence d'un homme en apparence respectable, père affectueux, commerçant d'un certain âge, brisé par une double vie vouée à la drogue et à la perversion.

Cet homme à l'âme dépravée, qui ne signait de son vrai nom nulle part dans le journal, se vantait de traquer ses victimes, puis de les assassiner et de les mutiler. Mais tout comme Jack l'Éventreur avait joué au chat et à la souris avec la police – en laissant des indices sur le lieu de ses crimes ou en envoyant des lettres à la presse –, l'auteur du journal y avait également semé des indices sur son identité. Dès la seconde page, par exemple, il écrivait :

Je rentrerai peut-être à Battlecrease.

« J'ai acheté tous les livres sur Jack l'Éventreur que je pouvais trouver, raconta Mike, et j'ai passé des heures à la bibliothèque pour essayer de voir si le journal correspondait à des faits établis. Et puis un jour j'ai lu un livre de Richard Whittington Egan intitulé *Meurtre, mutilation et mystère.* Il était consacré au crime à Liverpool, et le nom " Battlecrease House " figurait dans un compte rendu de l'affaire Maybrick. »

« Battlecrease » était le nom connu de beaucoup d'habitants de Liverpool comme celui d'une demeure qui fut le théâtre du tragique destin d'un couple. James et Florie Maybrick s'étaient installés dans cet hôtel particulier d'Aigburth, plaisant faubourg de Liverpool, durant ce qui allait être leur dernière et très agitée année de vie commune. Se pouvait-il, s'interrogea Mike, que le James Maybrick qu'on avait cru assassiné par sa femme fût lui-même l'un des meurtriers parmi les plus craints et les plus dangereux de l'histoire ? Se pouvait-il que le journal qui se trouvait désormais entre ses mains fasse le lien entre ces deux affaires abominables ?

Les recherches de Mike étaient tellement approfondies et détaillées qu'il pensa que, si un faussaire les avait récemment entreprises avec autant de soin que lui, la coïncidence était vraiment étrange. De plus pourquoi Tony ne voulait-il pas en tirer le moindre profit ? Mais s'il était authentique, comment avait-il pu rester ignoré pendant toutes ces années ? Et comment Tony en avait-il hérité ?

« Le lendemain, je suis allé chez Tony et je lui ai

demandé à quel drôle de jeu il s'amusait, déclara Mike. Mais il n'a rien voulu me dire, et il s'est contenté de répéter : " Je sais qu'il est authentique. Tâche d'en faire quelque chose. " Il n'a pas voulu me dire d'où venait le journal, ni depuis combien de temps il l'avait. Mais je lui ai fait confiance. Il n'avait pas de raison de me mettre dans l'embarras. »

Tony Devereux est mort d'une crise cardiaque avant que Mike n'ait eu le temps de lui poser plus de questions sur cette énigme. Désormais en proie à une véritable obsession, soir après soir, les noms mentionnés dans le journal venaient hanter Mike, tels des revenants arrachés aux griffes d'un sinistre passé victorien. Il y avait « Bunny », ainsi que Maybrick surnommait son épouse volage; George, l'ami loyal; Michael, le frère prospère mais perfide; Edwin, le frère en apparence loyal; Gladys et « Bobo », les enfants tant chéris; et Lowry, l'employé indiscret.

Alors, Mike poursuivit des recherches de plus en plus approfondies, avec l'intention d'écrire lui-même l'histoire du journal. A la bibliothèque, il passa des heures à visionner des articles de journaux microfilmés. Il lut et travailla toutes les nuits : « Depuis ce moment-là, je n'ai pas connu une seule nuit de sommeil complète. Le journal a presque détruit ma vie et mon mariage. Dieu merci, Anne a une patience d'ange et elle m'a épaulé tout le long du chemin. »

Mais finalement Mike s'aperçut qu'il n'était pas de taille à résoudre cette énigme. Il voulait tenir la promesse qu'il avait faite à Tony, mais il ne savait pas comment s'y prendre pour authentifier le journal, ou pour le faire publier. Il a donc téléphoné à une maison d'édition londonienne, et il a invité le directeur littéraire à se rendre à Liverpool pour lire le document. Les éditeurs londoniens ne s'enthousiasment pas facilement. Les personnes qui font la prétendue découverte du siècle sont en effet très nombreuses.

« Trouvez-vous un agent littéraire », a-t-il conseillé à

Mike. Et il lui recommanda Doreen Montgomery, de la Société Rupert Crew à Londres. C'est ainsi qu'un jour du printemps 1992, Mike a pris le train en gare de Liverpool à la station Lime Street... tout comme James Maybrick l'avait fait plus d'un siècle auparavant. Le jour même, Doreen Montgomery, mon agent littéraire depuis près de vingt ans, m'a demandé de rencontrer Mike. Elle avait des doutes sur cette incroyable histoire et souhaitait avoir l'avis d'une spécialiste en enquêtes-reportages.

Mike plaça le journal sur le bureau de Doreen, au milieu d'une pile de manuscrits, puis, non sans nervosité, nous regarda pendant que nous tournions lentement les pages, glacées d'horreur. Notre lecture terminée, nous avons ensuite discuté avec lui de ce que nous venions de découvrir, Doreen et moi nous efforçant de conserver notre sang-froid.

La logique nous dictait trois possibilités :

1) il s'agissait d'un faux, écrit peu de temps après les meurtres ou dans les années suivantes;

2) c'était le produit des fantasmes de James Maybrick, qui se prenait pour Jack l'Éventreur;

3) nous étions devant un authentique et James Maybrick était Jack l'Éventreur.

Doreen et moi restions sur nos gardes, pensant en particulier aux « carnets d'Hitler », qui avaient causé tant d'embarras en 1982. Après leur publication, des tests avaient en effet établi que le papier contenait des fibres de nylon et un produit chimique utilisé pour renforcer la blancheur. Or, aucune de ces deux substances n'avait été employée dans la fabrication du papier avant 1950.

Agissant par impulsion, Mike et moi avons porté le journal au British Museum, le meilleur endroit à mon sens où nous pouvions trouver un avis éclairé. Mais l'authentification du journal se révéla plus difficile que nous ne le pensions.

L'entrée principale du British Museum est monumentale et l'intérieur est également très impressionnant :

des millions de volumes tapissent les murs et un silence religieux enveloppe le visiteur. C'est donc là que l'authenticité du journal a été mise à l'épreuve pour la première fois, devant un aréopage d'historiens d'un âge respectable, spécialistes des manuscrits, qui en ont étudié les pages à la loupe.

« Fascinant, a déclaré Robert Smith, le conservateur de la section consacrée aux manuscrits du XIXe siècle. Tout à fait extraordinaire. Il a l'air authentique. Mais il faut que vous le fassiez examiner par un expert légal. Nous ne disposons pas du matériel nécessaire ici. »

Notre première réaction a alors été de nous rendre chez Jarndyce, la librairie spécialisée dans les livres anciens qui fait face au musée. Là, Brian Lake, qui se passionne tout particulièrement pour la littérature du XIXe siècle, a été du même avis que Robert Smith : « Cela me paraît intéressant, a-t-il dit, mais pour déterminer précisément à quand il remonte, faites procéder à une expertise légale. »

C'est ainsi que je me suis lancée dans une enquête scrupuleuse visant à déterminer de manière scientifique les origines du journal. J'ai décidé de consulter un éventail de spécialistes aussi vaste que possible, afin d'examiner tous les aspects du document. J'ai non seulement fait appel à un expert légal de premier plan pour qu'il étudie la composition de l'encre et du papier, mais j'ai aussi obtenu l'aide bénévole d'un expert en documents, d'un graphologue, d'un psychiatre et de spécialistes du corps médical. La première étape consistait à établir, aussi clairement que possible, que le journal remontait bien à l'époque victorienne et qu'il avait été donc rédigé il y a plus de cent ans.

Pour ce faire, je me suis adressée au Dr Nicholas Eastaugh, dont la spécialité est avant tout de dater les matériaux utilisés dans les tableaux de maîtres et les vieux manuscrits. Sa clientèle est internationale. Il a travaillé pour le Museum of London, la National Gallery, la Tate Gallery et Christie's.

Le Dr Eastaugh a examiné le journal dans son atelier de Teddington, dans le sud-ouest de Londres. Il s'agissait de tester l'encre pour évaluer son âge et, si possible, la date à laquelle elle avait été appliquée sur le papier, puis le papier lui-même, également ce qui subsistait des pages manquantes et enfin la poudre noire incrustée entre les pages du journal.

Pour ces tests, il a utilisé une microsonde à protons. Il nous a expliqué que cet appareil permet, « grâce à l'impact non destructeur d'un faisceau de protons sur une petite partie de page, de détecter les produits chimiques présents dans les encres, les papiers, les parchemins et les colorants testés ». Un dispositif semblable a été utilisé par le Crocker National Laboratory en Californie pour déterminer la manière dont la Bible de Gutenberg avait été imprimée, et pour établir que la carte du Vinland, en apparence d'origine médiévale, contenait en fait du titane, dont on ne s'est pas servi pour la fabrication du papier avant le début du XXe siècle.

Les premières conclusions du Dr Eastaugh furent les suivantes : « Les résultats des diverses analyses de l'encre et du papier réalisées jusqu'ici ne sont pas en contradiction avec la date de 1888-1889. »

Prise de confiance, j'ai alors porté mon attention vers l'homme qui était l'auteur du journal. Se pouvait-il qu'il soit un ennemi personnel de James Maybrick, cherchant à lui nuire ? Ou bien Maybrick lui-même, mais en proie à des hallucinations ? Quelle était l'intensité des tortures morales éprouvées par l'auteur de ces lignes ? Pour obtenir une réponse à ces questions, j'ai interrogé le Dr David Forshaw, spécialiste de la dépendance à l'hôpital psychiatrique Maudsley de Londres. A l'époque de Jack l'Éventreur, cet hôpital, connu sous le nom de Bedlam, était un célèbre asile d'aliénés.

David Forshaw a accompli trois années de recherche en psychiatrie légale à l'Institut de psychiatrie de Londres, il est détenteur d'un diplôme d'histoire de la médecine et il est l'auteur de nombreuses publications consacrées à la psychiatrie et à la dépendance. Il a passé plusieurs mois à examiner le journal et selon lui, si un faussaire avait voulu créer de toutes pièces ce journal faussement simple, il lui aurait fallu posséder une profonde connaissance de la psychologie criminelle et des effets de la toxicomanie. Forshaw pense que de toute façon l'auteur du journal s'est fondé sur une expérience personnelle.

La première expertise ne trouvait rien qui contredît que le journal était de l'époque victorienne. Quant à la seconde, elle reconnaissait dans ces pages le récit d'une tragédie vécue. Mais, comme je n'allais pas tarder à m'en apercevoir, les preuves les plus convaincantes émergeraient du texte lui-même : en effet, les événements rapportés dans ces pages coïncidaient de façon extraordinaire avec les méandres meurtriers de Jack l'Éventreur à travers les rues ténébreuses et mal famées de Whitechapel.

Pour me guider dans mes recherches, j'ai également consulté trois spécialistes de Jack l'Éventreur – Martin Fido, Paul Begg et Keith Skinner –, qui m'ont donné accès à leurs impressionnantes archives. Ensuite, j'ai fait appel à deux autres experts, Melvyn Fairclough et Martin Howells. Tous sans exception se sont voués à la recherche de la vérité au sujet de l'Éventreur, et tous se sont déclarés fascinés par le journal, en dépit d'un scepticisme de rigueur. Selon eux, rien n'empêchait de penser que James Maybrick pût être un suspect de plus, inconnu à ce jour.

Forte de ces réponses encourageantes, j'ai décidé d'en apprendre davantage sur l'auteur du journal. Pour ce faire, je disposais d'une source d'informations précieuses. En effet, le procès intenté contre l'épouse de Maybrick avait eu suffisamment de retentissement pour que les archives en aient été conservées, ainsi que divers documents biographiques, ces derniers certes peu nombreux et parfois contradictoires.

J'ai donc pris le chemin de Liverpool, où tout a commencé.

Chapitre 2

A Liverpool, d'interminables rangées de maisons victoriennes soigneusement entretenues s'alignent au sommet de la colline qui descend vers l'Albert Dock et la Mersey [1]. Mais jusqu'au fleuve, on n'aperçoit qu'un vaste périmètre de logements sociaux.

Derrière la façade aux carreaux luisants des pubs traditionnels se presse encore une foule bruyante qui se reflète dans des miroirs ouvrés comme des vitraux de cathédrale. Mais Liverpool, cité jadis prospère, doit aujourd'hui lutter pour survivre aux ravages de la pauvreté et du chômage, et les navires qui desservaient autrefois le port le plus industrieux de Grande-Bretagne voguent maintenant vers d'autres horizons.

Certes, la ville est entourée de parcs verdoyants et de faubourgs élégants. C'est là qu'ont survécu les hôtels particuliers richement décorés des marchands prospères de l'époque victorienne, qui conservent avec fierté le souvenir d'un passé empreint d'énergie et d'audace. Aujourd'hui, leurs propriétaires louent des chambres aux étudiants, et plusieurs de ces bâtisses ont été converties en maisons de retraite.

Le faubourg d'Aigburth se trouve au sud du centre-

1. Fleuve qui rejoint la mer d'Irlande à Liverpool.

ville, sur les rives de la Mersey. Et c'est à Aigburth que se dresse encore Battlecrease House. Sise bien en retrait au 7 Riversdale Road, cette imposante demeure aux murs beige rosé ne comporte pas moins de vingt pièces. De l'autre côté de la route se trouvent les terrains verdoyants du Liverpool Cricket Club, dont James Maybrick était membre. De Riversdale Road, qui part d'Aigburth Road et descend jusqu'à la Mersey, on aperçoit les montagnes lointaines du pays de Galles.

Lorsque Maybrick a visité ce qui allait devenir sa dernière demeure, il est probable qu'il avait eu vent des rumeurs qui hantaient le quartier : celles d'un meurtre commis dans cette maison quelques années plus tôt. Mais elles ne l'ont pas empêché de s'y installer, avec sa jeune épouse américaine et ses deux enfants. Bien mal lui en a pris, car en 1889, guère plus d'un an après, on se pressait devant la grille pour pointer un doigt curieux vers les fenêtres de la chambre du haut, où Maybrick lui-même avait trouvé la mort. Certains allaient même jusqu'à prélever une brindille sur la haie qui jouxtait la grille.

Jack l'Éventreur a frappé à un moment où les journaux étaient assoiffés de manchettes à sensation. Les progrès techniques et l'amélioration du système éducatif avaient conduit à une compétition impitoyable les quelque deux cents quotidiens britanniques de l'époque. Les rédacteurs en chef de Fleet Street n'ont pas tardé à comprendre que les crimes abominables de l'Éventreur et les pieds de nez qu'il adressait aux autorités, incapables de l'arrêter, représentaient une mine d'or.

D'où venait l'Éventreur ? Qu'est-ce qui le poussait à tuer, encore et encore ? Pourquoi mutilait-il ses victimes ? Pourquoi ne pouvait-il pas résister à l'envie de laisser des indices ? C'était l'étoffe dont le roman d'horreur gothique était fait. La barbarie de l'Éventreur surpassait tout ce que Bram Stoker avait pu imaginer dans *Dracula*, paru un an auparavant, ou Robert Louis Stevenson dans *Docteur Jekyll et M. Hyde*, dont l'adaptation théâtrale faisait frissonner le public du Lyceum Theatre à Londres.

Après la mort de Mary Jane Kelly, les meurtres ont cessé. Mais la terreur a persisté car, en dépit de la plus impressionnante chasse à l'homme jamais organisée en Grande-Bretagne, le tueur n'avait pas été capturé.

A ce jour encore, l'Éventreur continue d'alimenter toute une industrie fondée sur ses exploits macabres et sur les efforts inlassables déployés pour déterminer son identité et ses motifs.

Dans les années qui ont suivi les meurtres de Whitechapel, nombre de ceux qui avaient participé à la chasse à l'Éventreur ont pris la plume, qui pour révéler ses carnets personnels, qui pour présenter au monde des documents qu'on avait cru disparus à jamais. Chaque « découverte » a donné lieu à l'émergence d'un flot de nouvelles théories. C'est ainsi qu'en 1959, le journaliste Daniel Farson a mis au jour un mémorandum signé Sir Melville Macnaghten, qui était devenu en 1890 directeur adjoint du *Criminal Investigation Department* de Scotland Yard. Il existe deux versions de ce document, et une troisième a été évoquée. Celle qu'a vue Farson appartient à la fille de Macnaghten, Lady Aberconway. Sir Melville y nomme pour la première fois les trois hommes qui, explique-t-il, étaient soupçonnés par Scotland Yard en 1888. Il s'agit de John Druitt, d'Aaron Kosminski et de Michael Ostrog.

Il déclare en outre, sur la foi de sources apparemment officielles, que le meurtrier de Whitechapel avait frappé cinq fois, et cinq seulement. Pourtant, le public et les autres policiers pensaient alors qu'il s'était manifesté au moins à deux autres reprises. Daniel Farson a été le premier à publier cette information.

Dans les années 1970, plusieurs auteurs ont suggéré un nouveau suspect, le prince Albert Victor, duc de Clarence, petit-fils de la reine Victoria. Si tant de gens se souviennent de son inclusion parmi les suspects, c'est sans doute parce que le grand public est friand de scandales mettant en cause la famille royale.

C'est un article du Dr Thomas Stowell paru dans *The Criminologist* en novembre 1970 qui a enflammé les esprits. Stowell se fondait sur des documents privés de Sir William Gull, médecin personnel de la reine Victoria, qui avait traité le prince pour la syphilis et avait ensuite déclaré qu'il était décédé d'un ramollissement du cerveau. Ces documents n'ont jamais été examinés par des experts et ils ont aujourd'hui disparu. Toutefois, plusieurs journaux intimes et les bulletins quotidiens de la cour attestent qu'au moment des meurtres le prince Albert Victor se trouvait soit en Écosse, soit dans la retraite royale de Sandringham, dans le Norfolk.

C'est vers 1980 qu'ont été découvertes des notes prises au crayon par l'inspecteur principal Donald Swanson, qui avait joué lui aussi un rôle de premier plan dans l'enquête portant sur les meurtres de Whitechapel. Il s'agissait là de commentaires, rédigés aux alentours de 1910, dans les marges et sur les pages de garde de son exemplaire personnel des mémoires de Sir Robert Anderson, directeur adjoint de la *Metropolitan Police* à l'époque des meurtres de Whitechapel. Publiées par le *Daily Telegraph* en 1987, les notes de Swanson nommaient le suspect qui avait les faveurs d'Anderson : Aaron Kosminski. Toutefois, elles contenaient des imprécisions qui n'ont eu pour effet que d'attiser le débat, plutôt que d'y mettre un terme.

En 1987 également une grande enveloppe est parvenue à Scotland Yard : elle contenait, entre autres documents, une lettre signée « Jack l'Éventreur » qui avait disparu des années auparavant. Et en 1993, une lettre datant de l'époque des meurtres a été retrouvée : elle nommait l'auteur de la lettre adressée à Scotland Yard en 1987.

La plupart des toutes premières théories portant sur l'identité de l'Éventreur ont été facilement discréditées. Exemple typique, celle avancée par le premier livre à identifier un suspect – Alios Szemeredy. Ce prétendu chirurgien né en Amérique, décrit plus tard comme un fabricant de saucisses, s'était suicidé à Vienne en 1892. Cette théorie avait été suggérée à son auteur par une rumeur extravagante surprise dans la capitale autrichienne.

Aujourd'hui, après un siècle de recherches, les trois personnages soupçonnés à l'origine par la police – Druitt, Kosminski et Ostrog – continuent d'être chacun soumis à des investigations régulières par l'un ou l'autre membre d'un groupe d'auteurs qui partagent tous la même obsession : être le premier à découvrir la véritable identité de l'Éventreur. Druitt, le fils d'un chirurgien, lui-même décrit à tort comme un médecin, a débuté sa vie professionnelle en qualité d'avocat. Il était devenu maître d'école à l'époque des meurtres. On l'a retrouvé noyé dans la Tamise à Chiswick en décembre 1888, les poches remplies de pierres. Son corps avait séjourné dans l'eau pendant environ un mois. Mais pourquoi Druitt a-t-il été déclaré suspect par Sir Melville Macnaghten ? La principale raison pour laquelle le directeur adjoint du CID était parvenu à cette conclusion est que le corps de Druitt avait été découvert peu de temps après le meurtre de Kelly. Il en avait déduit que les facultés mentales de Druitt s'étaient détériorées sous le poids de la culpabilité. Il avait également affirmé que la propre famille de Druitt pensait que c'était lui l'assassin – mais sans preuve. Enfin, il prétendait avoir eu accès à des « informations de source privée » et à « certains faits », dont il n'a jamais révélé la nature exacte, en vertu desquels Druitt aurait été « sexuellement aliéné ».

Plus réservé, en 1903, l'inspecteur Abberline de la *Metropolitan Police*, qui avait été à la tête de l'équipe de détectives chargés de l'enquête sur les meurtres de Whitechapel, déclarait : « Je connais tous les détails de cette histoire, mais au bout du compte, qu'en est-il ? Simplement ceci : peu de temps après le dernier meurtre à Whitechapel, le corps d'un jeune médecin a été repêché dans la Tamise, mais rien à part le fait qu'il a été trouvé à un moment proche du crime ne permet de l'incriminer. »

Pour ce qui est d'Aaron Kosminski, Sir Robert Anderson affirmait que sa culpabilité « était sans nul doute un fait avéré ». Selon le directeur adjoint de la *Metropolitan Police*, Kosminski éprouvait une haine farouche envers les femmes et souffrait de tendances homicides. Il prétendait également qu'il était devenu fou à force de s'adonner aux « vices solitaires ». Kosminski a été envoyé à l'hospice de Stepney, puis, en 1891, à l'asile d'aliénés de Colney Hatch. Toutefois, dans les rapports de police qui l'incriminent, on relève des erreurs dans la liste des dates, des noms et des lieux censés prouver sa culpabilité.

Le dernier suspect, selon la police, était un escroc à la petite semaine d'origine russe : Michael Ostrog. Tout ce qu'on sait de lui ou presque, c'est qu'il avait pour habitude d'être cruel avec les femmes. Il est probable que les soupçons ont pesé sur lui parce qu'il avait coutume de se promener dans Whitechapel, les poches pleines de scalpels et autres instruments chirurgicaux. La police n'a jamais réussi à prouver qu'il se trouvait dans les parages des crimes. Et en dépit des affirmations contenues dans le rapport de Macnaghten, selon lesquelles Ostrog aurait été interné dans un asile après les meurtres, entre 1889 et 1893, aucune confirmation n'a jamais été trouvée dans les archives.

Les graviers crissaient sous mes pas lorsque j'ai remonté l'allée privée de Battlecrease House. Quand la porte s'est ouverte, je me suis trouvée face à Paul Dodd, instituteur de son état, qui a passé son enfance dans cet hôtel particulier. Il m'a fait visiter la maison, dont les pièces ont gardé tout leur cachet. La propriété a été la seule de la rue à échapper aux bombes durant la Seconde Guerre mondiale, mais elle a été endommagée par une mine, puis par une secousse sismique en 1984. Enfin, la chute d'un arbre a détruit la serre. Malgré cela, l'imagination n'a aucune peine à faire revivre le passé.

Lorsqu'on traverse le grand salon et la salle à manger, dont les fenêtres sont ornées de vitraux représentant des oiseaux aquatiques, on pénètre dans la salle de bal qui donne sur le jardin. Les frises du plafond, magnifiques, et la cheminée de marbre italien, dans lequel des grappes de raisin ont été gravées avec un talent exquis, sont restées intactes.

En haut du splendide escalier en chêne massif se trouvent les chambres réservées aux amis et au personnel, une nursery et la pièce où Maybrick est mort.

Plus tard, ce même jour, après une visite sur la tombe où Maybrick est enterré avec ses parents et son frère Edwin, je suis allée passer un moment dans le bar confortable du pub où Maybrick a pour la première fois songé au meurtre : le Poste House.

A la naissance de James, les Maybrick habitaient Liverpool depuis soixante-dix ans. Ils étaient venus du sud-ouest de l'Angleterre, et l'une des branches de la famille s'était installée dans les quartiers de Stepney et de Whitechapel, au cœur de l'East End londonien. Plus tard, lorsque la crise du chômage s'est aggravée, certains membres de la famille sont partis s'installer dans le port de Liverpool, plus prospère.

L'église paroissiale de St. Peter, au centre de Liverpool, est vite devenue le fief de la très respectable famille de James. Ainsi, l'orgue a été tenu par des Maybrick, certains d'entre eux étaient membres du conseil paroissial, et lorsque James est né, le 24 octobre 1838, c'est son grand-père qui était prêtre de la paroisse.

Le baptême, le 12 novembre de la même année, avait constitué un événement particulièrement heureux pour les parents. En effet, Susannah et William, graveur sur cuivre de son état, avaient perdu l'année précédente un fils âgé de quatre mois. Ils avaient décidé de respecter la coutume victorienne qui voulait qu'on donne au nouveau bébé le nom de son frère défunt. Le nouveau-né avait également un frère aîné, William, alors âgé de trois ans.

Lorsque James a fêté ses six ans, son grand-père était mort et son père l'avait remplacé comme prêtre de la paroisse. On aurait pu penser que le goût de la prêtrise continuerait de se transmettre de père en fils. Mais en dépit de leur participation active à la vie de St. Peter et de leur respect des conventions victoriennes, aucun des frères Maybrick n'est resté pratiquant.

La famille habitait alors au 8 Church Alley, étroit sentier situé dans l'ombre de St. Peter, qui menait jusqu'à la populeuse Church Street. A deux pas se trouvait la rue dont le nom jouerait plus tard un rôle si important dans la vie de Maybrick : Whitechapel. Ce Whitechapel, à l'inverse de son homonyme londonien mal famé, était une rue commerçante à la mode. Le Blue Coat Hospital, école destinée aux enfants pauvres de la ville, se trouvait également non loin. Lorsque James allait traîner dans Church Street, il s'attardait au Civet Cat, échoppe spécialisée dans la bimbeloterie qui vendait des jouets étrangers. Il lui arrivait aussi de rêver à des contrées lointaines en contemplant la vitrine de M. Marcus, le marchand de tabac, qui organisait des excursions à Londres dans des trains parés de drapeaux multicolores.

L'espace manquait dans la maison des Maybrick, et les conditions avaient empiré avec l'arrivée de trois autres enfants, Michael (né en 1841), Thomas (né en 1846) et Edwin (né en 1851). (Un autre fils, Alfred, était mort à l'âge de quatre ans, en 1848.) Après la naissance d'Edwin, la famille s'est donc installée dans une maison plus spacieuse sise au 77 Mount Pleasant, tout près de Church Alley.

Les Maybrick menaient une vie simple. Ils n'engagèrent une domestique qu'après le départ de James de la maison familiale. Le recensement de 1861 signale qu'elle se nommait Mary Smith. On en sait très peu sur l'enfance des garçons et sur leur scolarité. James était probablement inscrit au Liverpool College, tout comme Michael, mais les archives de cette école ont été perdues au cours de la Seconde Guerre mondiale.

Si l'on en croit un portrait paru plus tard dans *The New Penny Magazine*, c'était Michael le petit génie de la famille. Ses dons musicaux lui permettaient, paraît-il, de s'adonner à l'« invention harmonieuse ». Une de ses compositions a été interprétée à l'opéra de Covent Garden, à Londres, alors que son auteur était à peine âgé de quatorze ans. Forts d'un tel succès, William et Susannah ont encouragé Michael à aller étudier à Leipzig. De là, il est parti pour le conservatoire de Milan, où il a découvert qu'il possédait en outre une belle voix de baryton. Il a aussitôt rejoint les rangs de la Compagnie de l'Opéra Carl Rosa, avant d'entamer l'équivalent victorien d'une carrière dans la musique pop, et de partir en tournée dans les salles de concert britanniques et américaines. En guise de nom de scène, Michael a choisi Stephen Adams, et il s'est associé avec le librettiste Frederick Weatherly. Ensemble, ils ont écrit des centaines de chansons telles que « Nancy Lee » et « A Warrior Bold ». En 1888, Stephen Adams était devenu la coqueluche des Britanniques. C'est en 1892 que Michael a publié « The Holy City », véritable succès qui se vend encore aujourd'hui et qui a été suivi, ce qui ne manque pas d'ironie, par une chansonnette intitulée « We All Love Jack », c'est-à-dire « Nous adorons tous Jack ».

Mais le musicologue Tony Miall n'est guère impressionné par le talent de Michael Maybrick : « C'est l'une des personnalités musicales les moins engageantes de la période. Sa poursuite continuelle de la respectabilité et de l'argent entre en conflit avec l'image d'un artiste soucieux de promouvoir son art. On chercherait en vain chez lui la moindre trace de compassion. Ses relations avec sa famille étaient plus cérémonieuses que chaleureuses. On est porté à soupçonner que ses rapports avec sa femme étaient de la même eau – en résumé, il s'agissait d'un homme sans cœur. »

Ses frères auraient du mal à surpasser Michael. William est devenu graveur et apprenti doreur, mais on raconte qu'il a fini par répondre à l'appel de la mer, devenant ainsi la brebis galeuse de la famille. Thomas et Edwin se sont lancés dans le commerce. Quant à James Maybrick, il est parti travailler dans la capitale en 1860, peut-être pour y apprendre le commerce du coton. Jusqu'à présent, cette période de sa vie était restée mystérieuse.

En 1891, deux ans après le procès de Florie, Alexander William MacDougall, avocat écossais respecté, a publié un *Treatise on the Maybrick Case* (Traité sur l'affaire Maybrick) de 606 pages, dans lequel il affirmait : « Il existe une femme qui se fait appeler Mme Maybrick et prétend avoir été la véritable épouse de James Maybrick. Durant le procès, elle a séjourné au 8 Dundas Street, Monkwearmouth, Sunderland. Son adresse habituelle, où elle réside actuellement, est 265 Queens Road, New Cross, London, S.E. »

Qui était cette mystérieuse Mme Maybrick ?

Ainsi que l'exige la coutume britannique, il a fallu attendre le 2 janvier 1992 pour que les documents relatifs au recensement de 1891 soient rendus publics. C'est donc seulement à partir de cette date qu'il a été possible de vérifier l'affirmation de MacDougall et de découvrir le détail de la vie secrète de Maybrick à Londres. J'ai eu accès à ces documents, qui m'ont permis de déterminer le nom des habitants du 265 Queens Road.

Il s'agissait de Christiana Conconi, veuve de soixante-neuf ans, originaire de Durham, qui vivait de ses rentes ; de sa fille de dix-huit ans, Gertrude, dont le jeune âge a de quoi surprendre ; et d'une visiteuse de quatorze ans. Une autre personne se trouvait également dans la maison : la nièce de Christina, Sarah Robertson, célibataire, âgée de quarante-quatre ans.

Sarah était née à Durham, elle aussi. Sa tante Christina avait épousé un horloger nommé Charles James Case en

1847, puis s'était installée au 40 Mark Lane, près de la Tour de Londres. Il est probable que la jeune Sarah les a rejoints plus tard, pour travailler comme assistante dans le magasin.

Est-ce à ce moment-là que le destin a précipité Maybrick, jeune provincial qui explorait pour la première fois l'East End de Londres, où ses ancêtres avaient vécu, entre les bras de Sarah ? Whitechapel se trouve à deux pas de Mark Lane. En 1888, lorsque Maybrick a entamé la campagne meurtrière dont il fait la chronique dans son journal, il connaissait sans doute comme sa poche ces rues misérables, grouillantes du petit peuple de Londres.

Charles Case est mort en 1863, et Christina s'est remariée trois ans plus tard. Son nouveau conjoint était un commissaire de la Royal Navy, Thomas David Conconi. A leur mariage, l'un des témoins n'était autre que « Sarah Ann Maybrick ».

En 1868, Thomas Conconi a ajouté un codicille à son testament : « Au cas où mon épouse viendrait à décéder de mon vivant, je lègue mes meubles, couverts, linge de maison et porcelaine à ma chère amie Sarah Ann Maybrick, épouse de James Maybrick originaire de Old Hall Street à Liverpool et qui réside aujourd'hui au 55 Bromley Street Commercial Road, Londres. »

D'après les archives, c'est à cette adresse qu'habitaient alors les Conconi. Mais on n'a retrouvé aucun certificat de mariage attestant que James et Sarah étaient unis.

Bromley Street existe encore. Ses petites maisons à deux étages, avec leurs grilles noires bien lustrées, ont été restaurées en 1990. Mais le n° 55 avait été démoli après la Seconde Guerre mondiale, pour faire place à de nouvelles constructions. Whitechapel se trouve à dix minutes de marche.

Selon le recensement de 1871, qui la mentionne comme « épouse d'employé de négociant », Sarah Ann a continué de vivre avec les Conconi, mais le nom de Maybrick ne figure nulle part. A la mort de Thomas, en 1876, Sarah apparaît de nouveau, mais cette fois comme « S. A. Maybrick, nièce » sur le certificat de décès. En 1891, elle est recensée sous le nom de Sarah Ann Robertson, époque à laquelle elle vivait à Queen's Road, New Cross, ainsi que l'affirme MacDougall. Mais curieusement, lorsque Christiana meurt en mars 1895, l'« informatrice » mentionnée sur le certificat de décès n'est autre, une fois encore, que « Sarah A. Maybrick ». Et sur son propre certificat de décès, rédigé le 17 janvier 1927, elle apparaît comme « Sarah Ann Maybrick, aussi connue sous le nom de Robertson, célibataire vivant de ses rentes, domiciliée 24 Cottesbrook Street, New Cross ».

Quant à James Maybrick, les archives indiquent qu'il était revenu à Liverpool en 1871, après le décès de son père à l'âge de cinquante-cinq ans. Il travaillait désormais avec Gustavus A. Witt, courtier, à Knowsley Buildings, dans Chapel Street, prolongement de Tithebarn Street, qui donnait dans Old Hall Street. Deux ans plus tard, il travaillait toujours avec Witt dans les mêmes locaux trop exigus où s'entassaient trente négociants et courtiers en coton. C'est à cette époque que Maybrick a fondé Maybrick et Compagnie, Marchands de coton. Plus tard, il s'est associé avec son frère Edwin, tout en conservant le contrôle de l'entreprise.

C'était un univers très difficile, dont le magazine local *Porcupine* (le Porc-épic) avait brossé un portrait sans concession dans son édition du 30 avril 1870. Un article intitulé « Cotton Gambling » suggérait que le marché du coton donnait lieu à des jeux d'argent pas très honnêtes, et il décrivait le monde féroce et sans scrupule qui avait attiré le jeune Maybrick. Un négoce naguère encore plein de noblesse qui s'était fourvoyé, presque du jour au lendemain, pour cause d'une pénurie de coton consécutive à la guerre de Sécession. C'était devenu un négoce ouvert à « quiconque pouvait obtenir du crédit sur la base de sa réputation, fût-elle usurpée, fût-il sans le sou », rapportait le magazine.

A partir de 1868, le système « baissier » a fait son apparition sur le marché du coton. Ce système en vigueur à la Bourse consiste à « vendre du coton que l'on ne possède pas dans l'espoir qu'on pourra faire un profit plus élevé en l'achetant moins cher plus tard ». Il a introduit dans le marché un élément de risque qui l'apparentait au jeu. « Il est regrettable, notait *Porcupine*, que l'Association des courtiers en coton ait donné son aval à ce système de commerce, qui a eu pour effet de discréditer le marché. »

Maybrick était un opportuniste, il a su tirer profit de cette compétition acharnée. En 1874, à trente-six ans, il est parti installer une filiale de sa compagnie dans le port de Norfolk, en Virginie, qui connaissait une ascension fulgurante grâce au coton. Comme beaucoup d'autres, Maybrick s'est ensuite partagé entre la Grande-Bretagne et l'Amérique : il travaillait en Virginie durant la saison de la cueillette, de septembre à avril, puis retournait à Liverpool au printemps.

Norfolk avait été ruiné par la guerre de Sécession, mais les habitants avaient repris le dessus avec énergie. Toutefois, un quart de la superficie de la ville était réduit à l'état de marécage, en particulier autour du Dismal Creek Swamp, infesté de moustiques. Or, pour encourager les investissements étrangers, il était nécessaire d'approvisionner la ville en eau potable au moyen de canalisations. Le système de distribution d'eau a donc été modernisé, et la fin des travaux a coïncidé avec l'inauguration de la ligne de chemin de fer reliant Norfolk avec les États producteurs de coton du Deep South, le Sud profond. La ville s'est transformée alors en port international, dont près de la moitié des navires effectuaient la liaison entre Liverpool et l'Amérique.

L'année où Maybrick est arrivé à Norfolk, la bourse du coton y ouvrait ses portes, déclenchant un raz de marée commercial qui eut des répercussions des deux côtés de l'Atlantique. Les affaires étaient florissantes.

Trois ans plus tard, Maybrick vivait dans York Street avec Nicholas Bateson et un domestique noir nommé Thomas Stansell. C'est à ce moment-là qu'il a contracté la malaria. Une première ordonnance, qui prescrivait de la quinine, n'a produit aucune amélioration. Aussi le pharmacien de Main Street, Santo, en a-t-il délivré une seconde. Cette fois, arsenic et strychnine étaient recommandés. Ce serait pour Maybrick le début d'une longue déchéance.

« Il était très inquiet au sujet de sa santé, a rapporté Bateson lors de sa déposition pour la défense au procès de Florie. Il se frottait sans arrêt le dos des mains et se plaignait d'avoir les membres engourdis. Il craignait la paralysie. La dernière année où j'ai vécu avec lui, son état n'a fait qu'empirer. Il est devenu de plus en plus dépendant des médicaments. »

Lorsque son tour est venu de témoigner, Stansell s'est souvenu d'avoir effectué des commissions pour Maybrick. « Quand je lui ai apporté l'arsenic, il m'a dit d'aller lui faire du bouillon. [...] Il m'a demandé de lui donner une cuiller [...] il a ouvert le paquet et en a pris un petit morceau. Puis il l'a mis dans le thé et il a remué. »

Stansell s'est déclaré surpris par la quantité de cachets et de potions qui se trouvaient dans le bureau de Maybrick. « Je suis, lui a dit un jour le marchand de coton, une victime de l'intempérance. »

La compagne de Maybrick, à cette époque, s'appelait Mary Howard (aussi connue sous le nom de Hogwood). C'était la tenancière d'un des bordels les plus fréquentés de Norfolk. Après la condamnation à mort de Florie, Mary a fourni une déposition au Département d'État de Washington, dans laquelle elle déclarait : « J'ai connu feu James Maybrick pendant plusieurs années et jusqu'au moment de son mariage il venait chez moi deux ou trois fois par semaine lorsqu'il se trouvait à Norfolk, et il était souvent d'humeur fantasque. Il était fréquent qu'il prenne de l'arsenic deux ou trois fois par soirée. Avant de l'avaler, il disait toujours : “ Bon, je vais prendre ma dose du soir. ” Il tirait de sa poche une petite fiole dans laquelle il transportait son arsenic et, après en avoir placé une petite quantité sur sa langue, il avalait une gorgée de vin. En fait, il répétait ce manège si souvent que j'en étais venue à craindre qu'il ne meure tout d'un coup dans ma maison, et que certaines d'entre nous ne soient ensuite soupçonnées de meurtre. Quand il était ivre, James Maybrick versait la poudre dans le creux de sa main et la léchait avec sa langue. Je l'ai souvent mis en garde, mais il répondait : “ Oh, j'y suis habitué. Ça ne me fera pas de mal. ” »

L'arsenic est très répandu dans l'environnement naturel, où il est souvent associé avec les minerais métallifères. Il a causé la mort d'innombrables personnes, dont celle, dit-on, de Napoléon Bonaparte. L'empereur emprisonné à Sainte-Hélène aurait été empoisonné par les émanations provenant du papier peint de sa cellule, qui avait été appliqué à l'aide d'un mélange contenant de l'arsenic. Cette substance a pourtant rendu bien des services à travers les âges, notamment en médecine mais également en cosmétique. Au XVIe siècle, la reine Élizabeth Ire utilisait de l'arsenic comme produit de beauté, en l'appliquant sur son visage pour lui faire adopter un blanc mat du plus bel effet. Florie Maybrick elle-même employait une préparation à base d'arsenic pour embellir son teint.

En 1786, le Dr T. Fowler a rapporté les bienfaits de l'arsenic pour la fièvre et les maux de tête sporadiques. La « Médecine de Flower » était un fortifiant populaire à l'époque de Maybrick. Le mot grec pour arsenic – *arsenikos* – signifie mâle, et Maybrick, comme beaucoup d'hommes de son époque, croyait que l'arsenic accroîtrait sa virilité. C'est la raison pour laquelle il s'est mis à en consommer. Mais cette « drogue » a vite créé chez lui une dépendance fatale.

L'année 1880 a été cruciale pour Maybrick : à l'âge de quarante et un ans, il est tombé amoureux. Le printemps approchait et, comme chaque année, il avait réservé une place sur le *Baltic* pour rentrer à Liverpool. Propulsé par des hélices, le *Baltic* était l'un des fleurons de la flotte transatlantique à vapeur de la White Star Line, conçu « pour fournir le plus haut degré de confort à toutes les classes de passagers ». Le voyage s'effectuait en six jours et le billet coûtait 27 guinées [1].

C'est le 12 mars que le *Baltic* a quitté New York sous le commandement du capitaine Henry Parsell. Or, parmi les deux cent vingt passagers de première classe, se trouvait une « Belle du Sud » impulsive et cosmopolite : Florence Chandler, dite Florie. Agée seulement de dix-huit ans, elle était chaperonnée par sa mère, l'impressionnante baronne Caroline von Roques, grande voyageuse. Leur destination : Paris. Se trouvait également à bord un ami de ces dames, le général J. G. Hazard, originaire de Liverpool. C'est lui qui les a présentées à Maybrick dans le bar élégant du *Baltic*.

Maybrick a appris que la piquante Belle du Sud aux cheveux blond vénitien était issue de la haute société américaine. Elle était née le 3 septembre 1862, pendant la guerre de Sécession, dans une ville très sophistiquée : Mobile, dans l'Alabama. Depuis ce jour, sa vie avait été entièrement dominée par le coton. Il n'existait personne d'important, dans la haute société du Sud, qui ne fût un cousin de la mère ou du père de Florie – William Chandler, le premier mari de la baronne. Pour reprendre une expression anglaise, Florie et son frère aîné, Holbrook St. John, étaient nés avec une cuiller d'argent dans la bouche.

En 1863, le père de Florie est mort. Il n'avait pas quarante ans, et sa famille était convaincue, sans aucune preuve, que sa femme l'avait empoisonné. Sous la menace d'un procès, Mme Chandler a dû quitter Mobile. Six mois plus tard, elle était remariée avec un soldat d'exception, le capitaine du Barry. Mais un an plus tard, il devait lui aussi trouver la mort sur un vapeur en route vers l'Écosse. C'était inévitable, les mauvaises langues s'en sont saisies.

---

1. Pièce d'or retirée de la circulation en 1813. Mais on a continué, dans certains milieux professionnels, à fixer tarifs ou honoraires en guinées. *(N.d.T.)*

Florie s'était donc retrouvée sans père, menant une vie solitaire. Pendant que sa mère parcourait l'Europe, la jeune fille avait navigué d'institutions en pensionnats, faisant parfois escale chez un membre compatissant de la famille. Dix ans après le décès du capitaine du Barry, la mère de Florie avait épousé un officier de cavalerie prussien, le baron Adolph von Roques. Erreur funeste. En effet, non content de lui être infidèle, le baron la battait et avait fini par dilapider sa fortune.

Florie a dû considérer James Maybrick comme la conquête idéale : à ses yeux, il incarnait la figure paternelle qu'elle avait perdue, et c'était le type même de l'homme sûr de lui, habile en affaires, dont le goût du risque pimentait l'existence ordinaire. De son côté, il a dû imaginer qu'elle lui donnerait accès à une classe et à un style de vie dont sa naissance l'avait privé mais auxquels il aspirait. Elle ferait beaucoup pour sa réputation parmi les nantis de Liverpool soucieux de leur statut social, et lui apporterait peut-être en prime la fortune.

C'est avec une rapidité étourdissante que Maybrick a séduit Florie. Avant la fin du voyage il l'avait demandée en mariage et, lorsqu'ils mirent pied à terre à Liverpool, on parlait déjà d'une cérémonie en grande pompe l'été suivant. En proie à sa folie des grandeurs habituelle, le négociant en coton s'est alors mis en tête que le mariage aurait lieu en l'église St. James, nom on ne peut mieux choisi, à Piccadilly. Et c'est bien à St. James, dans l'un des quartiers les plus en vogue de Londres, que la cérémonie a eu lieu le 27 juillet 1881 sous les auspices du révérend J. Dyer Tivey. La mariée portait une robe plissée de satin et de dentelle couleur ivoire, son bouquet était composé d'ancolies blanches et de muguet. Le marié, son aîné de vingt-quatre ans, portait quant à lui un gilet de satin blanc dont les broderies représentaient des roses et du muguet, ainsi qu'une jaquette doublée d'ouatine.

Le frère de Florie, Holbrook St. John, était venu de

Paris pour la donner en mariage. Mais bien que les frères de Maybrick, Edwin, Thomas, et Michael aient été présents, James a dû être déçu de constater combien cette union suscitait peu d'enthousiasme parmi eux. Michael, qui dominait le trio, était sceptique. Plusieurs invités ont rapporté qu'il ne croyait pas un mot des belles paroles de la baronne. Celle-ci avait promis monts et merveilles à son futur gendre, sous la forme d'un héritage constitué de nombreuses propriétés. Mais Michael n'y voyait qu'une habile manœuvre de la future belle-mère pour finir ses jours dans un foyer britannique doté de tout le confort. (Toutefois, après le procès de Florie, elle a écrit au ministre de l'Intérieur, Henry Matthews, pour lui signifier que sa fille « n'avait certainement pas tué pour des motifs pécuniaires, car j'ai aidé la famille financièrement pendant des années ».)

A l'époque du mariage, Maybrick avait souscrit une assurance pour un montant de 2 000 livres, porté ensuite à 2 500 livres, dont Florie était la bénéficiaire. Il a aussi établi un fonds en fidéicommis de 10 000 livres, somme qui correspondrait aujourd'hui à quarante fois ce montant, mais n'a jamais versé un *penny*.

La maison de sa grand-mère à New York rapportait à Florie un petit revenu de 125 livres par an, et elle touchait également de temps à autre des revenus en provenance des terres de son père, près de Mobile. Mais les Maybrick étaient loin de posséder l'argent nécessaire pour entretenir la façade qu'ils souhaitaient présenter.

Depuis le départ, leur union était fondée sur la tromperie : le certificat de mariage lui-même révèle la vraie nature de Maybrick. Non sans prétention, il se décrit comme « *esquire* [1] », et son adresse n'est autre que le quartier huppé de St. James.

Comment Florie, qui n'était encore qu'une enfant, aurait-elle pu soupçonner que la vie de son mari reposait

1. Titre honorifique d'un *gentleman.* *(N.d.T.)*

sur l'hypocrisie, la bassesse, la duperie ? Et comment aurait-elle pu imaginer qu'il existait déjà une Mme Maybrick, qui vivait à Londres ?

Pis encore, comment aurait-elle pu deviner que l'homme qu'elle aimait allait bientôt devenir l'une des figures les plus terrifiantes des temps modernes ?

Chapitre 3

James Chandler, affectueusement surnommé « Bobo », est né huit mois après le mariage des Maybrick. Ce bébé souffreteux, prématuré, a valu à Florie un accouchement difficile.

Au printemps 1882, Maybrick est retourné en Amérique avec femme et enfant, et pendant les deux années qui ont suivi, ils se sont partagés entre Liverpool et Norfolk, où ils louaient une maison dans Freemason Street.

A 8 heures chaque matin, Maybrick partait à pied pour son travail. Mais plutôt que de se rendre tout droit à son bureau situé dans Main Street, il passait chez C.F. Greenwood, pharmacien de Freemason Street, pour acheter sa ration quotidienne d'arsenic.

Un jour, John Fleming, marin originaire de Halifax, en Nouvelle-Écosse, l'a surpris en train de verser la poudre grisâtre dans ses *hominy grits*, forme américaine du porridge. Plus tard, dans une déclaration écrite sous serment, Fleming a révélé que Maybrick lui avait tenu ces propos : « Vous seriez horrifié, je n'exagère pas, si vous saviez de quoi il s'agit. C'est de l'arsenic. Nous absorbons tous du poison, à plus ou moins forte dose. Par exemple, je vais maintenant avaler une dose d'arsenic qui suffirait à vous tuer. Je prends de cet arsenic une fois de temps en temps parce que je trouve qu'il me donne des forces. »

Après sa visite chez le pharmacien, Maybrick se rendait à la bourse du coton, où se mêlaient exportateurs, courtiers et acheteurs. Il déjeunait à 13 heures, et consacrait le reste de la journée à la correspondance et aux tâches administratives. Ensuite, il allait passer un moment dans l'un des nombreux clubs de Norfolk.

C'est à cette époque, raconte Florie dans une lettre écrite ultérieurement, que son mari a pris l'habitude de se frotter le dos des mains. Elle ignorait que la sécheresse de la peau et les démangeaisons sont l'un des symptômes d'une utilisation excessive de l'arsenic.

Maybrick n'était pas le seul dans son cas, loin de là. La mode de l'arsenic, et celle de la strychnine qui produisait des effets similaires, se répandaient à un rythme alarmant parmi les hommes aisés, tant en Grande-Bretagne qu'en Amérique. A l'époque du procès de Florie, le *Liverpool Citizen* aura ce commentaire : « Nous savons tous pertinemment que ces messieurs du négoce ont tout autant l'habitude de consommer ces drogues dangereuses, strychnine, arsenic et que sais-je encore, que de boire du champagne et de fumer du tabac. A ce qu'il paraît, il s'en absorbe assez à la bourse de Flags pour empoisonner tout Castle Street.

« Une fois qu'ils ont pris l'habitude d'absorber de l'arsenic, ils en demeurent esclaves à tout jamais. [...] Et lorsqu'ils sont sur la pente descendante, il ne leur est plus possible de faire machine arrière. D'après les toxicologues, s'ils ne parviennent pas à obtenir leur dose quotidienne, ils peuvent vraiment dire à juste titre que " les flammes de l'Enfer leur brûlent les entrailles ", car ils endurent alors les horreurs atroces de l'empoisonnement à petit feu. »

Peu à peu, le charbon en prenant la place du coton est devenu le premier produit d'exportation à Norfolk. Aussi, en mars 1884, James a-t-il décidé de rapatrier sa femme et le jeune Bobo à Liverpool. Là, ils ont loué une maison toute neuve, baptisée Beechville. Elle était sise dans South Road, dans le faubourg huppé de Grassendale.

James et Florie aimaient à se promener en voiture à cheval et à jouer au whist. Mais ils vouaient surtout une passion commune aux courses hippiques et se rendaient très souvent à Aintree, près de Liverpool. C'est là que se disputait le Grand National, course célèbre dans le monde entier.

Soucieux de leur statut social, les Maybrick avaient réussi à se faire accepter dans les salons Wellington de Mount Pleasant, fréquentés par la bonne société de Liverpool. A l'occasion des cinq bals annuels organisés dans ces murs, un tapis rouge était déroulé jusque sur le trottoir. Les dames descendaient des voitures à cheval « habillées avec la splendeur qui sied aux épouses et aux filles des hommes les plus riches du plus grand port de mer britannique ».

Maybrick était également membre du très coté Palatine Club. Dans son journal, il rapporte y avoir dîné avec son ami George (Davidson). Toutefois, le couple ne pouvait pas réellement prétendre appartenir à l'élite. Aussi, comme beaucoup d'Anglais de l'époque victorienne en quête d'un statut social plus élevé que le leur, Maybrick est-il devenu citoyen d'honneur de la ville. Mais il n'a jamais été mentionné parmi les notables dans les publications destinées à la fleur de la société.

Est-ce pour cette raison que ni son mariage ni son retour à Liverpool n'ont endigué sa toxicomanie, de plus en plus pernicieuse ? Il n'avait aucune difficulté à s'approvisionner, car son cousin William travaillait pour un pharmacien de gros, John Thompson. Mais en 1886, William a été renvoyé. Aux abois, Maybrick a supplié Thompson de le rétablir dans ses fonctions. Sans succès.

Il n'a pas tardé à trouver un fournisseur : il s'agissait d'Edwin Garnette Heaton, qui tenait une pharmacie dans Exchange Street East. Heaton servirait Maybrick pendant dix ans, période durant laquelle la dose prescrite est passée de quatre à sept gouttes – l'arsenic était communément administré en poudre, mais aussi sous forme de gouttes. Maybrick se rendait régulièrement à la pharmacie, jusqu'à cinq fois par jour, pour y obtenir ce que le pharmacien décrivait comme un « remontant » pour « exciter la passion ». Sept gouttes cinq fois par jour équivalaient pratiquement à un tiers de grain d'arsenic. Or, un grain suffit à tuer un homme. Quand Maybrick partait en voyage d'affaires, Heaton lui préparait huit ou seize doses, selon la taille de la bouteille que lui présentait son client.

L'arsenic altérait le comportement de Maybrick, ce qui finit par inquiéter le frère de Florie, Holbrook St. John, qui travaillait comme médecin à Paris. « Je ne prétends pas savoir à quels stratagèmes il se livre, a-t-il écrit, mais il a interdit à Florie de nous révéler quoi que ce soit au sujet de ses affaires et il la mène complètement en bateau. Nous ne pouvons malheureusement ni écrire à Florie, ni obtenir de ses nouvelles sinon par l'intermédiaire de James, et il lui dicte les lettres qu'elle envoie. Je regrette profondément cette attitude inattendue de Maybrick, qui se révèle être un tyran doublé d'une brute, mais puisque telle est la réalité nous devons nous protéger du mieux que nous le pouvons ».

En 1884, l'économie britannique a connu une brève période de déclin. Selon ses amis, Maybrick est alors devenu aussi inquiet au sujet de son argent qu'à propos de sa santé. Quant à Florie, à qui l'on n'avait jamais appris à tenir un budget, sa passion des beaux vêtements la poussait à l'extravagance. Elle les achetait en quantité chez Woolright's, le grand magasin chic de Bold Street, qui, avec son stock immense de fourrures, de bijoux et de tissus exotiques, attirait en foule les femmes élégantes.

Il n'est donc guère surprenant que certains membres de la famille aient commencé à perdre patience. Ainsi la baronne von Roques devait-elle écrire à son avocat new-yorkais : « Ma pauvre petite fille est complètement sous la coupe de son mari et il ne se révèle pas être un fils pour moi. »

En décembre de cette même année, le frère de Florie a contracté une tuberculose dont il est mort en quatre mois.

La coutume voulant que les femmes n'assistent pas aux enterrements, Maybrick s'est rendu seul à Paris, où avait lieu la cérémonie.

Florie avait peu d'amis proches. Aux yeux des dames de Liverpool, c'était une étrangère. Deux d'entre elles faisaient toutefois exception à la règle : Matilda Briggs, ancienne admiratrice de Maybrick, et sa sœur, Louisa Hughes, qui venaient souvent à Battlecrease House. Après le décès de son frère, Florie a même emprunté cent livres à Mme Briggs pour apaiser ses créanciers.

Le 20 juillet de l'année suivante, Florie a donné naissance à une fille, Gladys Evelyn. L'accouchement a eu lieu en présence du Dr Arthur Hoper, de Rodney Street, qui suivait les Maybrick depuis leur mariage.

Cette naissance n'a pas aidé à restaurer le bonheur conjugal. Et c'est en 1887 que Florie a découvert ce que d'autres savaient depuis déjà longtemps : il y avait une autre femme dans la vie de son mari. Dans son journal, Maybrick mentionne effectivement sa liaison avec une femme qui réside à Liverpool.

« Ce soir j'irai voir la mienne. »

Mais de qui s'agit-il ? Peut-être de Sarah Ann Robertson dont on perd la trace en 1886, et dont on ignore où elle se trouvait en 1887. Aussi est-il possible qu'elle ait suivi Maybrick à Liverpool, mais il est plus probable qu'il l'ait abandonnée à Londres. Dans ce cas, qui est cette autre femme ?

Ce dont on est sûr, c'est que le couple a décidé de faire chambre à part en 1887, à la demande expresse de Florie. William Stead, le rédacteur en chef du magazine hebdomadaire *Review of Reviews*, et Bernard Ryan, dans son livre *The Poisoned Life of Mrs. Maybrick* (la Vie empoisonnée de Mme Maybrick), l'affirment en effet tous les deux.

Non seulement Florie soupçonnait l'adultère, mais elle craignait aussi que son mari n'abusât de ses « médicaments ». Les amis qui rendaient visite à Maybrick lorsqu'ils venaient d'Amérique en voyage d'affaires avaient eux aussi remarqué la faiblesse croissante et le vieillissement prématuré d'un homme qui n'avait encore que quarante-huit ans.

Au printemps 1887, une épidémie de scarlatine s'est déclarée dans tout le pays et Bobo a contracté la maladie. Florie est restée à Liverpool pour veiller sur lui pendant que James emmenait leur fillette de neuf mois au pays de Galles, par crainte de la contagion. Tous deux y sont restés six semaines.

A son retour, Maybrick a réduit la somme qu'il versait à Florie pour la nourriture, les gages des domestiques et les autres dépenses du ménage. Au mois d'octobre suivant, les affaires de la famille ne s'étaient pas arrangées. D'après ce que Florie écrit à sa mère, Maybrick n'avait réalisé que 125 livres de profit en cinq ans, et son actif ne s'élevait plus qu'à 1 500 livres. Selon Florie, le capital avait été utilisé pour meubler la maison. « Je suis complètement épuisée et dans un tel état de nervosité et de surmenage que je ne suis bonne à rien. Chaque fois que retentit la sonnette de la porte d'entrée, je manque m'évanouir de crainte que ce ne soit un créancier et lorsque Jim rentre à la maison le soir c'est toute tremblante de peur que je scrute son visage pour voir si l'on est venu le voir au bureau à propos de mes notes [...] je passe ma vie à craindre quelque chose ou quelqu'un. Il n'y a aucun moyen d'endiguer le flot. La vie vaut-elle la peine d'être vécue ? Je ne demanderais pas mieux que d'abandonner la maison et d'aller m'installer ailleurs mais Jim dit que ce serait sa ruine. Car il faut préserver les apparences jusqu'à ce qu'il dispose d'un capital suffisant pour éponger son passif, car au moindre soupçon, tout le monde lui tomberait dessus immédiatement et comment Jim pourrait-il régler avec ce qu'il a maintenant ? »

Maybrick était loin d'être cohérent et était même parfois malhonnête dans la gestion des finances du ménage. A sa mort, il a laissé plus de 5 000 livres, l'équivalent d'environ 200 000 livres d'aujourd'hui. Il n'était donc pas devenu aussi pauvre que Florie le croyait. Ce qui explique qu'il ait pu se permettre certaines extravagances. Un beau jour, il avait ainsi décidé qu'il fallait une nounou aux enfants. Sans hésiter, il en avait engagé une sur-le-champ. Et bien qu'à l'époque le recrutement de domestiques de sexe féminin ait été l'affaire de l'épouse, mais certainement pas celle d'un homme seul, il s'était rendu seul à Birkdale, Southport, où Alice Yapp vivait avec ses employeurs. Ce faisant, Maybrick avait donc foulé aux pieds les conventions sociales. Les commères locales s'en sont donné à cœur joie. Et lorsque « Nurse Yapp », âgée de vingt-huit ans, s'est installée chez les Maybrick, le *Liverpool Echo* l'a présentée avec tact comme « une jeune femme plutôt avenante ».

La tension nerveuse éprouvée par Florie s'est encore intensifiée. Elle avait en effet maintenant perdu toute maîtrise de son existence. Les motifs d'inquiétude ne manquaient pas : ses dettes, la dépendance de son mari, sa santé et son infidélité. C'est dans cet état d'esprit qu'elle se trouvait lorsqu'elle a fait la connaissance d'Alfred Brierley.

Durant l'été 1887, les Maybrick organisent un dîner. Un négociant en coton nommé Alfred Brierley, qui ne manque pas de prestance, a été invité. Les locaux de sa compagnie, Brierley, Wood and Partners, sont situés dans Old Hall Street, à deux pas du bureau de Maybrick.

Brierley est né en 1851 à Rochdale, dans le Lancashire, et il a grandi entouré de ses dix frères et sœurs. Les Brierley sont de véritables piliers de leur communauté. Grâce au commerce du coton et à la sécurité que leur ont offerte l'Église anglicane et le parti conservateur, ils ont gravi les échelons de la société jusqu'à exercer une influence proportionnelle à leur fortune, c'est-à-dire considérable. Ils ont même donné leur nom à plusieurs rues.

A l'âge de trente-six ans, Brierley est toujours célibataire, séduisant et fort impressionnable.

Troublée par les manigances de son mari, Florie adorait

flirter. Cette femme pleine de vie avait toujours apprécié les attentions des hommes à son égard. Or, à Liverpool, en ces temps austères où la morale réprimait les pulsions, il en aurait fallu très peu pour qu'une pétulante Belle du Sud commette un écart. A Mobile, dans une Amérique déjà très libérée le samedi soir, il n'était pas rare qu'une jeune fille dépourvue de chaperon se joigne à un groupe d'amis des deux sexes sur un bateau, et qu'elle passe la nuit à danser et à boire. Elle dormait ensuite toute la journée du lendemain. Un tel comportement n'aurait jamais été toléré dans l'Angleterre victorienne.

On ne sait pas quels sentiments éprouvait réellement Florie envers Brierley, ni le moment précis où elle a cédé à ses inclinations. On constate, à la lecture du journal, que Maybrick souffrait d'une paranoïa croissante à propos des infidélités qu'il prêtait à sa femme.

C'est sans doute au début du mois de mars 1888 que les Maybrick ont quitté Grassendale pour Aigburth, à moins d'un kilomètre et demi. Ils se sont installés dans Battlecrease House, maison beaucoup plus imposante et mieux située, qu'ils ont prise à bail pour cinq ans. Ils étaient accompagnés de « Nurse Yapp », du jardinier James Grant, qui venait d'épouser l'ancienne femme de chambre, Alice, et de la domestique, Mary Cadwallader. Plus tard la même année, ils ont engagé une cuisinière, Elizabeth Humphreys.

Les voisins du couple dans Riversdale Road étaient des hommes d'affaires et des bourgeois aisés. Florie s'est empressée de meubler la maison avec style. Chaque pièce s'est retrouvée nantie de tapis en velours et de rideaux en panne rouge sombre, doublés de satin bleu pâle. Les meubles à dorures ont été recouverts de rouge sombre et de bleu.

Dans le cabinet privé de Maybrick, se trouvaient des fauteuils en cuir profonds et confortables. C'est là qu'il conservait le vin, les cigares, le tabac, les cartes à jouer et les jetons de poker. A l'étage, son vestiaire, dans lequel on parvenait en traversant la chambre principale, était constamment verrouillé.

Cet été-là, Battlecrease House allait recevoir une invitée, qui ne tarirait pas de souvenirs relatifs à la vie dans cette maisonnée. Une vie de plus en plus étrange. « Petite mademoiselle », c'est le sobriquet dont Maybrick avait affublé la jeune Florence Aunspaugh, turbulente petite Américaine de huit ans qui resterait avec la famille pendant que son père, Charles, collègue de Maybrick, se trouvait en Europe.

C'est à l'auteur Trevor Christie que Florence Aunspaugh, devenue une vieille dame, a conté ses souvenirs. La plupart des notes prises par Christie n'ont pas été publiées dans le livre qu'il a consacré à l'affaire Maybrick. Elles sont conservées dans les archives de l'Université du Wyoming, à Laramie. Ces témoignages de premier plan ont une valeur inestimable, car ils permettent d'éclairer un autre pan de la vie du couple.

« Battlecrease était un vrai palais, raconte Florence, dans le style typique des domaines anglais. Les terres devaient couvrir près de trois hectares, et elles étaient extrêmement bien entretenues. Il y avait de grands arbres, des buissons luxuriants et des plates-bandes magnifiques. Çà et là, on apercevait de petits recoins ménagés dans des rochers, et des pavillons recouverts de vieux lierre anglais et d'autres plantes grimpantes. Une serre se trouvait près de la maison et un couple de paons se promenait en liberté [...]. Un petit ruisseau naturel traversait le domaine; à un endroit, on l'avait élargi et on avait creusé pour former un petit lac [...]. Cet étang contenait des poissons. Des cygnes et des canards y nageaient. Je revois cette piscine comme si c'était hier, car je suis tombée dedans deux fois et c'est le jardinier qui m'en a sortie.

« M. Maybrick aimait beaucoup la chasse et il possédait pas mal de chiens [...]. J'ai vu six chevaux; il y en avait deux noirs, très beaux, qui étaient toujours attelés à la voiture, deux gris, qui étaient attelés à ce qu'ils appelaient le cabriolet, et deux chevaux de selle bais : M. Maybrick utilisait toujours le même, et Mme Maybrick le second. »

Aux yeux de la jeune Florence Aunspaugh, l'épouse de Maybrick ne manquait pas de séduction. « Ce qu'elle avait de plus beau, c'étaient ses cheveux. Ils étaient blonds, mais pas d'un jaune terne, passé. Non, une pointe de roux, juste ce qu'il faut, les faisait briller. Ils étaient dorés comme les blés.

« Et je n'ai jamais vu bleu plus beau que celui des yeux de Mme Maybrick. Ils étaient grands et ronds, d'un bleu si profond qu'ils en devenaient parfois violets; mais leur expression était des plus étranges [...]. Si vous la regardiez droit dans les yeux, ils semblaient sans vie, sans expression, comme si vous regardiez les yeux d'un cadavre. Complètement dépourvus de vivacité, de chaleur. Si vous continuiez à la regarder, les yeux semblaient changer et adopter l'expression d'un animal effrayé.

« Jamais on ne décelait chez elle la moindre expression d'intellectualité, que ce soit dans les yeux ou sur le visage, et pourtant elle dégageait un magnétisme et un charme [...] qui semblaient irrésistibles.

« Elle était très consciente de sa beauté et de sa séduction, et elle recherchait l'admiration, en particulier celle des représentants du sexe masculin. Elle donnait l'impression d'aimer se trouver tout près d'eux et de les toucher. Je l'ai vue tapoter le sommet du crâne d'un homme, poser un bras sur celui d'un autre, et placer la main sur le genou d'un troisième. Elle agissait ainsi devant M. Maybrick. Depuis que j'ai atteint la maturité, je me demande pourquoi il le tolérait, mais c'est un fait. »

Le James Maybrick qui avait survécu dans la mémoire de la jeune Florence Aunspaugh était austère et impressionnant, mais se laissait aussi aller à de brefs accès de tendresse envers ses enfants et elle-même.

« Après le petit déjeuner, M. Maybrick nous installait

sur ses genoux, son petit garçon et moi, et il nous parlait. Il me taquinait pour voir quel genre de réponse hardie je lui donnerais [...].

« Un jour, M. Maybrick a demandé à Nurse Yapp de nous habiller, le petit garçon et moi, avec des vêtements d'une élégance inhabituelle, car il souhaitait nous recevoir dans le petit salon un peu avant que le dîner ne soit annoncé [...]. Je ne crois pas avoir jamais été plus élégante [...]. La bonne du premier étage nous a fait descendre dans le hall d'entrée par le bel escalier. M. Maybrick nous attendait devant la porte qui s'ouvrait sur le petit salon. Il m'a prise par la main et m'a entraînée vers l'arche qui séparait les salons. Là, il a déclaré : “ Mesdames et messieurs, je veux vous présenter cette charmante petite mademoiselle qui vient des États-Unis. ”

« On ne pouvait pas dire qu'il était beau [...] mais il avait le front bien dessiné, un visage agréable, très intellectuel, et une expression ouverte, honnête. Ses cheveux tiraient sur le roux, il avait les yeux gris et le teint rubicond. Ses manières n'avaient rien d'abrupt ni de brusque, trait si caractéristique des Anglais, mais il faisait montre d'une grande culture et d'un raffinement exquis. C'était un hôte superbe.

« Mais il avait deux défauts malheureux : son naturel morose et son tempérament extrêmement colérique. Il s'imaginait aussi être affublé de tous les maux dont “ la chair avait hérité ”.

« Oui, M. Maybrick était dépendant de l'arsenic. Il en avait un besoin maladif, comme un drogué. Il en consommait dans la maison même. Il demandait sans arrêt au médecin de lui en prescrire et au pharmacien de lui concocter un fortifiant contenant de l'arsenic. Un jour, il a dit à ma mère : “ Ils m'en donnent juste assez pour aggraver ma souffrance, m'inquiéter et faire en sorte que j'en redemande, encore et encore. ”

« Il prenait toujours des comprimés de strychnine et se gavait de bouillon de viande à l'arsenic. Un jour, mon père a dit : “ Maybrick a une dizaine de pharmacies dans le ventre. ”

« Je l'ai vu en colère à plusieurs reprises, et deux fois il était furieux. J'étais la cause de son deuxième éclat [...]. Son bébé [Gladys] avait un petit lit avec des barreaux très hauts tout autour [...]. Un matin, le bébé pleurait et je me suis précipitée vers son lit pour le faire passer par-dessus les barreaux mais au bout d'un moment j'étais si épuisée que je ne pouvais plus le tenir et je l'ai laissé retomber [...]. Si j'avais réussi à sortir [Gladys] du lit et qu'elle était tombée par terre, elle se serait sans doute brisée les reins [...].

« La nurse est arrivée, folle de colère. Elle m'a saisie par la nuque, m'a secouée comme un prunier et m'a lancé : “ Si tu recommences, je te donnerai une tournée dont tu te souviendras toute ta vie. ”

« Durant cette petite scène, M. Maybrick est passé dans le couloir [...]. M. Maybrick était furieux [...] il a dit : “ Je vous ai vue attraper cette enfant par la nuque – vous auriez pu lui briser le cou. Cette enfant est loin de son père et de sa mère, elle se trouve dans ma maison et sous ma protection, et si je vous entends encore lui parler de cette façon-là je vous ferai rouler au bas de l'escalier et je briserai chacun de vos bon Dieu d'os. ” »

Il régnait à Battlecrease House une atmosphère étrange. Bien qu'elle ne soit encore qu'une enfant, Florence l'avait ressentie.

« Un courant de mystère semblait circuler partout, qui vous donnait un sentiment bizarre, le sentiment qu'il se passait quelque chose que vous ne pouviez pas comprendre. Dans le jardin, on voyait souvent les domestiques conversant à mots couverts. Si quelqu'un approchait, ils s'arrêtaient net et se dispersaient. »

Mme Briggs comptait parmi les personnalités qui jouaient un rôle de premier plan à Battlecrease House.

« C'était une femme qui avait à peu près le même âge que M. Maybrick, et on avait dit à mon père qu'elle avait été follement amoureuse de M. Maybrick et avait tout essayé pour l'épouser. Il est très évident qu'il ne partageait pas les mêmes sentiments à son égard. »

Il y avait aussi « Nurse Yapp », « une femme très efficace et très capable », mais aussi « on ne peut plus fourbe et déloyale ».

« Mme Briggs et Nurse Yapp méprisaient et haïssaient Mme Maybrick. Et le plus pathétique dans tout ça, c'est que Mme Maybrick n'avait pas l'intelligence nécessaire pour s'en rendre compte [...].

« Mme Briggs prenait toutes sortes d'initiatives dans la maison et avec les domestiques. Elle appelait M. Maybrick " James ". A table, il m'est arrivé de l'entendre dire des choses telles que : " James, tu ne penses pas qu'un toit sur la véranda attenante à ton cabinet particulier serait de beaucoup préférable [...]. James, je suggère que tu mettes ton gros manteau [...]. James, que dirais-tu d'un rôti de porc pour le dîner ? " Je ne l'ai pas entendue s'adresser une seule fois à Mme Maybrick.

« Quand M. et Mme Maybrick étaient absents, elle se rendait dans toutes les pièces de la maison. Dans la chambre de M. Maybrick et dans celle de Mme Maybrick. Seule une pièce lui était interdite : le cabinet particulier de M. Maybrick. Il y avait une serrure à barillet Yale sur la porte et elle n'était jamais ouverte, seulement quand il s'y trouvait. On n'y faisait jamais le ménage. Seulement quand il s'y trouvait. »

Thomas et Edwin, les frères de Maybrick, comptaient parmi les visiteurs réguliers à Battlecrease House, où il leur arrivait de passer la nuit. Michael venait moins souvent car il habitait Londres. Quant à William, le frère aîné, il ne venait apparemment jamais, bien qu'il habitât Liverpool.

Michael avait la réputation d'être le cerveau de la famille. Selon Florence Aunspaugh, « il possédait une propriété très prétentieuse qui surpassait celle de James sur tous les plans ». En 1888, il n'était toujours pas marié et c'est une gouvernante qui s'occupait de lui.

A la suite du procès et de la condamnation de Florie, le public s'est retourné contre Michael, estimant qu'il l'avait trahie. A Londres, le public le sifflait régulièrement. A tel point qu'il a été contraint de faire ses adieux à la scène, pour prendre sa retraite sur l'île de Wight. La mode de cette île avait terni depuis que la popularité croissante des casinos attirait la clientèle chic de l'autre côté de la Manche. Aussi Michael a-t-il pu y prendre un nouveau départ. Le gros poisson de naguère devait maintenant frayer avec le menu fretin.

Si l'on en croit Florence, le plus jeune frère, Edwin, était « l'un des hommes les plus beaux que j'aie jamais vus ». Il mesurait plus d'un mètre quatre-vingts, et sa silhouette bien proportionnée lui donnait fière allure. Ses yeux brun foncé, ses cheveux noirs ondulés et ses traits réguliers ajoutaient à son charme. Sans parler de sa voix magnifique – plus belle encore que celle de Michael – qu'il n'avait malheureusement jamais eu l'opportunité d'exploiter. A l'âge de trente-sept ans, lui aussi demeurait célibataire.

Les relations de James et d'Edwin avec Michael souffraient du pouvoir exercé sur eux par ce dernier. Dans son journal, Maybrick mentionne à plusieurs reprises la jalousie qu'il éprouve à l'endroit de Michael, qu'il appelle « le frère raisonnable ». La fille d'Edwin, Amy, a raconté des années plus tard que son père « ne laçait jamais ses chaussures sans consulter Michael ».

Toutefois, Maybrick était proche d'Edwin, avec lequel il a même travaillé. Edwin lui manquait beaucoup lorsqu'il s'absentait. Il est probable qu'il manquait aussi à Florie. Des rumeurs quant aux sentiments éprouvés par l'épouse volage envers son beau-frère circulaient depuis un bon moment à la bourse du coton. On soupçonnait même une liaison. Après la mort de Maybrick, les domestiques ont murmuré que des lettres adressées à Florie par Edwin avaient été retrouvées.

Charles Aunspaugh a confié à sa fille, Florence, que Michael avait détruit ces lettres. Cependant, elle se souvient d'un incident rapporté par son père, qui justifie les soupçons. « La première fois que mon père a noté que quelque chose ne tournait pas rond, c'est le soir du grand dîner. Vingt couples y assistaient, la table était donc très longue. La conversation s'était organisée en petits groupes. M. Edwin était assis près de Mme James Maybrick, et ils se parlaient en riant. Mon père a jeté un coup d'œil en direction de James et c'est à ce moment-là qu'il a entendu Mme Maybrick dire à Edwin, en riant : " Si je t'avais rencontré d'abord, les choses auraient peut-être été différentes. " »

Il s'agissait peut-être d'une plaisanterie sans conséquence. Toutefois, Maybrick l'a prise au pied de la lettre.

« Il a lâché son couteau, poursuit Florence, il a serré le poing et son visage s'est enflammé. Une seconde plus tard, il avait retrouvé son calme, ramassé son couteau, et l'incident a été oublié. »

Chapitre 4

Le Poste House, situé dans Cumberland Street près des docks de Liverpool, n'a guère changé depuis 1888. A l'époque, cet établissement était célèbre pour son ragoût, qui attirait les foules à l'heure du déjeuner. Aujourd'hui, les clients s'entassent dans ce qui est devenu un bar minuscule et mal éclairé.

Non loin du Poste House se trouve la rue commerçante où se pressait autrefois le Tout-Liverpool : Whitechapel. C'est dans cette rue, que Maybrick a cru apercevoir Florie avec Alfred Brierley, l'homme qu'il accusait secrètement d'être l'amant de sa femme.

Dans le journal, Brierley n'est jamais mentionné par son nom. Maybrick le surnomme « le maquereau », et lorsqu'il songe à Florie dans les bras de son amant, sa « Bunny chérie » devient « la garce » ou « la putain ».

Il écrit :

> J'ai mangé un morceau au Poste House c'est là que je me suis enfin décidé : ce sera Londres. Et pourquoi pas, n'est-ce pas un endroit idéal ? N'est-il pas vrai que je me rends fréquemment dans la capitale et n'est-il pas vrai que j'ai une raison légitime de le faire. Toutes celles qui vendent leurs marchandises sordides paieront, de cela je

ne doute pas. Mais moi, faudra-t-il que je paie ? Je ne le pense pas je suis trop malin pour ça. [...]
La garce et son maquereau regretteront amèrement le jour où je les ai vus ensemble pour la première fois.

Miné par une santé déclinante, par la toxicomanie et par le fait qu'il lui fallait désormais faire chambre à part, Maybrick éprouvait une jalousie insensée. Les coquetteries dépourvues de tact de Florie l'irritaient. Mais c'est l'amitié grandissante de cette dernière pour Brierley qui a fait germer l'idée du meurtre dans l'esprit de Maybrick.

Il avait un motif. Il lui fallait déterminer le lieu du crime.

J'ai dit ce sera Whitechapel et ce sera Whitechapel. [...]
Whitechapel Liverpool, Whitechapel Londres, *ha ha*. Personne n'aurait jamais l'idée de faire le rapprochement. Et en vérité parce qu'il n'y a aucune raison de le faire.

Toutefois, dans un autre paragraphe du journal il est mentionné que Thomas, le frère de Maybrick, lui a demandé de venir le voir à Manchester. Thomas résidait dans le faubourg de Moss Side et travaillait comme directeur de la *Manchester Packing Company*, firme spécialisée dans l'emballage. Maybrick avait accepté, bien que son esprit fût déjà encombré de préoccupations autres que commerciales.

Demain je me rends à Manchester. Prendrai un peu de mon médicament et réfléchirai sérieusement à la question. [...]
Je m'obligerai à ne pas penser aux enfants.
Le temps passe bien trop lentement, je dois encore rassembler le courage nécessaire pour entamer ma campagne.
J'ai longuement réfléchi à cette question et je ne peux toujours pas décider quand je devrais commencer.

> L'opportunité est là, de ce fait je suis certain. [...] Mon médicament me fait du bien, en fait, je suis sûr que je peux en prendre plus que n'importe quelle autre personne vivante.

Tout comme Maybrick s'était servi de Michael comme alibi à Londres, c'est Thomas qui justifiait son voyage d'affaires à Manchester. En un peu plus d'une heure, le train au départ de Liverpool l'a conduit de la gare d'Aigburth à Manchester. Et c'est finalement à Manchester qu'il allait commettre son premier meurtre. Il a évoqué cette expérience, qui ne lui avait à l'évidence pas donné la satisfaction escomptée.

> Oh mon Dieu je ne sais plus où j'en suis. La putain est maintenant avec son créateur et il peut se la garder. Je n'ai pas eu de plaisir à serrer, je n'ai rien ressenti. Ne sais pas si j'ai le courage de revenir à mon idée de départ. Il faisait froid et humide à Manchester tout à fait comme ici dans ce bouge. La prochaine fois, je leur balancerai de l'acide dessus.

D'après le Dr David Forshaw, ce type de fantasmes est courant chez les auteurs de crimes en série. Des études portant sur plusieurs patients psychopathes ont montré qu'ils nourrissaient des fantasmes sexuels de type sadique. « Avec le temps, explique le Dr Forshaw, les fantasmes s'accentuent à tel point qu'ils se mettent en situation de les réaliser. Par exemple en suivant des victimes potentielles. Des souvenirs puisés dans ces " coups pour rien " sont ensuite incorporés aux fantasmes, qu'ils viennent enrichir [...]. Inexorablement, la progression mène au passage à l'acte. Durant ce processus, les patients deviennent progressivement incapables de faire la différence entre la réalité et un monde de fantasmes [...] où ils étaient totalement maîtres de la situation. Le fait d'infliger la souffrance leur redonne la maîtrise de la situation [...], ce qui leur permet de compenser le sentiment d'inadéquation qu'ils éprouvent. »

Les recherches n'ont, jusqu'ici, pas permis de retrouver la trace du moindre meurtre à Manchester en février ou en mars 1888. Mais il est fort possible que la disparition d'une prostituée de province n'ait donné lieu à aucun procès-verbal. Henry Mayhew, dans son ouvrage *London Labour and the London Poor* (les Travailleurs et les pauvres à Londres) publié pour la première fois en 1851, estimait que quatre-vingt mille prostituées travaillaient rien qu'à Londres.

Maybrick n'avait aucune raison d'inventer ce meurtre pour son journal. Son récit semble être la description précise d'une mort qui, à la différence des assassinats ultérieurs commis par l'Éventreur, n'avait pas fait la une des journaux. Il a étranglé sa première victime, comme toutes celles qui ont suivi. Mais il ne l'a pas éventrée et n'en a tiré aucun plaisir : jusqu'à la parution en 1975 de l'ouvrage de Donald Rumbelow, *The Complete Jack the Ripper* (Les œuvres complètes de Jack l'Éventreur), personne n'avait suggéré que l'Éventreur tuait ses victimes par strangulation, et ne procédait qu'ensuite aux mutilations. Mais le journal est très clair sur ce point, lorsque Maybrick décrit la façon dont il a assassiné sa victime à Manchester.

Il a ressenti immédiatement le besoin de consigner ses pensées et ses actes sur le papier. Selon David Forshaw, son langage est celui d'un homme qui joue la comédie et se donne confiance de manière perverse en se faisant passer pour moins éduqué qu'il n'est. Il éprouve une délectation morbide à déformer la grammaire, à multiplier les solécismes et les jeux de mots. « Il n'est pas rare que des personnes intelligentes mais complexées adoptent une personnalité moins éduquée sur le papier », dit le Dr Forshaw. On relève en outre de nombreuses fautes d'orthographe, de grammaire et de ponctuation qui tranchent sur les habiles jeux verbaux qui parsèment le journal. Ces erreurs peuvent donc être dues à la personnalité « moins éduquée » que Maybrick avait adoptée, mais elles peuvent également provenir du manque d'instruction d'un homme sans prétention culturelle, parvenu tout seul à un statut social convenable.

Cette entreprise présentait des dangers, bien sûr, et Maybrick se sentait plus en sécurité pour écrire dans l'intimité de son bureau, loin des regards inquisiteurs des membres de sa famille et de ses domestiques. Lorsqu'il parle de « rentrer », il veut dire rentrer chez lui, à Battlecrease House, et rien ne vient contredire l'hypothèse selon laquelle Maybrick aurait rédigé l'intégralité du journal dans son bureau, peut-être en fin d'après-midi, quand le personnel était parti. Toutefois, il lui fallait faire preuve d'une extrême prudence pour protéger son secret d'une découverte accidentelle par des employés tels que le comptable, George Smith, ou le jeune commis, Thomas Lowry.

> Que Smith trouve ceci, et je suis fait avant que ma campagne commence.

> Je commence à croire qu'il n'est pas sage de continuer à écrire. Si je dois buter une pute alors rien ne conduira les autorités jusqu'à moi, mais pourtant il y a des moments où je sens une contrainte irrésistible qui me pousse à jeter mes pensées sur le papier. [...] Cependant, le plaisir d'écrire tout ce qui m'attend [...] m'excite tant. Et oh quels actes je m'en vais commettre. Car comment pourrait-on soupçonner que je puisse être capable de telles choses, car ne suis-je pas, comme tout le monde le croit, un homme doux, dont on a pu dire qu'il ne ferait jamais de mal à une mouche.

Ses craintes sont fondées, car Thomas Lowry, dix-neuf ans, fils d'un sabotier de Liverpool, semble, selon son journal, avoir fait de dangereuses découvertes :

> Si j'avais pu tuer ce salaud de Lowry sur-le-champ de mes propres mains, je l'aurais fait. Comment ose-t-il mettre ma parole en doute sur quelque sujet que ce soit, c'est moi qui devrais mettre sa parole en doute. Qu'il aille au diable au diable au diable devrais-je replacer les objets manquants ? Non ce serait un trop grand risque. Devrais-je détruire ceci ? Mon Dieu je vais le tuer. Ne pas lui donner de raison et lui ordonner séance tenante de laisser tomber l'affaire, voilà je crois la seule ligne de conduite que je puisse adopter. Je vais me forcer à penser à quelque chose de plus agréable.

Le lendemain, Maybrick, désorienté par les médicaments, se souvient à peine de ce qui s'est passé.

> J'en ai pris trop je n'arrive pas à penser aussi clairement que je le devrais. Je ne me rappelle presque rien de ce qui s'est passé hier. Grâce à Dieu je me suis arrêté à temps. Je vais montrer ma colère envers ce salaud d'une telle façon qu'il regrettera d'avoir jamais abordé le sujet. Personne, pas même Dieu lui-même ne me privera du plaisir d'écrire mes pensées. [...] J'ai mal à la tête, Dieu n'a pas le droit de me faire ça que le diable l'emporte.

On ignore jusqu'à quel point Lowry s'était ingéré dans les affaires de son patron. Mais son action lui avait fait courir un danger bien plus grand qu'il n'en avait conscience. Il en savait trop, mais que savait-il au juste ? On peut seulement se risquer à suggérer que Lowry avait posé des questions à Maybrick au sujet de documents ou d'objets qui avaient disparu du bureau et qui avaient peut-être un rapport avec le journal. Si c'est le cas, la réaction de Maybrick ne laisse pas de surprendre par sa démesure. Mais il se sent menacé à un moment critique – nous sommes en juin 1888 – et la préparation de son premier meurtre à Whitechapel le plonge dans la plus vive excitation.

Quels qu'aient été les « objets manquants » et le « sujet » en question, l'évocation spontanée et violente de Lowry est tout à fait convaincante de l'état de panique dans lequel il se trouvait.

De temps en temps, Maybrick se rendait à Londres. Des trains au départ de Liverpool assuraient une liaison régulière avec la capitale et l'express mettait environ cinq heures pour atteindre sa destination. L'ancien partenaire de Maybrick à Liverpool, Gustavus A. Witt, possédait une filiale à Londres. Elle était sise dans Cullum Street, à quatre cents mètres à peine de Mitre Square, où Maybrick tuerait pour la cinquième fois un peu plus tard cette même année. Mark Lane était encore plus proche de Cullum Street où le jeune Maybrick allait probablement faire la cour à Sarah Robertson.

Lorsqu'il se trouvait à Londres, il séjournait le plus souvent chez son frère Michael, qui habitait Wellington Mansions, dans le très huppé Regent's Park. Michael était membre du Constitutional Club, et aussi franc-maçon. C'est lui le fondateur de la loge Orpheus, pour les musiciens.

Maybrick n'était pas à l'aise en compagnie de son frère cadet, aussi arrogant que satisfait de lui-même, mais la maison de Regent's Park était confortable – et idéalement située.

> Je rendrai visite à Michael en juin prochain. Juin est un mois si agréable, les fleurs sont tout en bourgeons l'air est plus odorant et la vie est presque certainement plus rose j'attends sa venue avec plaisir. Un très grand plaisir.

Dans son journal Maybrick raconte qu'il est allé voir son frère avec l'idée d'entamer sa « campagne ». Mais les choses ne se sont pas passées comme prévu. Il n'était pas prêt à tuer. En effet, bien que l'envie de frapper soit devenue presque incontrôlable, il n'avait pas élaboré ses plans avec la minutie nécessaire. A tel point qu'il a été contraint de se servir de Michael comme d'un geôlier.

> Comment suis-je parvenu à me maîtriser, je n'en sais rien. Je n'ai pas tenu compte de la substance rouge, il y en a des litres selon mon estimation. A coup sûr, je vais être éclaboussé. Je ne peux pas laisser mes vêtements s'imbiber de sang, ça je ne pourrais l'expliquer à personne, surtout pas à Michael. Pourquoi n'y ai-je pas pensé plus tôt ? Je me maudis. Pour m'arrêter j'ai dû lutter jusqu'à mes dernières forces, et si je n'avais pas demandé à Michael de m'enfermer dans ma chambre par crainte d'une crise de somnambulisme, dont j'ai expliqué qu'elles étaient devenues fréquentes récemment, n'était-ce pas astucieux ? j'aurais commis mes sales actes ce soir-là.

En ce mois de juin, Maybrick était paniqué au sujet de sa santé. On le sait d'après le journal et les témoignages de médecins au procès de Florie. Une hypocondrie poussée à l'extrême alimentait sa soif de protection médicale et de drogue.

Entre fin juin et septembre, il a rendu visite une vingtaine de fois au Dr Hopper, le médecin de famille. Il se plaignait de violents maux de tête qui avaient débuté en juin, au moment des courses hippiques de Royal Ascot, et d'un engourdissement des pieds et des jambes.

On n'avait pas connaissance, à l'époque, des effets de l'empoisonnement chronique par l'arsenic et par la strychnine. Si le Dr Hopper avait pu bénéficier des avancées de la science moderne, il aurait compris que la santé de son patient présentait des symptômes alarmants, dus au volume et à la diversité des médicaments qu'il consommait.

Mais le médecin entretenait des doutes au sujet de

l'hypocondrie de Maybrick. En conséquence, il ne lui manifestait aucune compassion, et il était irrité par ce patient qui prenait de sa propre initiative, entre les visites, des remèdes conseillés par des amis. L'un de ces médicaments, le sirop Fellows, était une mixture contenant de l'arsenic, de la strychnine, de la quinine, du fer et des hypophosphites. En outre, lorsque les ordonnances du Dr Hopper ne produisaient pas l'effet escompté, Maybrick doublait la dose.

Autrefois, on prêtait beaucoup de vertus médicinales à la strychnine et on la trouvait dans le commerce, sous forme de cachet dont l'action était fortifiante et aphrodisiaque.

Un jour Maybrick a remis au Dr Hopper des ordonnances rédigées pour lui par un certain Dr Seguin, de New York, où Maybrick se rendait régulièrement en voyage d'affaires. Elles prescrivaient de la strychnine et de la *nux vomica*. Ce médicament à base de strychnine, très populaire auprès des Anglais de l'époque victorienne, était également utilisé comme aphrodisiaque. Le Dr Hopper a détruit ces ordonnances. « Je me suis dit qu'il devait avoir un sacré cafard », a-t-il déclaré au procès de Florie, avant d'ajouter que Maybrick « attachait trop d'importance à des symptômes insignifiants ».

En juillet, sur recommandation du médecin, Maybrick est allé faire une cure thermale à Harrogate Spa, dans le Yorkshire. Il a pris une chambre au Queen Hotel, établissement modeste. Son nom est dûment mentionné dans le « Registre des visiteurs », une rubrique régulière du journal local, « le bulletin d'Harrogate ». Il y est resté seul pendant quatre jours.

Chaque année le 1er août, les courses de Goodwood, dans le Sussex, étaient un rendez-vous obligé des Maybrick avec la bonne société. Cette année-là, ils y ont rencontré John Baillie Knight, ami d'enfance de Florie, qui était accompagné de ses tantes. Le soir, ils ont dîné ensemble à l'Exposition italienne de Londres.

C'est dans une pension de famille en Suisse que les

demoiselles Baillie avaient fait la connaissance de la baronne von Roques et de sa fille. Enfant, Florie avait séjourné chez elles à plusieurs reprises et elles lui avaient rendu visite à Liverpool après son mariage. D'après ce qu'elles ont confié plus tard à leur neveu, elles avaient noté une certaine tension entre James et Florie Maybrick. John Baillie et Florie ne se sont plus revus jusqu'en 1889, mais elle lui a écrit plusieurs fois. Dans ses lettres, elle lui a fait part de sa détresse au sujet des infidélités de son mari.

Le premier lundi d'août, jour férié en Angleterre, une prostituée répondant au nom de Martha Tabram a été assassinée dans le quartier de Whitechapel, à Londres. Elle avait passé la soirée à boire et à chercher des clients. A 4 h 50 le matin suivant, elle a été découverte gisant dans une mare de sang dans le George Yard Building. Elle avait reçu trenteneuf coups de couteau, principalement dans les seins, dans le ventre et dans les parties génitales.

Il est probable que Martha avait été assassinée par son dernier client, un soldat des régiments de la garde royale. Mais la presse et la police ont détecté des similitudes entre ce meurtre et celui d'Emma Smith, qui avait été assassinée et mutilée en avril, le lundi de Pâques, et ont conclu qu'elles avaient toutes deux étaient tuées par le même homme.

Puis en automne, lorsque Jack l'Éventreur a entamé sa campagne à Whitechapel, la presse et la police ont de nouveau établi un lien entre ces assassinats et ceux de Martha Tabram et d'Emma Smith.

L'hypothèse selon laquelle tous ces meurtres auraient été perpétrés par le même criminel ne sera pas contredite pendant soixante-dix ans.

Mais le journal ne mentionne ni le meurtre d'Emma Smith ni celui de Martha Tabram.

Plus tard en août, plusieurs semaines après son dernier séjour chez Michael, Maybrick retournerait à Londres. Mais cette fois, il louerait une chambre à Whitechapel.

Il était prêt à passer à l'acte.

Chapitre 5

> J'ai pris une petite chambre dans Middlesex Street, ce qui est une plaisanterie en soi. J'ai payé largement et je crois qu'on ne posera pas de questions. C'est en vérité un endroit idéal. J'ai marché dans les rues et je me suis plus que familiarisé avec elles. [...] Je n'ai pas de doutes, ma confiance est au plus haut. Je suis excité d'écrire ces lignes, la vie est douce, et ma déception s'est dissipée. La prochaine fois, c'est sûr.

Middlesex Street, mieux connue sous le nom de Petticoat Lane, est fameuse pour son marché dominical. Après les deux premiers meurtres de l'Éventreur, la police a conclu que le tueur devait avoir disposé d'une cachette dans Whitechapel – mais personne n'avait encore découvert où. Le fait que Middlesex Street soit mentionnée dans le journal est une précieuse indication.

Non loin de là, selon le plan des pas-de-porte commerciaux de 1888, vivaient Mme Polly Nathan, qui tenait le *fish and chips* [1], Solran Berlinski, marchand de chiffons, George Bolam, *nourrisseur*, Isaac Woolf, négociant en cartes à jouer et Samuel Barnett, qui avait créé avec sa femme Henrietta des cantines pour les pauvres. Samuel Barnett n'était autre

1. Établissement qui vend des frites et du poisson frit. Très populaire, encore aujourd'hui. *(N.d.T.)*

que le pasteur local, et il prônait ce qu'on appelait alors le « socialisme dans la pratique ».

Mais pourquoi le choix de Middlesex Street constituait-il « une plaisanterie en soi » ? A cause des trois dernières lettres de son nom ? Ou de son surnom, Petticoat Lane [1], qui remontait au moins à l'époque des Tudor ? Parce que Middlesex Street donnait dans Liverpool Street ? Une autre explication est possible : Middlesex Street était une artère commerçante fréquentée par la communauté juive, et donc le foyer de l'agitation antisémite. Or, dans le journal, Maybrick ne fait pas mystère de son inimitié pour les juifs.

> Pourquoi ne pas laisser les juifs souffrir ? Ils ne m'ont jamais été sympathiques, il y en a bien trop à la bourse pour mon goût.

Vers la fin de sa vie, cependant, il s'en est voulu d'avoir nourri ces préjugés. Après avoir rencontré un ancien collègue à la bourse, il écrit en effet :

> J'ai éprouvé du regret car n'était-il pas juif. J'avais oublié combien j'ai d'amis juifs. Je me venge sur les putains, pas sur les Juifs.

Mais outre l'aspect ironique de son nom le choix de Middlesex Street présentait des avantages pratiques pour Maybrick :

La frontière entre le champ d'action des deux forces de police rivales, la *Metropolitan Police* et la *City Police*, passait par cette rue. Maybrick pouvait donc créer la confusion et narguer la police en commettant ses forfaits d'un côté, puis de l'autre de cette limite administrative. Il en jouera particulièrement dans le cas du meurtre de Catharine Eddowes.

De plus Middlesex Street se trouvait à une distance très

1. L'allée des jupons. *(N.d.T.)*

commode du bureau du collègue de Maybrick, Gustavus A. Witt.

Avant le XIXe siècle, Whitechapel offrait l'image d'un quartier de marchands respectables et de prospérité tranquille. Mais en 1888, les conséquences du déclin étaient visibles partout. D'arrière-cours miteuses en boyaux nauséabonds et jonchés de détritus, les alentours de Middlesex Street alliaient surpopulation et violence. On y trouvait des centaines de pensions où, pour trois *pence* la nuit, on pouvait s'acheter un lit dans une chambre misérable et sans chauffage. Ceux qui n'avaient pas d'argent dormaient dans les caniveaux ou dans les cages d'escalier. Des familles entières s'entassaient dans une pièce minuscule, avec un lit pour tout mobilier. Partout flottaient des remugles putrides d'urine et de moisissure.

Au moins mille deux cents « infortunées » – terme employé à l'époque pour désigner les prostituées – battaient le pavé. Comme tant de femmes victoriennes appartenant à la classe ouvrière, la plupart étaient vieilles avant l'âge, usées par des conditions de vie inhumaines, la pauvreté, les coups et la boisson.

Le 18 août, moins de deux semaines avant que Maybrick ne frappe pour la première fois à Whitechapel, son frère Edwin est parti pour l'Amérique à bord du *SS Adriatic*. Selon le Dr Forshaw ce détail est significatif : en l'absence de son cadet dévoué, Maybrick avait la bride sur le cou. Plus personne n'était là pour vérifier ses dires quand il affirmait se rendre à Londres pour affaires.

Toutes les conditions étaient maintenant réunies pour le passage à l'acte.

A 0 h 30, le vendredi 31 août, Mary Ann Nichols, plus connue sous le nom de Polly, quitte le Frying Pan, pub de Brick Lane, à Whitechapel. On a refusé de l'accueillir au 18 Thrawl Street, mais loin d'être découragée, elle a lancé : « J'aurai vite assez d'argent pour m'offrir un pieu. » Et de faire admirer son nouveau chapeau, avec lequel elle espère attirer les hommes. Elle semble encore jeune pour une femme dans sa quarantaine et elle sera décrite par le Dr Ralph Llewellyn qui procédera à l'autopsie, comme « très saine ».

Trois personnes au moins vont apercevoir Polly Nichols arpentant les rues obscures, dans l'espoir de trouver un client. L'horloge de l'église paroissiale St. Mary Matfellon vient de sonner la demie de 2 heures lorsqu'elle s'engage en titubant dans Whitechapel Road, où elle va parcourir un kilomètre et demi avant de rencontrer Maybrick.

Tous deux quittent la rue principale et empruntent Buck's Row, petite sente pavée sans éclairage. Une rangée de nouveaux cottages d'ouvriers, serrés les uns contre les autres, fait face à des entrepôts. Là, Maybrick plaque Polly Nichols contre une grille, à l'entrée d'une vieille écurie, et il l'étrangle. Puis il la pousse à terre et lui tranche la gorge jusqu'aux vertèbres.

L'obsession de décapiter qui poursuivait Maybrick apparaît constamment dans son journal – et les rapports des médecins légistes de l'époque le confirment, de profondes entailles à hauteur du cou ont été observées à chaque meurtre.

> J'ai montré à tout le monde que je ne plaisante pas, le plaisir était bien supérieur à ce que j'avais imaginé. La putain n'était que trop heureuse de faire son boulot. Je me rappelle tout et ça m'excite. Il n'y a pas eu de cri quand j'ai coupé. J'étais plus que contrarié quand la tête n'a pas voulu se détacher. Je crois qu'il me faudra plus de force la prochaine fois. J'ai frappé profondément en elle. Je regrette de n'avoir pas eu la canne, il aurait été délicieux de l'enfoncer en elle bien à fond. La garce s'est ouverte comme une pêche bien mûre. J'ai décidé que la prochaine fois j'éventrerai complètement. Mon médicament me donnera de

la force et à la pensée de la putain et de son maquereau, je redoublerai d'énergie.

Frustré parce qu'il n'avait pas réussi à enlever la tête de sa victime, l'Éventreur a ensuite déchiré sa jupe avant de l'éventrer et de taillader ses entrailles.

Quand il en a eu terminé, il s'est éclipsé en silence. Aucun des résidents ou des veilleurs de nuit du voisinage n'a rien entendu.

Comme chaque matin, Charles Cross, charretier de son état, emprunte Buck's Row pour se rendre à son travail lorsqu'il aperçoit ce qu'il prend d'abord pour une bâche. Il s'agit en fait de Polly Nichols. Le corps est encore chaud. Le chapeau neuf doublé de velours noir se trouve juste à côté.

Quelques heures plus tard, à la morgue, deux indigents de l'hospice voisin reçoivent l'ordre de nettoyer le cadavre. C'est seulement à ce moment-là qu'on découvre que Polly Nichols a été mutilée.

L'enquête criminelle est confiée à l'élégant coroner Wynne Edwin Baxter. Il revient tout juste d'un périple en Scandinavie et se présente au Whitechapel Working Lads Institute vêtu d'un pantalon à carreaux noirs et blancs, d'un gilet blanc et d'un foulard cramoisi.

On a demandé au Dr Llewellyn de quitter son cabinet de Whitechapel Road pour venir examiner le corps. Il observe une blessure d'environ six ou sept centimètres sur la partie gauche de l'abdomen. Les tissus ont été profondément transpercés. Plusieurs autres incisions sont visibles en travers de l'abdomen, ainsi que trois ou quatre coupures du côté droit. Toutes ont été pratiquées avec un couteau.

Ce rapport va donner à croire que le meurtrier se tenait devant sa victime, qu'il a immobilisé sa mâchoire de la main droite et tranché la gorge de gauche à droite en tenant son couteau de la main gauche. Mais pareille technique aurait requis un contorsionniste.

Pour leur part, les auteurs de *The Jack the Ripper A-Z* (Jack l'Éventreur de A à Z) suggèrent qu'« il se tenait devant ses victimes, ainsi qu'il convient pour un rapport sexuel en position debout ; qu'il plaçait les deux mains autour de leur cou, ce qui lui permettait de les réduire au silence instantanément et de leur faire perdre connaissance rapidement ; qu'il les poussait au sol avec la tête à sa gauche et leur tranchait la gorge en amenant le couteau vers lui. Le sang des carotides jaillissait donc en direction opposée, ce qui lui évitait d'être éclaboussé. Cela suggère également qu'il était droitier ».

De retour chez lui à Liverpool, Maybrick a parcouru les journaux avec avidité pour y lire le récit de son deuxième meurtre. Il n'a pas été déçu.

> J'ai eu l'impression de devoir attendre longtemps avant de lire le récit de mon triomphe, mais ce n'était pas le cas. [...] Ils ont tous bien écrit. La prochaine fois ils en auront beaucoup plus à écrire, je n'ai aucun doute là-dessus. [...] Je resterai calme et ne manifesterai aucun intérêt pour mon acte, si d'aventure quelqu'un le mentionnait, mais je rirai sous cape, oh comme je rirai.

Un journaliste du *Star* a passé au peigne fin tous les pubs et tous les asiles de nuit en quête d'un portrait du tueur. Il a prétendu avoir interrogé une cinquantaine de femmes en trois heures, et chacune lui avait donné une description identique : celle d'un homme que les riverains avaient surnommé « Tablier de cuir » : il était âgé d'environ quarante ans, petit, doté d'un cou de taureau et d'une moustache noire, et il avait un faciès de type sémite. Ses mouvements étaient « silencieux et sinistres », ses yeux luisaient et il avait un « sourire repoussant ».

En réalité, le Juif polonais qu'on avait surnommé « Tablier de cuir » – un finisseur de bottes, de son vrai nom

John Pizer – était innocent de ce meurtre-là, bien qu'il ait été reconnu coupable de deux ou trois agressions mineures dans le passé. En effet, la nuit du meurtre de Polly Nichols, il se trouvait dans Seven Sisters Road, à Holloway, dans le nord de Londres, où il admirait le rougeoiement produit dans le ciel par deux incendies qui s'étaient déclarés sur les docks. Il a été aperçu sur place non seulement par le patron d'une pension de famille, mais aussi par un policier. Ainsi, en dépit de l'acharnement mis par le sergent William Thick à l'arrêter, on n'a pas pu établir de lien entre Pizer et le meurtre. Les journaux ont été condamnés à lui verser des dommages et intérêts.

Mais l'appétit du sensationnel, tendance nouvelle à l'époque, avait été aiguisé et cette affaire a servi à alimenter un filon malsain. Les lecteurs se trouvaient confrontés à des mots qu'ils n'avaient jamais rencontrés dans leurs journaux, ainsi qu'à des illustrations représentant des corps mutilés avec une précision choquante. Le public victorien, corseté par les impératifs moraux en vigueur à l'époque, se délectait de ces détails d'une dépravation effroyable.

La presse américaine elle-même exploitait sans vergogne cette affaire, qu'elle comparait à un récit d'Edgar Allan Poe, *le Double Assassinat de la rue Morgue*. Elle décrivait un homme de petite taille aux yeux noirs pleins de malice, qui se déplaçait en silence et « courait d'une façon bizarre ». Un journaliste du *New York Times* à l'imagination débordante a même expliqué que, après avoir été attaquée, Polly Nichols s'était enfuie en courant et qu'on l'avait retrouvée à plusieurs rues de là, presque décapitée.

Jack l'Éventreur est apparu à un moment où la Grande-Bretagne traversait une période socialement agitée. Non sans humour, l'écrivain irlandais George Bernard Shaw l'a décrit comme un « génie indépendant qui, en étripant cinq femmes, a réussi à rallier les journaux à la cause des oppressés ».

En outre, la première campagne électorale pour les

County Councils [1] battait son plein dans la capitale et les radicaux cherchaient à obtenir le contrôle de l'East End. Or, les gros titres consacrés aux crimes de l'Éventreur mettaient l'accent sur le chômage et les conditions de vie déplorables qui prévalaient parmi les démunis de Londres. Ses actes terribles ont ainsi contribué à l'adoption ultérieure de réformes sociales nécessaires, ainsi qu'à l'amélioration des procédures policières.

C'est pure coïncidence, bien sûr, si la pièce tirée du *Dr Jekyll et M. Hyde* de Robert Louis Stevenson était à l'affiche à ce moment précis. Cette pièce était plus proche de la vérité qu'on aurait pu l'imaginer. Le Dr Jekyll, homme respectable et vieillissant, découvre une potion capable de libérer des sensations enfouies au plus profond de sa personnalité : il se sent jeune, marche d'un pas alerte, et rêve de plaisirs secrets. Mais cette potion réveille aussi en lui l'« esprit de l'Enfer » et le pousse à commettre des meurtres dans les rues de Londres.

Une semaine après avoir massacré Polly Nichols, James Maybrick préparait son prochain meurtre.

1. Divisions administratives. *(N.d.T.)*

Chapitre 6

La notoriété dont Maybrick jouit désormais le rend plus hardi. Ainsi, il ne peut résister à l'envie de discuter du meurtre de Polly Nichols avec son meilleur ami, George Davidson. Tous deux évoquent l'excellent travail des forces de police locales et conviennent que des crimes tels que celui de Whitechapel ne pourraient jamais survenir à Liverpool, où les femmes peuvent se promener dans la rue en toute sécurité. Cette conversation suggère ensuite à Maybrick le commentaire suivant :

> Et en vérité elles le peuvent car je ne vais pas jouer à mes petits jeux devant ma propre porte *ha ha.*

Il se trouve alors dans un tel état d'exaltation qu'il envisage de répéter son crime dans les plus brefs délais.

> Je ne laisserai pas passer trop de temps avant ma prochaine. En vérité, j'ai besoin de répéter mon plaisir dès que possible. Le Maquereau peut l'avoir avec plaisir et je prendrai mon plaisir dans mes pensées et mes actions. Je serai malin. Je ne passerai pas chez Michael lors de ma prochaine visite. Mes frères seraient horrifiés s'ils savaient, en particulier Edwin après tout n'a-t-il pas dit que j'étais l'un des hommes les plus gentils qu'il ait

jamais rencontrés. J'espère qu'il apprécie les fruits de l'Amérique. Pas comme moi, car mon fruit à moi est bien aigre. [...]
Le gentleman aux gentilles pensées va bientôt frapper de nouveau. Je ne me suis jamais senti aussi bien, en fait, j'en prends plus que jamais et je sens la force s'accumuler en moi. La tête viendra la prochaine fois, et aussi les mains de la putain. Et si je les laissais dans différents endroits un peu partout dans Whitechapel ? Elles courent elles courent la tête et les mains, comme le furet *ha ha.* Peut-être que j'en emporterai un morceau avec moi pour voir si ça a bien le goût de bacon frais grillé.

Le week-end suivant, c'est-à-dire le vendredi 7 septembre, il repart pour Londres. Dans le train, il griffonne quelques vers maladroits.

Une sale putain cherchait à gagner de l'argent.
Une autre sale putain cherchait pareillement.

Ces deux lignes évoquent la rencontre de Maybrick avec Polly Nichols. Il est à ce point satisfait du résultat qu'à la suite de tous les meurtres à venir, il écrira des poèmes fourmillant de références à des détails significatifs pour lui. Les vers deviennent rapidement une obsession. Il s'acharne à les corriger et à les récrire jusqu'à ce qu'il soit enfin satisfait du résultat. Ils l'aident à se convaincre de sa supériorité intellectuelle, notamment vis-à-vis de son frère cadet, celui qui reçoit tous les honneurs. A plusieurs reprises dans le journal, Maybrick exprime la crainte respectueuse mêlée de jalousie que lui inspire Michael.

[...] si Michael peut réussir à faire rimer des vers, alors je peux faire mieux, beaucoup mieux il ne me surpassera pas. Réfléchis imbécile, réfléchis. Je maudis Michael d'être si malin, je le surpasserai, j'en fais mon affaire. Un drôle de petit poème verra le jour, *je le veux.*

En réalité, Maybrick s'intéresse très peu à la carrière de son frère, et il ignore que si ce dernier écrit effectivement la musique des chansons qu'il interprète, il n'est pas l'auteur des paroles.

En proie à un profond complexe d'infériorité, Maybrick cherche à prouver au monde qu'il est capable de prouesses intellectuelles et physiques hors de pair. Il lui faut se rassurer en se répétant à l'envi qu'il est « malin » : ce mot n'apparaît pas moins de vingt-cinq fois dans le journal.

La seconde victime de l'Éventreur à Whitechapel se nomme Annie Chapman. Elle est âgée de quarante-sept ans. Cette fille de cavalier de la Garde a quitté son mari et ses deux enfants. Elle a survécu en vendant des fleurs, et parfois son corps.

Minée par une maladie des poumons et du cerveau, elle n'a plus que quelques semaines à vivre. Ses amis décriront cette femme courtaude et robuste, mais à la silhouette harmonieuse, comme une personne sérieuse qui ne buvait que le samedi soir.

Il est environ 23 h 30, en ce vendredi 7 septembre, lorsque Timothy Donovan, le concierge de la pension Crossingham, fait entrer Annie Chapman dans la cuisine. Elle sort de sa poche une boîte contenant deux cachets, mais la boîte se brise et elle replace hâtivement les cachets dans une enveloppe ramassée par terre. Puis elle annonce au concierge qu'elle sort gagner un peu d'argent.

Mme Elizabeth Darrell sera la dernière personne à voir Annie Chapman, devant le 29 Hanbury Street, entre 5 h 00 et 5 h 30. Annie est en conversation avec un « miséreux ». Mme Darrell entend ce dernier demander : « Tu veux bien ? » « Oui », répond Annie.

Mais l'homme en question n'est autre que Maybrick. Il s'engouffre avec la prostituée dans le passage étroit qui mène dans la cour intérieure du n° 29, maison délabrée où logent dix-sept personnes. C'est là que Maybrick saisit Annie à la gorge et l'étrangle. Puis, tailladant de la gauche vers la droite, il s'efforce de la décapiter, mais il n'y parvient pas.

Par Dieu, comme j'aurais voulu pouvoir prendre la tête.

Il l'éventre, retire les intestins et les place sur l'épaule gauche de sa victime, puis il arrache l'utérus et une partie de l'abdomen.

A 5 h 30 environ, Albert Cadosh, charpentier qui réside dans la maison voisine, part travailler. Soudain, il perçoit des bruits de voix dans la cour. Il croit entendre quelqu'un dire « non », puis un coup sourd contre la palissade. Mais il n'y prête guère attention et poursuit son chemin. Personne d'autre ne passera par là jusqu'à 6 h 45.

C'est l'heure à laquelle John Davis se réveille. Aussitôt, il descend dans la cour et c'est lui qui découvre le cadavre mutilé d'Annie Chapman.

« Je ne peux pas décrire ce qui se trouvait à côté d'elle, déclarera-t-il. C'était une partie de son corps. »

Très vite, une foule en proie à la plus vive excitation se rassemble autour du cadavre. On recouvre les restes d'un grand sac avant de les emporter. Mais les rares possessions de la victime demeurent à l'endroit où Maybrick les avait abandonnées : un morceau de mousseline, une brosse à dents, un peigne de poche. « Dans la robe de la morte se trouvaient deux *farthings*, si bien astiqués qu'on se demande si la dame n'avait pas dans l'idée de les faire passer pour deux demi-souverains », écrira l'*Evening News* dans son édition du 8 septembre. Ces pièces n'ont plus jamais été mentionnées, pas même durant l'enquête criminelle.

A l'écart des objets ayant appartenu à la victime, se trouve également dans la cour du 29 Hanbury Street une enveloppe déchirée. Celle qu'Annie Chapman avait ramassée dans la cuisine de la pension Crossingham. Au recto, l'inspecteur Joseph Chandler remarque que la lettre « M », écrite selon lui par un homme, a été laissée en évidence. Le cachet de la poste indique que la missive a été expédiée de Londres, le 28 août 1888. Au dos de l'enveloppe, l'inspecteur aperçoit le sceau du *Sussex Regiment*. Le 14 septembre, il va interroger les hommes du 1er bataillon de ce régiment, basés à Farnborough, dans le Hampshire. Mais sans succès : ce type d'enveloppe est en vente partout, et n'importe qui aurait donc pu l'envoyer.

Entre-temps, Maybrick est retourné à Liverpool. Il observe à distance les efforts maladroits de la police, qui a passé Whitechapel au peigne fin dans l'espoir de retrouver la trace de l'Éventreur. Trois jours après le meurtre d'Annie Chapman, voici ce qu'il écrit dans son journal :

> Les cachets sont la réponse
> finir avec les cachets. En vérité, n'est-ce toujours pas ce que je fais oh quelle farce.

A l'évidence, la découverte des cachets de sa dernière victime a amusé Maybrick. Il ignorait qu'elle se trouvait au seuil de la mort, et en avait sans doute conclu qu'elle se droguait, tout comme lui. Mais le sens des vers suivants est obscur :

> * [1] Laissé deux
> Pas de cachet, laissé que deux
>
> En vérité, ne suis-je pas un type malin ? Ça me fait rire de penser qu'ils ne comprendront jamais pourquoi j'ai agi ainsi.

1. * : Ligne biffée dans le manuscrit original.

Le meurtrier a-t-il retiré de l'enveloppe les cachets d'Annie Chapman pour y substituer deux des siens ?

Quant au « M » figurant au recto de l'enveloppe, voici ce qu'en dit Maybrick :

* Lettre M c'est vrai
Avec M ha ha
Attrapera Jim le malin

Il semblerait que l'enveloppe ait donné à Maybrick l'idée de laisser l'initiale de son nom de famille sur le lieu de ses crimes. A l'origine, le nom et l'adresse complète du destinataire devaient apparaître, mais il a dû la déchirer de façon à ne laisser subsister qu'un « M ».

Mais une autre question se pose : au dire de ses amis, Annie Chapman portait trois bagues de cuivre. Que sont-elles devenues ? Maybrick affirme les avoir arrachées des doigts de sa victime parce qu'elles lui rappelaient l'alliance de sa femme.

Commencer par les bagues
Une bague, deux bagues
garce, il m'a fallu un moment pour les arracher. Aurais dû les enfoncer dans la gorge de la putain. Par Dieu, comme j'aurais voulu pouvoir prendre la tête. Lui en ai voulu à mort de les porter, ça me rappelle trop la putain.
Une bague. Deux bagues
Une bague, deux bagues...

Mais voici ce qu'écrit le journaliste Oswald Allen dans la *Pall Mall Gazette* : « Un des aspects les plus curieux de ce crime, c'est que le meurtrier avait retiré des bagues en cuivre, ainsi que plusieurs articles sans valeur trouvés dans les poches de la victime, et les avait disposés avec soin aux pieds de celle-ci. »

Au fil de témoignages contradictoires, on s'est mis à évoquer « un tas de bagues et de pièces ». Or, il n'y avait jamais eu que trois bagues, et elles avaient disparu car Maybrick les avait emportées avec lui.

L'autre aspect distinctif du second meurtre de Whitechapel, c'est que la victime avait été éventrée. Selon le Dr George Baster Phillips, chirurgien de la police qui était présent à l'autopsie de quatre des victimes, le meurtrier ne pouvait être qu'un médecin. Depuis cette déclaration, les prétendues prouesses médicales du tueur ont fait l'objet d'innombrables analyses. Mais aujourd'hui, la plupart des médecins s'accordent à reconnaître que si l'utérus et le col avaient été détachés d'un coup net à travers le vagin, le reste de l'« opération » avait été exécuté sans art.

Le coroner, Wynne Baxter, a proposé une théorie ingénieuse qui lui avait été inspirée par un article paru dans la presse : un Américain s'était rendu dans plusieurs hôpitaux londoniens avec l'intention d'exporter des utérus préservés. Selon le coroner, ce macabre commerce pouvait avoir motivé le crime. Mais la presse médicale a été prompte à réfuter cette idée.

On en savait très peu, à l'époque, sur la psychologie des auteurs de crimes en série. La psychiatrie était une nouvelle discipline, et la médecine légale n'en était qu'à ses débuts. Certes, les hauts fonctionnaires de la police n'ignoraient pas la motivation sexuelle qui se cachait derrière les crimes de Whitechapel, mais ils n'abordaient pas le sujet avec leurs subordonnés. Ainsi, personne n'aurait imaginé que le fait d'ôter les organes féminins revenait à exercer un contrôle sur la victime, ni que les actes de cannibalisme représentaient la perversion ultime de l'« exercice du pouvoir » par le criminel. Dans un passage du journal, qui prête à confusion, Maybrick rapporte qu'il était si furieux d'avoir oublié sa craie et de n'avoir donc pas pu laisser d'indice – preuve tangible de son « pouvoir » – qu'il est finalement revenu sur ses pas et s'est vengé sur le cadavre.

> J'en ai emporté avec moi. C'est devant moi. J'ai l'intention de le faire frire et de le manger plus tard *ha ha*. A cette seule pensée, j'en ai l'eau à la bouche.

A la suite du meurtre d'Annie Chapman, seize hommes d'affaires de l'East End ont constitué le Comité de vigilance de Whitechapel. Sous la houlette de leur président, le maçon George Lusk, ils ont exigé que les rues soient mieux éclairées et mieux surveillées par la police.

Peu de temps après, *The Times* a émis une nouvelle théorie, celle que le tueur n'appartenait peut-être pas à la classe ouvrière, comme on l'avait pensé jusqu'alors, mais qu'il habitait dans un quartier tout à fait respectable. Quant au sentiment populaire, sans aucun doute fondé sur le sectarisme, il prétendait que seul un étranger avait pu commettre de tels crimes. Or, à Whitechapel, étranger était synonyme de juif.

> J'ai tout lu de mes actions j'ai de quoi être fier, je n'ai pas pu m'empêcher de rire, ils me présentent comme gaucher, médecin, employé d'abattoirs et juif. Très bien, s'ils insistent pour dire que je suis juif, juif je serai. Pourquoi ne pas laisser les juifs souffrir ? Ils ne m'ont jamais été sympathiques.

Cet extrait du journal, tout comme les vers qui suivent, indique que Maybrick avait prévu d'utiliser l'antisémitisme comme diversion. Une fois que la police se serait lancée sur une fausse piste, il commettrait un autre meurtre.

> Les Juifs et les Docteurs
> Seront accusés.

Le 22 septembre, le magazine *Punch* a publié une caricature qui n'a pas manqué d'amuser Maybrick. Elle représentait un policier les yeux bandés aux prises avec quatre malfrats. La légende était la suivante : « Faites trois tours sur vous-même et attrapez qui vous pourrez [1]. »

Cette caricature a donné lieu dans le journal de Maybrick à une série de jeux de mots à partir de son nom, et il a finalement eu l'idée de tracer la lettre « M » sur ses victimes, ou tout à côté.

> Je ne pouvais plus m'arrêter de rire quand j'ai lu *Punch* tout le monde pouvait voir les trois premières lettres de mon nom. Ils ont raison ils sont aveugles.
>
> Je ne peux pas m'arrêter de rire ça m'amuse tellement vais-je leur écrire pour leur donner un indice ?
>
> May s'en vient puis s'en va
> au cœur de la nuit noire
> il embrasse les putains
> et puis leur fait très peur
>
> Les Juifs et les Docteurs
> seront accusés
> mais c'est juste May
> qui joue à son vilain petit jeu

C'est alors que se produit chez Maybrick un soudain changement, comme en témoigne le journal :

> Je mène une bataille en moi-même. Mon désir de vengeance est irrésistible. La putain a détruit ma vie. J'essaie autant que possible de conserver toutes les apparences de la respectabilité. [...] L'excitation que j'éprouve à les découper me manque. Je crois sincèrement que j'ai perdu la raison.

1. Référence au *blind man's buff*, c'est-à-dire colin-maillard. *(N.d.T.)*.

Lorsqu'il s'aperçoit de la réaction provoquée dans le public par son second crime à Whitechapel, Maybrick cède à la mégalomanie qui se faisait jour en lui. Déjà, quelques mois auparavant, durant ses vacances à Battlecrease House, Florence Aunspaugh avait entendu « Nurse Yapp » décrire son maître comme Sir James. A l'évidence, ce titre usurpé l'avait flatté.

C'est ainsi qu'il se décrit dans le journal comme « Sir Jim ». Et à deux reprises, il se surnomme « Sir Jack ». Jack est une forme familière de James, dérivée du français Jacques. On imagine son plaisir lorsqu'il a découvert que ce prénom était formé des deux premières lettres de James et des deux dernières lettres de Maybrick. Il s'en servira pour façonner son pseudonyme, duquel il signera le journal et les lettres qu'il adressera à la presse et à la police à partir de septembre 1888.

> Avant que j'en aie terminé, toute l'Angleterre connaîtra le nom que je me suis donné. C'est en vérité un nom à garder en mémoire. Il sera, avant longtemps, sur les lèvres de tout le monde dans le pays. Peut-être que sa gracieuse Majesté l'entendra prononcer. Je me demande si elle me fera chevalier [1] *ha ha.*

C'est à ce moment précis, dans le journal, que l'inspecteur Abberline est mentionné pour la première fois.

> Abberline le dit, il n'a jamais été stupéfait,
> Que j'aie accompli mon œuvre avec tant d'honneur.

Abberline est l'incarnation des forces qui s'opposent à Maybrick : la police, dont les représentants sont comparés dans le journal à des « poulets sans tête ». Tout d'abord, Maybrick s'amuse de leurs efforts malheureux pour le capturer. Mais peu à peu, le ton change et Abberline devient le « pour-

1. Il serait alors effectivement devenu *Sir* James. *(N.d.T.).*

suivant », puis le « bourreau » qui vient le hanter durant ses nuits de cauchemar.

Malgré ses railleries cruelles et les images grotesques qui lui servent à décrire les efforts infructueux de la police, Maybrick révèle une surprenante vulnérabilité! Mais ses moments de faiblesse sont très naturels et donnent à ses confidences un aspect d'une réalité pathétique.

> Je me suis rendu sur la tombe de ma mère et de mon père. J'ai hâte que nous soyons réunis. Je crois qu'ils savent quelle torture la putain me fait subir.

A l'égard de ses enfants, il n'éprouve qu'amour et tendresse. Mais, il le sait, la « drogue » détermine de plus en plus ses actes, et il en vient à craindre que ses enfants eux-mêmes ne soient en danger.

> Je commence à moins penser aux enfants, mais une partie de moi me le reproche.

Pour Florie, cependant, il n'éprouve aucun attendrissement. Lorsqu'il lui laisse l'opportunité de voir son « maquereau », c'est uniquement dans le but de s'exciter à la pensée de ce qu'ils font ensemble. Son imagination alimente alors des crises de fureur auxquelles Florie doit s'habituer.

> La putain a vu son maquereau aujourd'hui ça ne m'a pas dérangé. J'ai imaginé que j'étais avec eux, cette seule pensée m'excite. Je me demande si la putain a jamais eu de telles pensées?

En ce même mois de septembre, Maybrick a souscrit la première et la plus importante de deux polices d'assurance. Il s'agissait d'une assurance-vie contractée sur sa tête auprès de la Mutual Reserve Fund Life Association de New York, pour un capital de 3 000 livres. Il est probable qu'il avait trompé la société en question, car plusieurs de ses amis avaient remarqué une dégradation alarmante de son état physique. Il vieillissait rapidement et Charles Anspaugh doutait de le voir terminer l'année. La peur de la maladie et de la mort qui obsédait Maybrick était maintenant justifiée.

Mais sa « campagne » se déroulait selon ses plans. Il jouissait de la publicité immense dont il faisait l'objet. Qu'on pût le prendre pour un juif comblait son sens de l'ironie. Qu'on pût le comparer à un médecin flattait son *ego* abusé par la drogue. C'étaient autant d'encouragements à poursuivre son action.

Mais la prochaine fois, il n'oublierait pas la craie.

Chapitre 7

Settles Street, le 29 septembre au soir, vers 23 heures. Devant le pub Bricklayers Arms, une femme cherche un abri car la pluie est battante. Il s'agit d'Elizabeth Stride, dite « Long Liz », originaire de Suède. Elle est âgée de quarante-quatre ans et sa longue silhouette osseuse ne passe pas inaperçue dans le quartier. Un moment plus tard, John Gardner et son ami Best, tous deux manœuvres, la voient dans les bras d'un homme d'allure respectable, portant jaquette et pardessus. Le vieux Matthew Packer dira plus tard qu'un homme accompagnant Elizabeth Stride est venu acheter des raisins dans son magasin de Berner Street.

Ce soir-là, une conférence animée a eu lieu dans les locaux de l'*International Workingmen's Educational Club*, au premier étage du 40 Berner Street. La plupart des quelque cent cinquante juifs qui fréquentent ce club sont déjà rentrés chez eux. Mais quelques membres se sont attardés et les accents d'un air folklorique russe flottent dans l'atmosphère pluvieuse.

A 0 h 30 environ, l'agent William Smith fait sa ronde : il aperçoit à son tour Elizabeth Stride. Elle se trouve en compagnie d'un homme bien habillé, qui porte un manteau noir, un chapeau de feutre, un col blanc et une cravate. L'agent remarque également une fleur rouge accrochée à la veste d'Elizabeth Stride.

Au 36 Berner Street, Mme Fanny Mortimer vient d'entendre passer l'agent Smith. Elle se rend sur le pas de sa porte et perçoit les accords qui proviennent du club, deux maisons plus loin.

Sur le côté du n° 40, un passage sombre conduit jusqu'à une cour sans éclairage, où travaille Arthur Dutfield, fabricant de charrettes et de fourgons. Mme Mortimer déclarera ensuite qu'elle n'a vu personne entrer ou sortir de cette cour.

Cinq minutes plus tard, Israel Schwartz passe devant la porte à claire-voie qui ouvre sur le passage. Cet homme n'a pas témoigné durant l'enquête, bien que la police ait accordé foi à son récit, publié dans le *Star* et l'*Evening Post.* Mais personne n'y a plus prêté attention jusqu'à la parution en 1976 de l'ouvrage de Stephen Knight, *Jack the Ripper : The Final Solution* (Jack l'Éventreur : la solution finale).

Schwartz a prétendu qu'il marchait de l'autre côté de la rue et avait vu un homme accoster une femme qui se tenait devant la porte à claire-voie. L'homme l'avait fait tomber puis l'avait poussée à l'intérieur du passage. « Elle a crié trois fois mais pas très fort. » D'après Schwartz, l'homme en question était âgé d'une trentaine d'années, il avait une petite moustache brune et portait une casquette noire à visière.

Cette description correspondait à Aaron Kosminski, Juif polonais. Le Dr Robert Anderson, directeur-adjoint du *Criminal Investigation Department* (CID), chargé de l'enquête sur l'Éventreur entre octobre 1888 et 1892, n'a pas tardé à se convaincre de la culpabilité de Kosminski. Il se fondait sur les déclarations d'un témoin cette fois anonyme, selon lui « le seul homme à jamais avoir vu de près le meurtrier ».

Mais dans l'entretien qu'il accorde au *Star* le 10 octobre, Schwartz ajoute les précisions suivantes : pratiquement au même moment, il aperçoit un autre homme sortant du cabaret situé au coin de Fairclough Street. Cet homme reste tapi dans l'ombre, en silence. Il épie Schwartz et le prend

Les sites principaux du Journal

Echelle :
0,3 cm = 10 km

Le Londres de James Maybrick

Le frère de James Maybrick, Michael, résidait à Regent's Park. Sarah Robertson vécut à New Cross, à Sydenham et Tooting, mais également à Whitechapel.

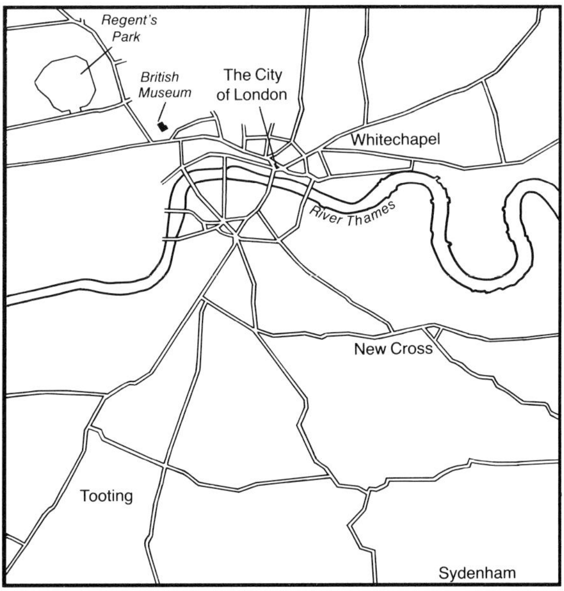

A gauche : La jeune Florence Chandler, avant son mariage avec Maybrick en juillet 1881.
(Richard Whittington Egan)
Ci-dessous : La mère de Florence Maybrick , la baronne Caroline von Roques.
(Richard Whittington Egan).
Ci-dessous : Embarquement, à Liverpool, sur le *SS Celtic*, qui ressemble au *SS Baltic* sur lequel James Maybrick a rencontré pour la première fois Florence Chandler.
(Smith Gryphon)

A gauche : Le terrain du Club de cricket de Liverpool, en face de Battlecrease House, dont Maybrick était membre. (Smith Gryphon)
A l'extrême gauche : La station d'Aigburth. (Smith Gryphon)

Ci-dessus : Battlecrease House aujourd'hui. (Smith Gryphon)
A droite : La pièce qui fut la chambre des enfants Maybrick. (Richard Whittington Egan)

Ci-dessus : Les membres de l'Association des marchands de coton, à Liverpool, en 1887. (Smith Gryphon)
Ci-contre : Lord Street, à Liverpool, citée dans le Journal. (Smith Gryphon)

A droite : Une esquisse contemporaine représentant Alfred Brierley, dont la liaison avec Florence Maybrick provoqua la violente colère de son mari.
(Richard Whittington Egan)

Ci-dessus : Le “Poste House” à Liverpool. (Smith Gryphon)
A gauche : Victoria Street, à Liverpool, dessin datant de 1880. Sur la gauche, on peut voir l'entrée du “Poste House” qui existe encore aujourd'hui.
(Liverpool Record Office)

A droite : Bromley Street où vivait Sarah Robertson. La maison qui se trouvait au numéro 55 a été démolie.
(Tower Hamlets Local History Department)

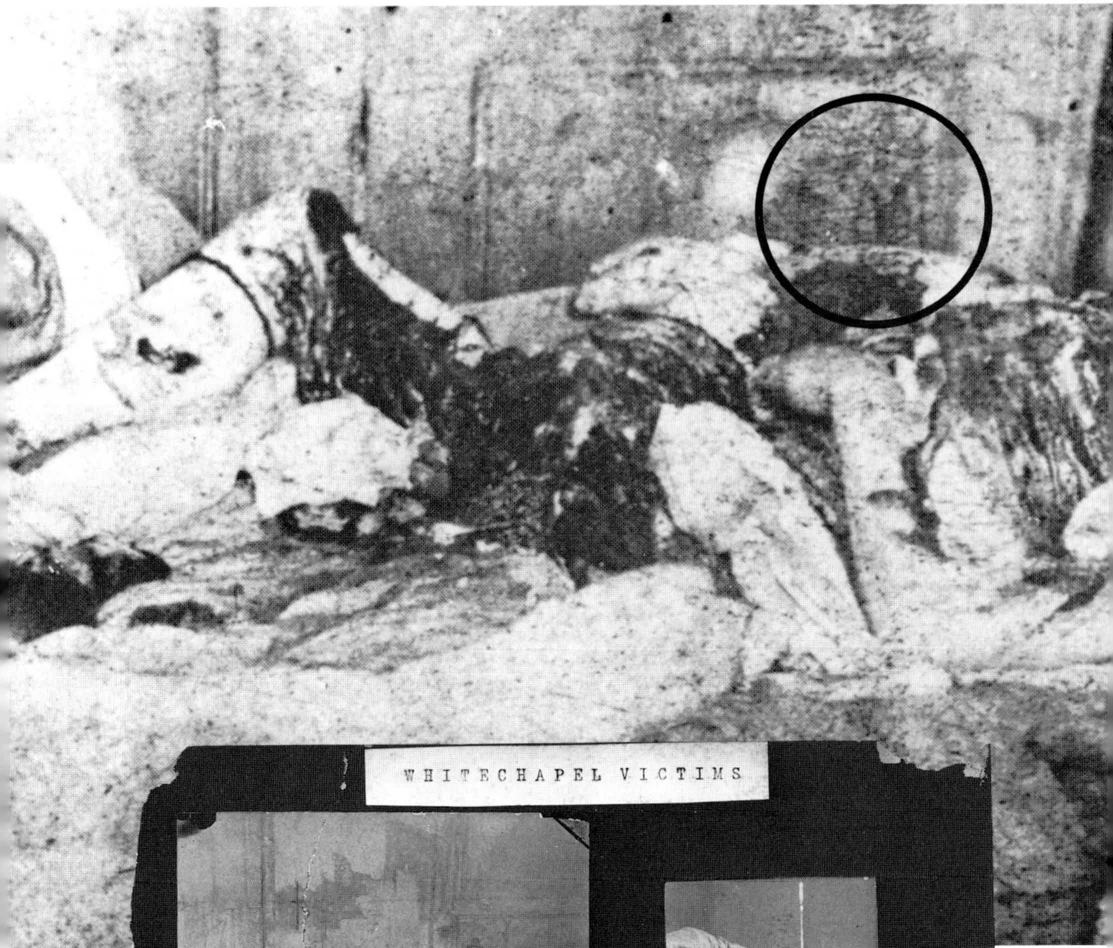

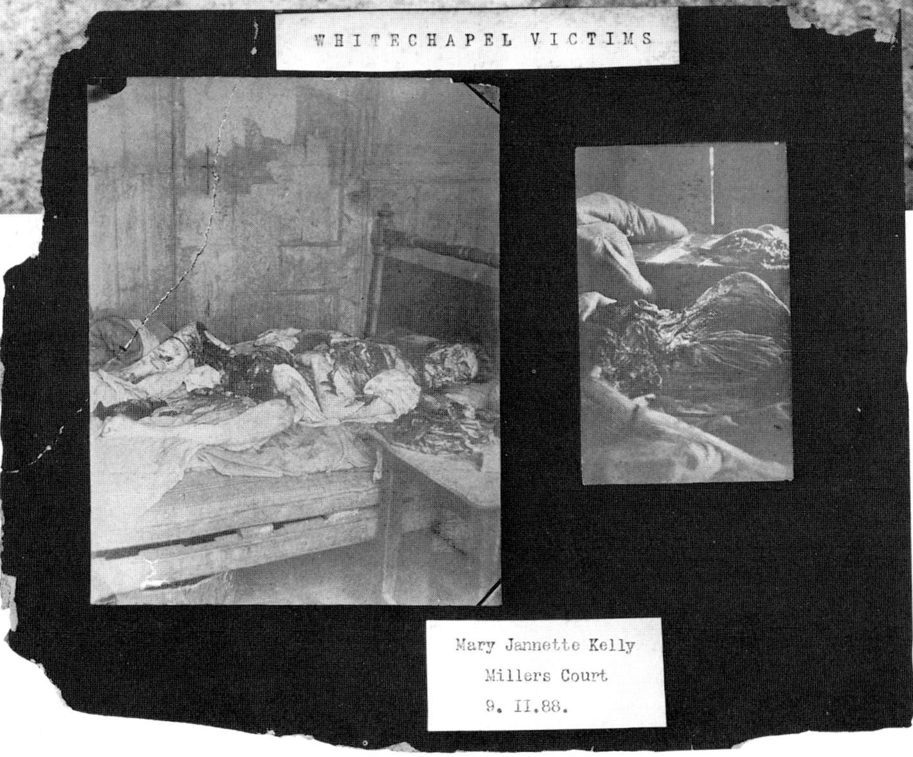

Les cinq victimes assassinées à Whitechapel. (archives de la Metropolitan Police)
Mary Kelly, la dernière prostituée assassinée par Jack l'Eventreur. Sur le mur, juste au-dessus de son corps, on peut lire les deux lettres: "F" et "M". La photo de droite, reproduite ici pour la première fois, est prise sous un autre angle. On peut voir, sur la table, un empilement de chairs provenant de son abdomen et de ses cuisses. (Public Record Office - Kew)

En haut : Un agrandissement de la même photographie montre plus clairement les lettres "F" et "M" (entourées). (Public Record Office-Kew)

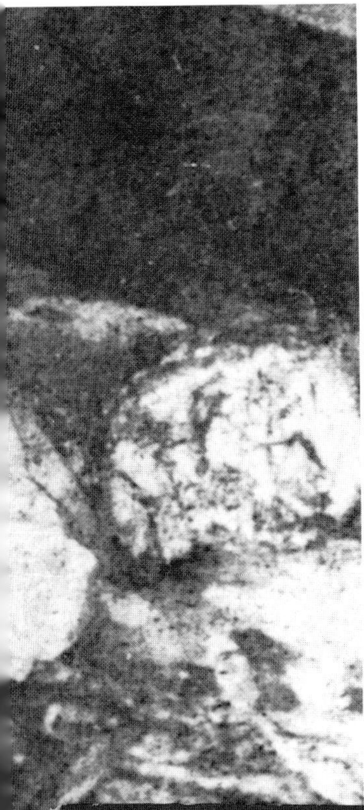

Ci-dessus : La foule Victorienne matinale se pressant au marché de Middlesex Street, connue à cette époque sous le nom de Petticoat Lane. C'est là que l'auteur du Journal loua une chambre à l'automne 1888.
(Tower Hamlets Local History Department)

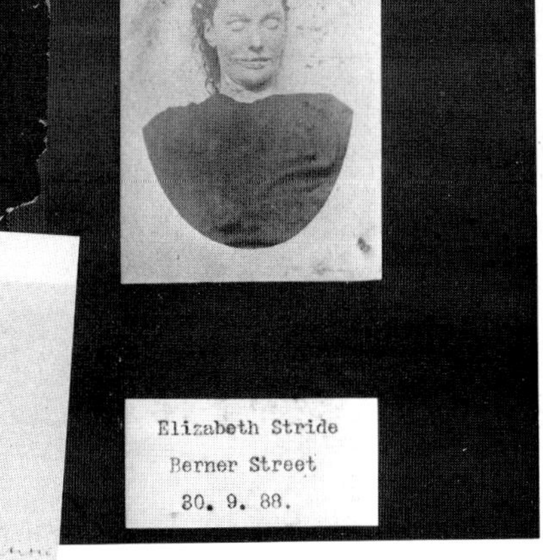

Les quatre premières victimes, Mary (Polly) Nicholls, Annie Chapman, Catharine Eddowes et Elizabeth Stride. (Public Record Office - Kew)

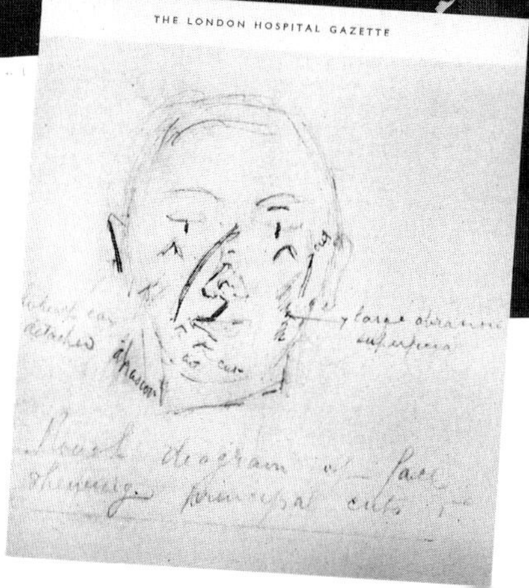

A droite : Un dessin fait au moment du meurtre de Catharine Eddowes montre sur chaque joue, une blesssure en forme de V qui, inversés et mis ensemble, forment un “M”.
(London Hospital)

A droite : Mike Barrett , le propriétaire du Journal, avec sa femme Anne et sa fille Caroline. (Smith Gryphon)
Ci-dessous : Le journal de Jack l'Eventreur. Cette sorte de petit registre servait, à l'époque victorienne, à conserver des souvenirs. (Duocrave)

A gauche : L'immeuble dans lequel se trouvait la société de Maybrick. Il a été détruit en 1970. (Richard Whittington Egan)

Ci-dessus : Un portrait de James Maybrick avec "une moustache élégante" telle que celle décrite par ceux que la police considéra comme des témoins des meurtres de Jack l'Eventreur. (Detective Magazine)

A droite : un portrait-robot dessiné par la police et diffusé le 6 octobre 1888. (British Library)

25. Sept. 1888.

Dear Boss

I keep on hearing the police have caught me but they wont fix me just yet. I have laughed when they look so clever and talk about being on the right track. That joke about Leather Apron gave me real fits. I am down on whores and I shant quit ripping them till I do get buckled. Grand work the last job was, I gave the lady no time to squeal. How can they catch me now. I love my work and want to start again. You will soon hear of me with my funny little games. I saved some of the proper red stuff in a ginger beer bottle over the last job to write with but it went thick like glue and I cant use it. Red ink is fit enough I hope ha. ha. The next job I do I shall clip the ladys ears off and send to the police officers just for jolly wouldnt you. Keep this letter back till I do a bit more work, then give it out straight. My knife's so nice and sharp I want to get to work right away if I get a chance. Good Luck.

Yours truly

Jack the Ripper

Dont mind me giving the trade name

wasnt good enough to post this before I got all the red ink off my hands curse it. No luck yet. They say I'm a doctor now ha ha

The Boss
Central News
Office
London City.

POST CARD
THE ADDRESS ONLY TO BE WRITTEN ON THIS SIDE

Central News Office
London City E.C

Fac-simile de l'affiche, distribuée par la police, qui reproduit la lettre du 25 septembre 1888, commençant par "Cher patron", où apparaît pour la première fois le surnom de "Jack l'Eventreur", avec la carte postale de "Jack le Malin", presque sûrement écrite de la même main. La police croyait que les deux documents avaient été écrits par Jack l'Eventreur.

(Public Record Office-Kew)

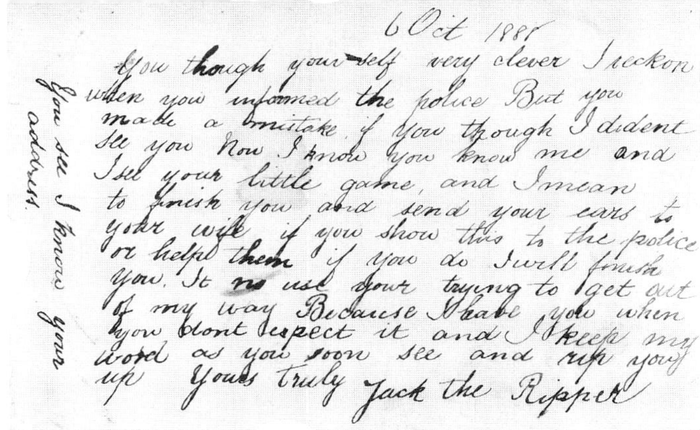

Ci-dessus à gauche : Un message encore jamais publié adressé au “Cher patron” et une enveloppe, d’une calligraphie très surchargée. Il est improbable que ce soit par pur hasard que le premier fait relaté sur le support de ce message commence par le mot “Liverpool”. (Public record Office - Kew)

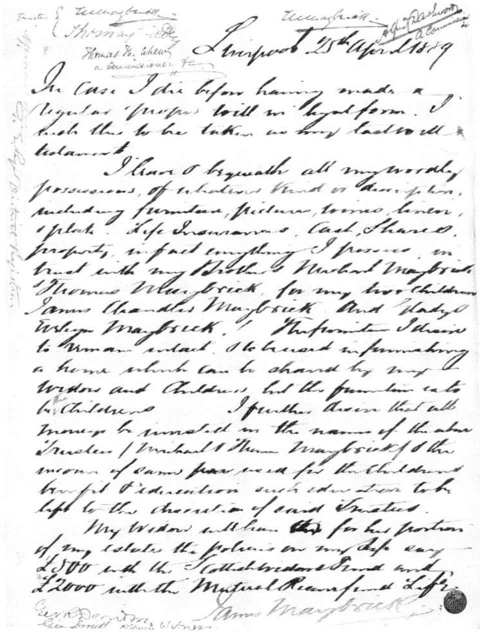

Ci-dessus : Un autre message, encore jamais publié, supposé de la même main que celui commençant par “Cher patron”, dans lequel l’auteur menace un témoin d’un des meurtres commis le 30 septembre. (Public record Office-Kew)

A gauche : La première page du dernier testament présumé de James Maybrick, apparemment écrit de sa propre main. Cependant, un avocat contemporain réputé ayant étudié ce document est convaincu que Maybrick ne peut l’avoir écrit lui-même. Entre autres, parce que le prénom de sa fille est mal orthographié deux fois-Eveleyn à la place d’Evelyn-ce qui ne semble pas une erreur propre à un père. (Sommerset House)

Page de gauche : Florence Maybrick à l'époque de son mariage. (Richard Whittington Egan)

Ci-dessus : Un dessin contemporain de Battlecrease House ; on y voit Florence Maybrick et ses deux enfants. (R. Whittington Egan)

Ci-dessus : Les enfants Maybrick, Gladys Evelyn et James Chandler, affectueusement surnommé "Bobo". (Richard Whittington Egan)
A gauche : Michael Maybrick, le frère chez qui séjournait souvent James Maybrick lorsqu'il se rendait à Londres. Il fut un auteur à succès de chansons populaires sous le pseudonyme de Stephen Adams. (Richard Whittington Egan)

A gauche : L'hôtel d'Aigburth dans lequel s'est déroulée l'enquête sur James Maybrick. (Richard Whittington Egan)

Page de droite : Croquis faits pendant le procès de Florence Maybrick, accusée du meurtre de son mari. (British Library)

Le comptoir de chez Wokes, la pharmacie de Grasendale où Florence Maybrick acheta le papier tue-mouche qui eut de si terribles conséquences. (Richard Whittington Egan)

La bouteille de jus de viande Valentine et la bouteille contenant un mélage de jus de viande et d'eau dans laquelle la moitié d'un grain d'arsenic a été découvert. (Richard Whittington Egan)

THE MAYBRICK MURDER TRIAL.

La petite maison, à South Kent, dans le Connecticut, où Florence Maybrick est morte.
(Richard Whittington Egan)

Ci-dessous : A South Kent, une croix très simple indique la tombe de Florence Maybrick morte en 1941 à l'âge de 79 ans.
(Richard Whittington Egan)

A droite : Le caveau de famille dans lequel repose James Maybrick dans le cimetière d'Anfield à Liverpool.
(Richard Whittington Egan)

Saint George's Hall, à Liverpool, où s'est déroulé le procès de Florence Maybrick.
(Richard Whittington Egan)

soudain à partie en le traitant de « Lipski » – le dénommé Lipski n'était autre qu'un juif reconnu coupable de meurtre l'année précédente. Même en tenant compte de la mauvaise visibilité et de la circonspection avec laquelle il convient de traiter toute identification visuelle, la description donnée par Schwartz du second homme correspond aussi bien à celui aperçu devant le pub Bricklayer's Arms qu'à celui qui a acheté du raisin : il était vêtu d'un pardessus noir et portait un chapeau de feutre à large bord. Mais surtout, il avait un couteau à la main.

Cependant, l'inspecteur Abberline, dans le rapport qu'il adresse au ministère de l'Intérieur le 1er novembre, affirme que Schwartz, qui ne parle pas anglais et a besoin d'un interprète, a déclaré que le second homme allumait sa pipe et n'avait pas de couteau. Cette confusion montre combien la véridicité des archives d'époque est aléatoire. Mais le second homme pourrait bien être Maybrick.

En l'entendant, l'agresseur s'enfuit et Schwartz part dans la direction opposée, car il ne veut pas être impliqué. C'est l'opportunité dont Maybrick avait besoin. Il est probable qu'il attend un moment, pour s'assurer que Schwartz est bien parti. Puis il se dirige alors vers Elizabeth Stride et, prétextant peut-être de vouloir lui venir en aide, il l'entraîne jusqu'au fond du passage, dans la cour d'Arthur Dutfield. Cet espace clos attire Maybrick, qui a le goût du risque. Le passage ne comportait qu'une seule issue : si quelqu'un arrive, Maybrick sera pris au piège. Mais d'un autre côté, il a l'avantage de se trouver caché.

Il n'y a pas une minute à perdre. Il saisit Elizabeth Stride par son écharpe, incline sa tête en arrière et l'étrangle avant même qu'elle n'ait le temps de pousser un cri. Puis il lui tranche la gorge. Elle serre encore dans sa main un petit paquet de cachous. A l'époque, les fumeurs en mâchaient pour chasser de leur haleine le goût du tabac – Maybrick lui-même s'en servait. Plus tard, il se souviendra de cette odeur.

Je sentais encore son haleine sucrée.

La femme est morte, mais l'Éventreur n'a pas eu le temps de mutiler son corps. En effet, il est maintenant 1 heure et Louis Diemschutz, vendeur de bijoux de pacotille, pénètre dans la cour avec sa charrette et son poney. Soudain, l'animal fait un brusque écart vers le mur gauche pour éviter un obstacle. Diemschutz se penche et tâte de son fouet une masse informe. C'est le corps d'Elizabeth Stride.

Diemschutz a interrompu Maybrick, mais il était trop tard pour que la vie de sa victime soit épargnée. L'effroi du bijoutier a toutefois permis la fuite de l'Éventreur. Blotti dans la pénombre, envahi par la panique, il écrira dans son journal :

> A mon grand étonnement je ne peux pas croire que je n'aie pas été pris [...] j'ai imaginé que mon cœur avait quitté mon corps. Sous l'effet de ma peur, j'ai imaginé que mon cœur faisait des bonds dans la rue et que je le suivais au comble du désespoir. J'aurais vraiment adoré couper la tête de ce damné cheval et l'enfoncer aussi loin que possible dans la gorge de la putain. Je n'ai pas eu le temps d'éventrer complètement la garce, je maudis ma déveine. Je crois que l'excitation d'être pris m'a excité encore plus que de découper la putain elle-même. En écrivant ces mots je trouve impossible de croire qu'il ne m'a pas vu, selon mon estimation j'étais à moins de quelques mètres de lui. L'imbécile a paniqué, c'est ce qui m'a sauvé. Ma satisfaction était loin d'être complète, damné salaud, je l'ai maudit encore et encore, mais j'ai été malin, ils n'ont pas pu me surpasser. *Personne* ne le pourra jamais.

Il ne faut que quelques minutes aux policiers pour parvenir sur les lieux. Il fait tellement sombre qu'ils doivent griller des allumettes pour examiner le cadavre.

A une exception près, tous les meurtres de Whitechapel tombaient sous la juridiction de la *Metropolitan Police*. Fondée en 1829, elle était responsable de tout Londres, à l'exception de la *City*[1]. Sa zone d'exercice était scindée en divisions. Celle de Whitechapel était la Division-H. Bien que ni la *Metropolitan Police*, ni la *City Police* n'aient réussi à capturer l'Éventreur, c'est la « *Met* » qui essuyait la plupart des critiques de la presse.

Ses responsables étaient placés sous l'autorité du ministère de l'Intérieur, dont les fonctionnaires jouissaient d'un pouvoir considérable et prenaient nombre des décisions pour lesquelles la police était ensuite blâmée par le public. Ainsi, ce sont eux qui ont interdit qu'une récompense du gouvernement soit offerte à quiconque fournirait des informations conduisant à l'arrestation du criminel. Et c'est le ministre de l'Intérieur, Henry Matthews, homme plein d'humour et rompu aux arcanes de la justice, qui a provoqué la démission de deux responsables de la *Metropolitan Police* – ironie du sort, le même Matthews se retrouverait lui-même sur la sellette un an plus tard, à la suite du meurtre présumé de James Maybrick.

L'un de ces responsables était Sir Charles Warren. Membre de la religion réformée et ancien soldat, il menait ses troupes avec une précision toute militaire. La presse ne lui avait jamais pardonné sa réaction musclée à une manifestation de masse contre le chômage, un an auparavant. Le 10 septembre, voici ce qu'écrivait le *Star* : « Comble de maladresse et de sottise, Sir Charles Warren, dont le nom suffit à hérisser le peuple de Londres, a récemment transféré la totalité des détectives de l'East End à l'Ouest et l'équipe du West End à l'Est. » Il n'aurait pas agi autrement s'il avait souhaité que les hommes de terrain ignorent tout de leur nouveau secteur.

Le plus célèbre des policiers ayant enquêté sur l'Éventreur est l'inspecteur Frederick George Abberline, sans

1. Centre des affaires (1,5 km^2). (*N.d.T.*)

doute parce qu'il savait très bien se mettre en valeur. Mais le fait est qu'il connaissait à la perfection son secteur et les malfrats qui y sévissaient. Maybrick ne s'y trompe pas, qui le choisit comme cible de ses sarcasmes.

Oh M. Abberline, c'est un malin petit monsieur.

Au moment où Maybrick s'enfuyait de la cour où il venait d'assassiner Elizabeth Stride, Catharine Eddowes, fille d'un ferblantier de Wolverhampton, était relâchée après avoir passé quelques heures au poste de police de Bishopsgate, dans la *City*. Ce jour-là, elle avait dû mettre en gage une paire de bottes pour pouvoir s'offrir une tasse de thé. A 20 h 30, elle était ivre et se trouvait en garde à vue. Elle a quitté le poste de police à 1 heure. A cette heure-là comme le lui a fait remarquer l'agent George Hutt, les débits de boisson étaient fermés. « Bonne nuit, vieille branche », lui a-t-elle répondu, avant de tourner à gauche en direction de Houndsditch.

Quelques minutes plus tard, elle devait se trouver à l'entrée de Duke Street, au bout de laquelle se trouvait Church Passage, qui menait à Mitre Square.

A ce moment, Maybrick vient de quitter Berner Street, il tourne dans Commercial Road, puis prend encore à gauche dans Whitechapel High Street, en direction de Middlesex Street. Toutefois, il ne retourne pas dans sa chambre, mais poursuit son chemin jusqu'à Aldgate. Ce faisant, il traverse la frontière qui sépare les juridictions respectives de la *Metropolitan Police* et de la *City Police*.

Malade de frustration, il avance à grandes enjambées, mais pas suffisamment vite pour attirer l'attention. Un quart d'heure plus tard, il croise Catharine Eddowes à hauteur de Church Passage. A 1 h 35, on les aperçoit marchant côte à côte.

De nouveau, Maybrick attire sa proie dans un recoin obscur. Mais cette fois, il donne libre cours à sa frénésie. Il pousse violemment Catharine Eddowes, qui s'écroule sur le sol, puis il l'étrangle et lui tranche la gorge. Ensuite, en proie à une fureur incontrôlable, il lacère et mutile le visage de sa victime, entaille les paupières, les joues et la lèvre supérieure, découpe le bout du nez et le lobe de l'oreille droite. Enfin, il l'éventre, arrache les organes internes, les intestins, et détache le côlon, qu'il place à côté du cadavre. Avant de partir, il grave deux « V » renversés, un sous chaque œil. Les rapports de l'époque parlent de triangles. Personne ne s'apercevra qu'à eux deux, ils forment un « M ».

On parvient à distinguer cette lettre sur une photographie découverte dans le sous-sol du London Hospital et publiée pour la première fois en 1966, dans la *Hospital Gazette.* Elle illustrait un article du Pr Francis Camps, spécialiste de pathologie. Un croquis d'époque représentant le visage mutilé de Catharine Eddowes accompagnait également cet article. Là aussi, le « M » est clairement visible.

Maybrick ne laisse lui-même planer aucun doute sur ce point dans son journal :

> Son nez m'agaçait alors je l'ai découpé, essayé d'arracher ses yeux, laissé ma marque, pas pu enlever la tête des garces.

En fouillant dans les poches profondes de sa victime, Maybrick trouve, entre autres, quelques petites boîtes et un peigne. L'étui à cigarettes en cuir rouge laissé à côté du corps est sans doute celui du meurtrier. Il n'est guère probable qu'il ait appartenu à une prostituée dans la misère.

Comme il ne trouve rien d'intéressant, il remet tout en place et s'enfuit en emportant l'utérus et un rein. Lorsque l'agent Edward Watkins découvre le corps, il est 1 h 45. Le chirurgien de la police, le Dr F. Gordon Brown, arrivera sur les lieux juste après 2 heures.

Si l'on compare les circonstances du crime et la liste des biens de Catharine Eddowes telle qu'elle a été dressée par la police avec les passages du journal qui sont consacrés à ce meurtre, on voit surgir des indices révélateurs.

Une seule putain pas bien, décidé que Sir Jim en frapperait une autre.
Je n'ai montré aucune peur et en vérité aucune lueur.
Bon sang, la boîte métallique était vide. [...]

Du sucre et du thé doux,
auraient pu servir à payer mes petits honoraires
Mais à la place j'ai dû m'enfuir et j'ai montré mon plaisir
En mangeant du rognon froid pour dîner

salaud
Abberline
bonnet
cache tout
indice
malin
vous en dirai plus [...]

Sir Jim faire un faux pas
peur
l'avoir près
le racheter près
cas
séance tenante

Il croit que je vais faire un faux pas
mais je n'ai pas peur
* Je ne peux pas le racheter ici [...]

Ne suis-je pas un type malin

Voici maintenant la liste des biens de Catharine Eddowes établie par la police :

« une très vieille jupe d'alpaga verte
très vieille jupe bleue en loques
tricot de corps d'homme blanc
ni culotte ni corset
une paire de bottes d'homme à lacets
1 boîte en fer-blanc contenant du thé
1 boîte en fer-blanc contenant du sucre
1 petit peigne fin
1 étui à cigarettes en cuir rouge à garnitures métalliques
1 morceau de vieux tablier blanc
1 boîte en fer-blanc couleur moutarde contenant des tickets de prêteur sur gages
1 boîte d'allumettes en fer-blanc, vide »

Trois journaux seulement ont rapporté qu'on avait trouvé un peu de fibre de coton dans l'une des boîtes. Ce détail ne figure pas dans la liste établie par la police. S'agissait-il du « très bon indice » dont parle Maybrick ?

Quant à la boîte d'allumettes en fer-blanc vide, cet objet en apparence sans intérêt est le plus important du lot. Mais aucun des journaux ne l'a mentionné à l'époque du meurtre. Quant à la liste de la police, qui n'a été accessible au public qu'en 1984 et se trouve aujourd'hui dans les *City of London Archives*, elle a été publiée pour la première fois dans les ouvrages de Donald Rumbelow et de Martin Fido, tous deux parus en 1987. Comment Maybrick aurait-il pu en connaître l'existence, si ce n'est parce qu'il se trouvait sur place, et parce qu'il se rappelait avoir cherché dans la boîte une allumette pour voir sa victime.

A la morgue, Joseph Lawende, vendeur de cigarettes juif, a identifié Catharine Eddowes d'après ses vêtements. Il a également décrit aux enquêteurs un homme qu'il avait aperçu sur le lieu du crime. Sa description a été publiée dans un article de *The Times*, le 2 octobre : il s'agissait d'un homme d'environ trente ans, mesurant un mètre soixante-dix, avec une moustache blonde et une casquette de toile.

Il ne faut pas longtemps pour aller de Mitre Square, où Catharine Eddowes avait été retrouvée, jusqu'à Middlesex Street. Toutefois, Maybrick ne pouvait pas emprunter la route directe. En effet, les commerçants ne tarderaient pas à envahir Middlesex Street pour installer leurs étalages : le dimanche était jour de marché.

Il s'est donc engagé dans Stoney Lane, il a traversé la rue principale, et il a pris une petite rue parallèle qui donnait dans Goulston Street.

Est-ce un besoin soudain de se cacher qui a poussé Maybrick à s'engouffrer dans l'entrée du n° 108-09 ? Quelques marches sans éclairage menaient à un palier bien à l'abri des regards. C'est là qu'il a essuyé son couteau ensanglanté et ses mains maculées de fèces sur un lambeau du tablier de Catharine Eddowes. Et c'est là qu'il a utilisé la craie. Le message qu'il a rédigé sur la porte d'entrée était appelé à devenir l'un des indices les plus déconcertants de tous ceux laissés par l'Éventreur. Il a suscité la controverse pendant plus d'un siècle.

C'est l'agent Long qui l'a découvert pendant sa ronde. A 2 h 55, il a remarqué le morceau de chiffon en haut des marches. Puis il a aperçu le graffiti et s'est douté que l'Éventreur avait dû passer par là. Il a recopié l'inscription telle quelle, mais il a admis plus tard qu'il avait pu commettre une erreur dans l'orthographe du mot « juifs ». Voici ce qu'il avait noté :

> Les Juifs sont les hommes qui ne seront pas blâmés pour rien.

Mais les archives de la *City Police* contiennent un message différent :

Les Juifs ne sont pas les hommes qui seront blâmés pour rien.

Goulston Street, où l'inscription avait été trouvée, se trouvait sous la juridiction de la *Metropolitan Police*, à l'inverse de Mitre Square, le lieu du crime, qui était du ressort de la *City Police*. Il s'ensuivit, de l'aveu même de la police, une confusion catastrophique.

Le *Criminal Investigation Department* de la *City Police* ordonna que le message fût photographié, puis effacé. Mais le *superintendent* Thomas Arnold, responsable du secteur de Goulston Street, craignait que cette inscription antisémite ne suscite des troubles parmi les résidents. Et lorsque le responsable de la *Metropolitan Police*, Sir Charles Warren, arriva sur place à 5 heures, il se déclara du même avis qu'Arnold et entreprit d'effacer lui-même les mots tracés à la craie.

Quant à Maybrick, il aura ce commentaire dans son journal :

> Je n'ai pas pu m'empêcher de rire, ils me présentent comme gaucher, médecin, employé d'abattoirs et juif. Très bien, s'ils insistent pour dire que je suis juif, juif je serai.

Puis il prédit :

> Les Juifs et les Docteurs
> Seront accusés

Dans son rapport au ministère de l'Intérieur, en date du 6 novembre 1888, Sir Charles Warren a fourni une copie de l'inscription incriminée. La forme et la disposition des mots ont été exactement reproduites, aussi est-il raisonnable d'assurer qu'il s'agit d'une copie de bonne qualité. Elle comporte un détail frappant : l'orthographe du mot juifs. En anglais, juifs s'orthographie « *Jews* ». Or, Maybrick a écrit « *Juwes* ». Cinq lettres au lieu de quatre, la place du « e », après le w qui ressemble à un « m » renversé sont autant d'indices qui suggèrent que Maybrick avait pris le risque d'inscrire son prénom sur le mur de Goulston Street, et qui plus est de s'identifier avec un juif. Il semble donc qu'il ait été désireux de faire accroire au public qu'un juif était responsable des meurtres de Whitechapel. S'agissait-il là de « ma drôle de petite blague juive » ?

Maybrick n'allait pas en rester là. En effet, c'est le lendemain, lundi 1er octobre, que le monde découvrirait le surnom qu'il s'était donné : Jack l'Éventreur.

Chapitre 8

La lettre, datée du 25 septembre, fut publiée dans la première édition du *Star* le 1er octobre. C'est peut-être la missive la plus célèbre de l'histoire du crime.

Sans elle, les meurtres de Whitechapel auraient sans doute été relégués parmi les nombreux crimes tout aussi horribles dont le *Black Museum* de New Scotland Yard et la *Chamber of Horrors* de Madame Tussaud perpétuent le souvenir.

C'est dans cette lettre rédigée à l'encre rouge que le meurtrier révèle le pseudonyme qu'il a choisi.

Cher Patron,
Je n'arrête pas d'entendre que la police m'a attrapé, mais elle n'est pas encore près de me régler mon compte. J'ai ri quand ils ont l'air si malins et disent qu'ils sont sur la *bonne* piste. Cette plaisanterie à propos de Tablier de cuir m'a fait me tordre. J'en ai après les putains et je n'arrêterai de les éventrer que lorsque je serai bouclé. Beau travail que le dernier. Je n'ai pas donné à la dame le temps de crier. Comment peuvent-ils m'attraper maintenant. J'adore mon travail et je veux recommencer. Vous entendrez bientôt parler de moi et de mes drôles de petits jeux. Pendant mon dernier travail, j'ai mis de côté un peu de la véritable substance

rouge dans une bouteille de soda au gingembre pour écrire avec mais elle est devenue aussi épaisse que de la colle et je ne peux pas m'en servir. L'encre rouge fait l'affaire j'espère ha ha. Le prochain boulot que je ferai je couperai les oreilles de la dame et je les enverrai aux officiers de la police juste pour la rigolade vous ne trouvez pas. Gardez cette lettre jusqu'à ce que je fasse encore un peu de travail, puis faites-la connaître tout de suite. Mon couteau est si épatant et si tranchant que je veux me mettre au travail tout de suite si l'occasion se présente. Bonne chance.

Votre humble serviteur
Jack l'Éventreur

Si ça ne vous dérange pas je donne ma raison de commerce.

La feuille avait été tournée à 90° et un second post-scriptum avait été ajouté :

N'était pas une si bonne idée de poster ceci avant que j'aie enlevé toute l'encre rouge de mes mains maudit sort. Pas encore eu de chance. Ils disent que je suis médecin maintenant. *ha ha*

La lettre a été transmise au quartier général de la police à Scotland Yard le samedi 29 septembre. Le rédacteur en chef du *Star* avait joint la note suivante à l'attention du *Chief Constable* Adolphus Williamson : « Le rédacteur en chef présente ses compliments à M. Williamson et se permet de l'informer que le document ci-joint a été reçu il y a deux jours par *Central News*, qui l'a traité comme une plaisanterie. »

Le texte de cette lettre a été publié dans l'édition de 2 heures du *Liverpool Daily Post* et dans l'édition de 5 heures du *Daily News* de Londres le lundi 1er octobre.

Ce même lundi matin, *Central News Agency* a reçu une carte postale écrite au crayon rouge. Elle avait été postée le 1er octobre dans l'East End et mentionnait les deux meurtres qui s'étaient produits en l'espace de moins d'une heure à Whitechapel le 30 septembre. Et voici le texte :

> Je ne me payais pas votre tête cher vieux Patron quand je vous ai donné le tuyau, vous entendrez parler du travail de Jacky l'Insolent demain double événement cette fois numéro un a poussé quelques cris pas pu finir. Pas eu le temps de prendre les oreilles pour la police. Merci d'avoir gardé ma dernière lettre jusqu'à ce que je me remette au travail.
>
> Jack l'Éventreur

Le texte de cette carte a été publié dans l'édition de 13 heures du *Star* le 1er octobre.

Dans la journée du dimanche, quelques heures après le crime, très peu de gens étaient au courant que l'une des oreilles de la victime de Mitre Square avait été partiellement coupée. Ce détail n'a été rendu public que dans les journaux du lundi. Or, du fait que les deux envois y faisaient référence et contenaient les mêmes tics d'écriture et la même signature, on en a déduit à l'époque qu'ils devaient émaner de la même personne. Dans *The Criminologist* d'août 1968, un graphologue canadien, C.M. Macleod, a eu ce commentaire à propos d'un article du Pr Camps, qui reproduisait des extraits de la lettre : « S'il n'existait qu'un seul authentique Jack l'Éventreur, je voterais pour l'auteur [de la lettre commençant par " Cher Patron "]. Il fait montre d'une énergie extraordinaire dans l'ensemble de son écriture, qui progresse avec une détermination brutale, mais aussi d'un grand art de la dissimulation lorsqu'il souligne. [...] Je dirais qu'il est assez intelligent et qu'il a suffisamment de maîtrise de lui-même pour exercer un emploi régulier qui lui fournirait une excellente couverture pour ses crimes. »

Mais une autre théorie apparaît dans la plupart des livres récents : la carte postale aurait été écrite par un imposteur. En effet, à l'époque, les services postaux étaient fort efficaces et les distributions plus fréquentes qu'aujourd'hui. Ainsi, il aurait été possible pour l'imposteur en question de lire le compte rendu du crime dans l'édition de 5 heures et d'envoyer une carte postale à temps pour qu'elle soit publiée dans l'édition de la mi-journée. Mais cette théorie omet un détail qui fait figure de preuve indiscutable : l'auteur de la carte n'aurait pas pu copier l'écriture et la signature de la lettre adressée au « Cher Patron ». En effet, à ce stade, la lettre n'était apparue que sous sa forme imprimée. C'est seulement deux jours après qu'un fac-similé de la lettre a été publié.

A 0 h 45 le dimanche matin, juste après la mort d'Elizabeth Stride et de Catharine Eddowes, un petit couteau d'une largeur de deux centimètres et demi à bout arrondi a été trouvé devant le magasin de M. Christmas dans Whitechapel Road. D'après le chirurgien de la police, le Dr George Bagster Phillips, il aurait pu s'agir de l'arme des crimes et il aurait pu appartenir à Elizabeth Stride. En effet, beaucoup de prostituées portaient des couteaux pour se défendre.

C'est dans ce quartier que la lettre adressée au « Cher Patron » avait été postée. Il s'agit là d'un détail très important, qui permet d'établir un lien entre la lettre et le couteau. Mais il a échappé aux chercheurs qui, jusqu'à maintenant, pensaient que le couteau avait été retrouvé deux jours avant les meurtres.

En outre, le Dr Bagster Phillips a déclaré que le couteau qui avait tué Elizabeth Stride n'était pas l'arme longue, étroite et à bout pointu qui avait mutilé les quatre autres prostituées de Whitechapel, mais plutôt une arme très similaire à celle retrouvée dans Whitechapel Road. La plupart des spécialistes modernes apportent leur aval à cette conclusion. Il se peut donc très bien que le meurtrier ait utilisé le couteau appartenant à Elizabeth Stride.

Partant, il est révélateur que l'auteur du journal ne s'y trompe pas. Maybrick confirme qu'il a utilisé un second couteau appartenant à Elizabeth Stride.

> * mon couteau étincelant
> * le couteau de la putain

A elles seules, la lettre et la carte postale ont suscité quelque deux mille messages rédigés dans le même style. Aucune étude approfondie de cette correspondance n'a été réalisée à ce jour.

Mais à l'époque, nombre de policiers chargés de l'enquête étaient convaincus de leur authenticité. A telle enseigne qu'ils ont imprimé une affiche sur laquelle figurait un fac-similé de la carte et de la lettre à l'encre rouge, affiche qui a été distribuée à tous les postes de police du pays le 3 octobre.

C'est sans doute l'inspecteur-chef Henry Moore qui faisait la liaison entre Abberline à Whitechapel et l'inspecteur-chef Swanson à Scotland Yard. En 1896, il a rédigé un rapport où il laissait entendre que ceux qui participaient à l'enquête avaient pris les lettres au sérieux et croyaient que l'auteur de la lettre adressée au « Cher Patron » et de la carte postale était bel et bien Jack l'Éventreur. Cette suggestion a été réfutée par Sir Robert Anderson vingt ans plus tard.

Le directeur-adjoint de la *Metropolitan Police* en 1888 a en effet écrit dans son autobiographie, publiée en épisodes dans *Blackwood's Magazine* en 1910, que « la lettre de Jack l'Éventreur qui est conservée au *Police Museum* de Scotland Yard est l'œuvre d'un journaliste londonien plein d'initiative ». Il est toutefois douteux qu'Anderson fasse référence à la lettre adressée au « Cher Patron ». En effet, Anderson omet de mentionner la carte postale qui l'avait suivie de près. En outre, il ne semble pas que la lettre en question ait été conservée au *Police Museum*. Enfin, rien ne permet d'affirmer qu'Anderson ne fait pas référence à une autre lettre signée Jack l'Éventreur. Or, il en existe au moins une autre qui a été rédigée avant le 25 septembre. Dans une note de bas de page, Anderson ajoute : « Je serais presque tenté de divulguer l'identité [...] du journaliste qui a écrit cette lettre. » Pour se prémunir contre d'éventuelles attaques consécutives à ces révélations, il précise : « ... pourvu que les éditeurs en prennent la responsabilité en cas de procès en diffamation. » A l'évidence, les éditeurs en question n'ont pas estimé qu'ils pourraient choisir la seule ligne de défense acceptable en cas de procès en diffamation, à savoir affirmer que cette accusation était fondée.

Deux décennies plus tard, un ancien journaliste du *Star*, Best, alors âgé de soixante-dix ans, a révélé à un collègue qu'il avait écrit toutes les lettres « pour donner un coup de pouce à la profession ». Il a prétendu avoir agi en connivence avec un journaliste de province. Ils avaient utilisé une plume Waverley aplatie pour donner l'illusion que le niveau d'alphabétisation de l'auteur des lettres était faible.

C'est en 1993 qu'on a retrouvé une lettre rédigée en 1913 par le détective inspecteur John Littlechild, responsable de la *Special Branch* l'année des meurtres. D'après les renseignements dont nous disposons à ce sujet, il y nomme les journalistes qui auraient écrit les lettres signées Jack l'Éventreur, y compris la lettre adressée au « Cher Patron » et la carte postale mentionnant « Jacky l'Insolent ». Des recherches sont actuellement en cours pour vérifier l'authenticité de cette lettre.

Le 4 octobre, voici ce qu'écrivait le *Daily Telegraph* : « Le texte de la carte postale semble avoir été griffonné à la hâte et la main n'est pas aussi ferme que celle de l'auteur de la lettre, mais il n'y a guère de doute que les deux missives ont été écrites par la même plume. »

Sue Ironmonger, l'experte qui a examiné ces documents, ne peut affirmer avec certitude que l'auteur de la carte et celui de la lettre sont bien une seule et même personne. Elle continue d'examiner ces missives et toutes les autres lettres de l'Éventreur qui sont conservées au *Public Record Office* de Kew. Mais elle ne pense pas que le journal et la lettre adressée au « Cher Patron » soient de la même main.

Il n'en demeure pas moins que le langage utilisé dans la lettre rappelle celui qui prévaut dans le journal. « J'en ai après les putains », « la substance rouge » et les « drôles de petits jeux » sont autant d'expressions qui semblent sorties tout droit de l'esprit torturé de Maybrick, de même que les interjections moqueuses – « *ha ha* ».

Lorsqu'on lui a demandé son avis au sujet du mystère de l'Éventreur, Sir Arthur Conan Doyle a répondu qu'il chercherait un tueur ayant séjourné en Amérique. Là encore, il se fondait sur le langage utilisé pour étayer sa théorie. Or, des américanismes tels que « *Dear Boss* » pour « Cher Patron », « *fix me* » pour « régler mon compte » et « *shan't quit* » pour « je n'arrêterai pas » auraient pu être des expressions familières pour Maybrick, non seulement parce qu'il avait vécu à Norfolk, mais aussi parce que son épouse était américaine.

De surcroît, il revendique dans le journal la paternité de ces deux missives et d'autres messages adressés à la presse.

> Avant ma prochaine en adresserai un autre à Central en souvenir de moi.

Deux lettres encore plus convaincantes que celle adressée au « Cher Patron », mais dépourvues de dates, ont été postées de Liverpool. Malheureusement, elles ont aujourd'hui disparu des dossiers de Scotland Yard. En 1966, dans un article publié dans la *London Gazette*, le Pr Camps affirmait qu'elles avaient été reçues avant la publication de la lettre adressée au « Cher Patron ». Toutes deux ont été publiées pour la première fois en 1927, dans le livre de J. Hall Richardson intitulé *From City to Fleet Street* (De la *City* à Fleet Street). La première prédit les assassinats sur le point de se produire à Londres.

> Prenez garde je serai à l'œuvre les 1er et 2 courants dans Minories à minuit et je donne aux autorités une chance mais il n'y a jamais de policier près de l'endroit où je travaille. Bien à vous Jack l'Éventreur.

L'expression « courant » était employée dans le commerce pour signifier « de ce mois ». Mais utilisée en septembre, elle ne pouvait pas faire référence au mois d'octobre. Le recours au jargon administratif constituait peut-être un signe de fierté pour un homme d'affaires comme Maybrick, par ailleurs manquant d'éducation, mais en l'occurrence il l'avait utilisé à mauvais escient.

Cependant, Catharine Eddowes a bien été retrouvée morte près de Minories le 30 septembre. Ainsi, la lettre en question ne comportait peut-être pas d'erreur. En effet il se peut que, à l'instar des terroristes d'aujourd'hui, Maybrick ait souhaité prouver l'authenticité de son message à la police sans pour autant lui donner suffisamment d'indications pour que le crime soit empêché ou le meurtrier arrêté.

La seconde « lettre de Liverpool » revêt une importance similaire.

> Quels imbéciles que ces policiers. Je leur donne même le nom de la rue où j'habite. Prince William Street.

Prince William Street se trouve dans l'un des quartiers les plus pauvres de Liverpool, Toxteth. En 1888 s'y alignaient des logements ouvriers utilisés par « nos sœurs désillusionnées du trottoir ».

Maybrick connaissait bien Prince William Street. Cette rue se trouvait en effet à quelques mètres de la route principale entre Aigburth et son bureau.

La police a répondu de façon massive au double meurtre. Quelque quatre-vingt mille prospectus demandant des informations ont été distribués, deux mille pensionnaires ont été interrogés lors d'une enquête de porte en porte et des policiers en civil se sont mêlés aux clients des pubs de l'East End et des pensions.

Le 2 octobre, l'*Evening News* ne croyait pas si bien dire lorsqu'il a publié le commentaire suivant : « On commence à penser que le meurtrier ne fréquente pas les pensions ordinaires, mais qu'il occupe une chambre simple ou trouve refuge dans un entrepôt vide. On suppose qu'il réside quelque part entre Middlesex Street et Brick Lane. »

Mais quatre jours plus tard, le *Liverpool Echo* apportait ce correctif : « Il ne peut exister aucun doute que la police est sur le point de conclure que le meurtrier de Whitechapel ne se trouve pas dans ce quartier et qu'il n'y habitait pas au moment des meurtres. »

Et le *Liverpool Daily Post* de renchérir le 11 octobre, sous la manchette « Un indice aurait été trouvé à Liverpool » : « Un détective du *Criminal Investigation Department* s'est récemment rendu à Liverpool et y a retracé les mouvements d'un homme, mouvements qui se sont révélés de nature plutôt mystérieuse. La taille de cette personne et sa description physique sont connues avec certitude et elle était entre autres en possession d'un sac de cuir noir. Cette personne a soudainement quitté Liverpool pour Londres et a logé pendant un certain temps dans un hôtel de première catégorie bien connu de West End. »

L'article continuait en affirmant que l'homme en question avait l'habitude de se rendre dans les quartiers les plus démunis de l'East End et qu'il laissait dans son hôtel son sac de cuir noir, contenant des articles vestimentaires et des gravures obscènes.

« Il a été suggéré que cette personne mystérieuse serait originaire d'Amérique. »

Le lendemain, les autorités ont réfuté la totalité de cet article. Il est vrai qu'elles avaient tout intérêt à ce que leurs soupçons ne soient pas ébruités.

Quant aux rares témoins à charge, ils jouissaient de la

protection de la police. La *Metropolitan Police* assurait celle d'Israel Schwartz, témoin essentiel de l'attaque perpétrée sur Elizabeth Stride, et la *City Police* surveillait Joseph Lawende, dont la description de l'homme qu'il avait vu discuter avec Catharine Eddowes ressemblait à celle de Maybrick.

C'était une mesure nécessaire. En effet, le 6 octobre, une lettre menaçante, bourrée de fautes d'orthographe, a été postée dans le nord-ouest de Londres. L'écriture est nette et bien lisible, du même style que celle de la lettre adressée au « Cher Patron ».

> 6 octobre 1888
> Vous pensiez que vous étiez très malin j'imagine quand vous avez informé la police. Mais vous avez fait une erreur si vous pensiez que je ne vous est (*sic*) pas vu. Maintenant je sais que vous me connaissez et je vois clair dans votre petit jeu, et j'ai l'intention de vous faire la peau et d'envoyer vos oreilles à votre femme si vous montrez ceci à la police ou si vous les aidez si vous le faites je vous ferai la peau. C'est pas la peine que vous essayez de m'éviter. Parce que je vous ai quand vous ne vous y attendez pas et je tiens parole comme vous verrez bientôt et vous éventrerai. Votre humble serviteur Jack l'Éventreur.

Cette lettre est demeurée dans les dossiers du ministère de l'Intérieur au *Public Record Office*, où personne ne s'en est soucié jusqu'à ce que mon éditeur, Robert Smith, la consulte pour les besoins de la présente enquête. (Elle est reproduite dans ce livre, de même que la lettre adressée au « Cher Patron » et la carte postale de « Jacky l'Insolent ».) On peut imaginer qu'elle était destinée à Schwartz ou à Lawende. Elle a été envoyée depuis le quartier où se trouvait l'appartement de Michael Maybrick, à Regent's Park. On le sait, Maybrick y séjournait souvent.

Anna Koren et Sue Ironmonger s'accordent à dire que cette lettre est écrite de la même main que celle adressée au « Cher Patron ». Le langage employé contient la même vindicte et la même fureur que celles manifestées par Maybrick, dans le journal, envers celui qu'il soupçonne de l'avoir aperçu.

> Bon sang bon sang bon sang ce salaud m'a presque attrapé, qu'il soit maudit qu'il aille au diable, la prochaine fois je le découperai en morceaux, je le jure devant Dieu. Quelques minutes et je l'aurais fait, *salaud*. Je m'en vais le dénicher, lui donner une leçon.

Ce même jour, le 6 octobre, le *Daily Telegraph* a publié un portrait et une description de l'homme que la police recherche. Ils ont paru dans le *Liverpool Echo* deux jours plus tard. La ressemblance avec Maybrick est indéniable. Ces deux images sont reproduites dans ce livre. Selon la description des journaux, l'homme en question avait de l'éducation et des moyens, il était âgé d'une quarantaine d'années et portait des vêtements sombres et un foulard de soie foncée autour du cou. « Son chapeau était probablement un melon " raide " de couleur presque noire et son apparence était parfaitement respectable. Il se comporte de façon calme et posée, et rien chez lui ne trahit le monomaniaque, si ce n'est un mélange de nervosité et de ruse dans l'expression des yeux. »

Le 6 octobre était un samedi, le jour de la semaine qui semble avoir joué un rôle clé dans les cinq meurtres de Whitechapel. Maybrick est-il revenu chez Michael après le double meurtre et, choqué par ce qu'il a lu dans les journaux du matin, a-t-il ressenti le besoin d'écrire à Joseph Lawende, Israel Schwartz ou un autre témoin tout aussi inquiétant ?

Lawende avait vu Maybrick avec Catharine Eddowes. La *City Police* le considérait donc comme un témoin essentiel et l'a protégé de la presse avant l'enquête criminelle, les

4 et 11 octobre. Et l'avocat de la *City* a même adressé cette requête au coroner : « A moins que le jury ne le souhaite, j'ai une raison spéciale pour ne pas donner de détails relatifs à l'apparence de l'homme. » Le coroner a donné son accord et Lawende n'a décrit que les vêtements du suspect. En effet, s'il pouvait identifier l'Éventreur, ainsi que le pensait la police, et si Maybrick avait vu le portrait publié dans les journaux, ce dernier aurait pu menacer le témoin.

De retour dans sa famille après le double meurtre du 30 septembre, Maybrick a observé et attendu. Comme toujours, à la pensée de Florie et de son amant, il était à la fois excité et enragé. Homme solitaire, au corps et à l'esprit malades, il s'est de nouveau tourné en quête de réconfort vers son meilleur ami, George Davidson.

> Ce soir, je fêterai ça en invitant George à dîner. Je suis de bonne humeur, crois que je vais autoriser la salope à prendre du plaisir avec son maquereau, remarquerai qu'une soirée en ville lui fera du bien, suggérerai un concert. Je ne doute pas que la voiture conduira la garce tout droit chez lui. J'irai me coucher en pensant à tout ce qu'ils font. A la pensée de cette excitation, je ne tiens pas en place.

Le 12 octobre, le *Manchester Guardian* a publié le récit troublant d'un événement qui avait eu lieu à Liverpool. « Mercredi soir, une jeune femme marchait dans Sheil Road, à Liverpool, non loin de Sheil Park. Elle a été arrêtée par une femme d'une soixantaine d'années qui, avec agitation et excitation, lui a enjoint de ne pas pénétrer dans le parc. Quelques minutes plus tôt, a-t-elle expliqué, elle se reposait sur un banc lorsqu'elle avait été accostée par un homme d'allure respectable vêtu d'un manteau noir, d'un pantalon clair et d'un chapeau de feutre mou, qui lui avait demandé si elle connaissait quelque femme de mauvaise vie dans les parages, avant de sortir immédiatement après un couteau muni d'une lame longue et fine et de déclarer qu'il avait l'intention de tuer autant de femmes à Liverpool qu'à Londres, ajoutant qu'il enverrait les oreilles de sa première victime à l'éditeur d'un journal de Liverpool. La sexagénaire, qui tremblait violemment en racontant son histoire, a affirmé qu'elle avait eu si peur qu'elle se rappelait à peine comment elle avait échappé à cet homme. »

Elle n'a jamais su qu'elle s'était sans doute trouvée en face de Jack l'Éventreur en personne.

Le 15 octobre, les journaux de Leeds ont rapporté que Jack l'Éventreur avait été vu à Chorley, petite bourgade située à quelques kilomètres au nord de Liverpool. Le jour suivant, George Lusk, président du Comité de vigilance de Whitechapel, a reçu une boîte en carton de sept centimètres sur huit. A l'intérieur se trouvait la moitié d'un rein humain conservé dans de l'alcool, ainsi qu'une lettre à peine intelligible qui a disparu depuis.

De l'enfer.
M. Lusk,
Mossieur
Je vous envoie la moitié du Rei que j'ai pris à une femme et cansarvé pour vous j'ai frit ltre morceau et l'ai mangé c'était très bun. Je vous enverrai peut-être le coutea sanglant qui l'a retiré si vous atadez seulement un peu plu longtemps

signé

Attrapez-moi quand vous pourrez Monchieur Lusk.

Les experts médicaux qui ont examiné le rein en question ont exprimé des avis divergents. Le pathologiste de la *City*, le Dr Sedgwick Saunders, a déclaré à l'époque qu'il n'appartenait pas à Catharine Eddowes et qu'il s'agissait probablement d'un spécimen dérobé dans un hôpital. Pour sa part, le Dr Openshaw, conservateur du *Pathology Museum* au London Hospital, a déclaré qu'il s'agissait bien du rein d'une femme de quarante-cinq ans atteinte du mal de Bright.

Dans son journal, Maybrick met un terme à la controverse, lorsqu'il indique qu'il a mangé l'autre rein de Catharine Eddowes.

> Du sucre et du thé doux,
> auraient pu servir à payer mes petits honoraires
> Mais à la place j'ai dû m'enfuir
> et au fait j'ai montré mon plaisir
> En mangeant du rognon froid pour dîner

David Forshaw estime possible que Maybrick, à l'instar d'autres auteurs de crimes en série, ait mangé certaines parties de ses victimes pour affirmer son pouvoir absolu sur elles. Il est également possible que l'Éventreur ait cru que le fait de manger des restes humains lui conférerait une parcelle de force qui appartenait à la personne décédée.

Pendant l'été, Florie était allée voir le Dr Hopper. Elle lui avait fait part de son anxiété. Son mari prenait « des médicaments très puissants qui avaient sur lui des effets néfastes » et, après chaque dose, il paraissait encore plus mal en point. Elle a supplié le médecin de parler à son mari et de le convaincre d'arrêter. Ces conversations ont fini par tomber dans l'oreille de Maybrick. Voici ce qu'il écrit en octobre, à la veille de son cinquantième anniversaire.

> La putain a informé le crétin bavard. J'ai l'habitude de prendre des médicaments puissants. J'étais furieux quand la garce me l'a dit. Si furieux que je l'ai frappée ha. La putain m'a suppliée de ne pas recommencer. Ça m'a donné du plaisir, un très grand plaisir. Si je n'avais pas mon travail, j'aurais découpé cette garce en morceaux sur-le-champ. [...] Il s'est écoulé trop de temps

depuis ma dernière, je n'ai pas été bien. J'ai eu mal dans tout mon corps. [...] Visiterai bientôt la cité des putains, très bientôt. Je me demande si je pourrais en buter trois ?

Lorsqu'il était nerveux, Maybrick ne pouvait plus réprimer son tempérament violent. Et s'il venait effectivement de frapper Florie pour la première fois, ainsi qu'il l'indique, ce ne serait pas la dernière.

Michael, lui aussi, s'inquiétait au sujet de la santé de son frère. Selon le journal, il lui a écrit plusieurs lettres en octobre et lui a notamment posé des questions sur ses crises de « somnambulisme » Il est possible que Michael ait déjà entretenu des soupçons au sujet de son frère et que le terme de « somnambulisme » ait servi d'euphémisme pour désigner des activités beaucoup plus occultes.

Maybrick a beaucoup souffert en octobre. Il n'a pu s'approvisionner en médicaments que de façon intermittente, et il n'en a pas tiré la force dont il avait besoin pour commettre ses meurtres. Aucun meurtre n'a eu lieu ce mois-là, aussi n'avait-il aucune raison de consigner ses pensées par écrit. Il n'a pas repris la plume pendant trois ou quatre semaines. C'est à la fin du mois qu'il écrit :

Il s'est écoulé trop de temps depuis ma dernière, je n'ai pas été bien.

Il est possible que le fait de fêter son cinquantième anniversaire, le 24 octobre, l'ait quelque peu déprimé. Il avait besoin de retrouver un meilleur moral. Durant la première semaine de novembre, il s'est donc rendu à Londres où il a séjourné dans l'appartement de Michael, à Regent's Park. Il avait prévu de se rendre à Whitechapel le jeudi de cette même semaine mais il a souffert d'une crise terrible, qui a peut-être confirmé les craintes de son frère.

J'ai été forcé de refréner mon plaisir en prenant la dose la plus forte que j'ai jamais prise. La brûlure cette nuit-là a pénétré mon esprit. Je me rappelle vaguement avoir placé un mouchoir dans ma bouche pour étouffer mes cris. Je crois que j'ai vomi plusieurs fois. La douleur était intolérable, je tremble rien que d'y penser. Plus jamais.

Je suis convaincu que Dieu m'a placé ici-bas pour tuer toutes les putains, car c'est ce qu'il a dû vouloir, ne suis-je pas toujours là. Rien ne m'arrêtera maintenant. Plus j'en prends plus je me renforce.

Michael avait dans l'idée qu'une fois mon travail terminé je rentrerais à Liverpool le jour même. Et en vérité, c'est ce que j'ai fait un jour plus tard *ha ha*.

Le vendredi 9 novembre, toute l'Angleterre allait être horrifiée par la bestialité incroyable de l'un des meurtres les plus abominables jamais commis.

Chapitre 9

Mary Jane Kelly avait environ vingt-cinq ans, le même âge que Florie Maybrick. Et comme Florie, mais à l'inverse des autres victimes de l'Éventreur, elle était jolie et elle avait les cheveux roux. Lorsque Maybrick l'a aperçue dans Commercial Street, la ressemblance avec son épouse a dû le frapper. C'est sans doute la raison pour laquelle il l'a attaquée avec une telle férocité.

Le jeudi 8 novembre, Mary Jane avait passé l'après-midi et le début de la soirée avec des amis, puis elle était rentrée chez elle, au 13 Miller's Court. Elle louait une chambre minuscule au rez-de-chaussée de l'immeuble, qu'elle partageait avec Joe Barnett, concierge au chômage.

Ce soir-là, Lizzie Albrook, une voisine plus jeune, était venue bavarder un moment avec elle. Kelly lui avait donné ce conseil : « Quoi que tu fasses, ne tourne pas mal et ne deviens pas comme moi. » Puis Mary Jane s'était mise à chanter à tue-tête, importunant les voisins.

Au petit matin, George Hutchinson rentre d'un voyage dans l'Essex lorsqu'il aperçoit un homme s'approchant de Mary Jane, qui cherche des clients. Hutchinson connaît bien Mary Jane et va même parfois jusqu'à lui donner de l'argent. Voici ce qu'il racontera aux policiers de Commercial Street : « A environ 2 heures, le 9 [novembre], juste avant d'arriver au croisement de Flower Street et de Dean Street, j'ai rencontré la femme qui a été assassinée. [...] Un homme qui arrivait en sens inverse a tapoté l'épaule de Kelly, il lui a chuchoté quelque chose et tous deux ont éclaté de rire. Je l'ai entendue lui répondre d'accord et l'homme a ajouté vous ferez l'affaire pour ce que je vous ai dit : il a ensuite placé le bras droit autour des épaules de Kelly. Il tenait aussi un petit paquet dans la main gauche, avec une espèce de lanière tout autour. Je me suis adossé au bec de gaz du pub Queen's Head, et je l'ai observé. »

La description de cet homme par Hutchinson est si détaillée qu'elle éveille les soupçons. S'étaient-ils rencontrés avant ? Aux policiers qui l'ont interrogé, Hutchinson a parlé d'un homme d'apparence « étrangère », au profil sombre, portant un long manteau sombre avec un col et des parements en astrakan, une veste et un pantalon sombres, un chapeau de feutre sombre « rabattu au milieu », des bottines claires à boutons avec des guêtres sombres, un col de lin et une cravate noire ornée d'une épingle en fer à cheval. Une grosse chaîne en or était visible sur son gilet, et la chaîne de sa montre était ornée d'un sceau d'où pendait une pierre rouge. Il portait une paire de gants blancs et un petit paquet. Il était âgé de trente-quatre ou trente-cinq ans, mesurait un mètre soixante-dix, avait le teint pâle et l'ombre d'une moustache.

Les épingles de cravate en forme de fer à cheval et les grosses chaînes en or étaient populaires à l'époque. Une photo de Michael Maybrick portant semblable épingle est parue à plusieurs reprises dans les magazines. Sur la photographie reproduite dans ce livre, James porte lui aussi une grosse chaîne en or et une épingle de cravate dont la forme ressemble à celle d'un fer à cheval.

Lorsque Maybrick a quitté l'appartement de son frère Michael pour aller travailler, il portait sans doute les vêtements respectables d'un homme d'affaires.

« Ils sont alors tous deux passés devant moi et l'homme

a baissé la tête, avec son chapeau rabattu. Je me suis incliné pour le regarder dans les yeux. Il m'a lancé un regard mauvais. Elle a dit allez chéri viens avec moi, je te promets que tu auras tout le confort. Ils se sont engagés dans Dorset Street. Je les ai suivis. Ils se sont arrêtés au coin de Miller's Court et sont restés là environ trois minutes. Il lui a dit quelque chose. Puis il a passé un bras autour des épaules de Kelly et l'a embrassée. Elle a dit qu'elle avait perdu son mouchoir. Il a sorti le sien, qui était rouge, et le lui a donné. Ils ont alors remonté Miller's Court ensemble. Je me suis approché pour voir s'ils étaient encore là, mais je ne les ai pas aperçus. Je suis resté là pendant trois quarts d'heure, pour voir s'ils ressortaient. Comme ce n'était pas le cas, je suis reparti à 3 heures. »

C'est Mary Jane qui a ouvert la voie. Le passage qui menait à sa chambre était trop étroit pour qu'on y marche côte à côte. Quant à sa chambre, elle ne mesurait que dix mètres carrés, et la jeune femme avait à peine assez de place pour ouvrir la porte : le lit et une petite table occupaient en effet la quasi-totalité de l'espace disponible. La fenêtre située à côté de la porte était cassée.

A 4 heures, des voisins ont entendu crier « au meurtre », mais ils n'ont rien fait. Ce genre de cri était fréquent dans le quartier.

C'est sans doute le moment où Maybrick est passé à l'action. La faible lumière d'une seule bougie ne suffisant pas à éclairer la pièce, il a fait brûler un chapeau et quelques vêtements dans la cheminée. Et c'est devant les flammes qu'il a accompli son « travail ». Quand il en a eu terminé, il ne restait plus rien d'identifiable de la jeune femme qu'il avait rencontrée quelques heures plus tôt. Des voisins l'ont entendu quitter la chambre vers 5 h 45.

A 10 h 45, Thomas Bowyer est passé pour encaisser le loyer de Mary Jane Kelly. Tout de suite, il a appelé à l'aide John McCarthy, l'épicier du quartier qui était aussi le propriétaire de la chambre de Mary Jane. Mais c'est seulement à

13 h 30 que la police a enfin forcé la porte d'entrée à l'aide d'un manche de pioche.

Le massacre qui a été perpétré cette nuit-là dépasse l'imagination. Il déclencherait chez Maybrick lui-même une série de cauchemars qui le hanteraient pendant le restant de ses jours. Les blessures infligées à Mary Jane étaient si abominables que personne n'a été en mesure de déterminer avec certitude si la jeune femme s'était ou non débattue. Nick Warren, rédacteur en chef de *Ripperana*, a fait observer que les coupures visibles sur les mains indiquaient que la jeune femme avait essayé de repousser son agresseur. Mais pour sa part, le chirurgien de la police, le Dr Thomas Bond, a déclaré : « Le coin du drap situé à droite de la tête de la femme était saturé de sang et avait été tailladé à plusieurs reprises, ce qui indiquerait que le visage était recouvert d'un drap au moment de l'attaque. »

Le Dr Bond a ajouté : « Il est très probable que le meurtrier est un homme d'apparence tranquille et inoffensive, sans doute d'âge moyen et bien habillé. »

Un photographe de la police a immortalisé la scène, et dès l'année suivante, dans *Vacher l'Éventreur et les crimes sadiques*, J.A.E. Lacassagne publiait une reproduction de ce cliché. Mais c'est seulement en 1988 que l'écrivain et spécialiste du crime Simon Wood a mentionné en privé à l'un de nos consultants qu'on distinguait une initiale sur l'une des photos du cadavre de Mary Jane Kelly. Et de fait, au-dessus du lit, on aperçoit la lettre « M » – la marque de Maybrick. Sur le côté, on aperçoit une autre lettre : « F ».

Une initiale ici et une initiale là
désigneront la mère putain.

Je l'ai laissée sur place pour les imbéciles mais ils ne la trouveront jamais. J'ai été trop malin. L'ai laissée *devant* pour que tous les yeux les voient. Devrais-je leur écrire pour leur dire ? Ça m'amuse.

Elle m'a rappelé la putain. Si jeune pas comme moi.

Après avoir choisi quatre prostituées beaucoup plus âgées et bien moins séduisantes que Florie, Maybrick avait opté pour une femme du même âge que son épouse, et presque aussi jolie. Et Mary Jane Kelly avait payé pour les écarts de conduite de Florie Maybrick, la « mère putain ».

Maybrick a identifié la prostituée avec sa femme : c'est pourquoi il a barbouillé ses initiales sur le mur. La forme du « M » majuscule, dont la première moitié est plus petite, est la même que dans le journal.

Cette photo de Mary Jane Kelly a été publiée dans un grand nombre d'ouvrages, et pourtant personne n'a jamais identifié l'indice ainsi laissé. Il faut toutefois préciser que la photo n'est suffisamment bien reproduite que dans l'ouvrage de Stephen Knight, *Jack the Ripper : The Final Solution*. Ailleurs, il est presque impossible de distinguer les initiales de Florie Maybrick. L'original de la police ainsi qu'un agrandissement de cette photo figurent dans la section iconographique de ce livre.

Les mutilations infligées à Mary Jane Kelly sont détaillées dans un rapport du Dr Bond, qui a disparu vers 1911 et n'a été retrouvé qu'en 1987. « Toute la surface de l'abdomen et des cuisses a été enlevée et la cavité abdominale a été vidée de ses viscères. Les seins ont été découpés, les bras mutilés par plusieurs blessures et le visage a été tellement tailladé qu'on ne reconnaît aucun des traits. Les tissus du cou ont été tranchés tout autour de l'os.

« Les viscères ont été trouvés en différents endroits : l'utérus, les reins et un sein sous la tête, l'autre sein à côté du pied droit, le foie entre les pieds, les intestins sur le côté droit et la rate sur le côté gauche du corps. Les lambeaux de chair prélevés sur l'abdomen et sur les cuisses se trouvaient sur une table. »

Dans le rapport d'autopsie, le chirurgien de la police ajoute : « Le visage était entaillé de tous les côtés, une partie du nez, des joues, des sourcils et des oreilles avait été enlevée. »

Les souvenirs conservés par Maybrick de cet accès de frénésie destructrice coïncident à un détail près : l'endroit où il a placé les seins de la victime.

> Je n'ai rien laissé de la garce, rien. J'en ai disposé un peu partout dans la pièce, j'avais du temps devant moi, comme l'autre putain j'ai découpé le nez de la garce, complètement cette fois. Je n'ai rien laissé de son visage, pas le moindre souvenir. [...] J'ai trouvé que c'était une bonne farce de découper ses seins, les ai embrassés un moment. Le goût du sang était doux, le plaisir irrésistible, faudra que je recommence, ça m'a tellement excité. Les ai laissés sur la table avec une partie du reste. Pensé qu'ils seraient à leur place là. Il leur fallait un boucher alors j'ai dépiauté tout ce que je pouvais, et ri pendant que je le faisais. Comme les autres garces, elle s'est fendue comme une pêche mûre.

Les pathologistes consultés affirment qu'à ce stade il aurait été difficile de faire la différence entre la chair des seins et celle de l'abdomen. Selon David Forshaw, l'extase éprouvée par le meurtrier au moment du carnage a temporairement oblitéré certains souvenirs. Mais quelques jours plus tard, lorsque Maybrick, d'humeur plus paisible, évoque le meurtre dans un poème, il est plus près de la vérité.

* Leur goût était si doux
* J'ai pensé les laisser près des pieds de la putain

Il est déçu de n'avoir pas réussi, tout comme lors des précédentes mutilations, à décapiter sa victime.

Un de ces jours, j'emporterai la tête avec moi, *je le ferai.*
Je la ferai bouillir et la servirai pour mon dîner.

Ce passage est suivi d'une énumération qui semble de prime abord quelque peu décousue. En réalité, il ne faut pas la lire de gauche à droite, mais de haut en bas. Les mots racontent alors les événements survenus cette nuit-là.

clé	fendre
fuir	initiale
chapeau	
mouchoir	maquereau
caprice	s'occuper de la putain
Mère	lumière
père	feu

* Avec la clé j'ai pris la clé des champs
J'avais la clé,
Et avec elle j'ai pris la clé des champs
* les vêtements j'ai brûlés
* avec le chapeau
Le chapeau j'ai brûlé
la lumière j'ai cherché
* Pour l'amour de la mère putain
Et j'ai pensé à la mère putain. [...]
Un mouchoir rougi
conduisait au lit
et j'ai pensé à la mère putain

La question de la clé soulève une interrogation. La police a dû forcer la porte d'entrée de la chambre de Mary Jane Kelly. Ensuite, tous les journaux ont rapporté que la clé avait été perdue, ce qui confirme l'affirmation de Maybrick, selon laquelle il l'aurait emportée. Mais quelques jours après, un journal a rapporté que la clé se trouvait désormais en possession de la police.

Maybrick avait-il verrouillé la porte en partant, puis jeté la clé une fois qu'il se trouvait en sécurité ?

Enfin, deux autres détails du journal sont très troublants. Dans les dernières pages, lorsque Maybrick, sur le point de mourir, songe aux actes qu'il a commis, il évoque Mary Jane Kelly et mentionne son nom. C'est la seule fois qu'il mentionne le nom d'une de ses victimes. Cela signifie-t-il qu'à ses yeux, seule Kelly, substitut de Florie, possédait une identité ?

> Ce soir je prierai pour les femmes que j'ai massacrées.
> Que Dieu me pardonne pour les actes que j'ai commis
> sur Kelly   pas de cœur   pas de cœur.

Dans son rapport d'autopsie, retrouvé en 1987, le Dr Bond déclare : « Le péricarde était ouvert et le cœur absent. »

Or, ni la police ni les journaux n'ont mentionné que le cœur manquait. Maybrick écrit alors :

> Oh M. Abberline, c'est un malin petit monsieur
> il garde pour lui tout ce qu'il peut

Quelques jours plus tard, Hutchinson a rapporté aux journalistes qu'il avait entrepris de retrouver le tueur de Mary Jane le dimanche suivant, c'est-à-dire le 11 novembre. Et en dépit d'un épais brouillard il était sûr d'avoir vu de nouveau l'homme qu'il avait aperçu avec Mary Jane. Il se trouvait cette fois dans Middlesex Street.

Après la publication de ce témoignage, l'agence de la *Press Association* a signalé que la police avait changé de tactique. Sur la base des déclarations de Hutchinson, de Lawende et de Schwartz, elle possédait en effet désormais la description la plus détaillée dont elle ait jamais disposé. « On suppose, indiquait l'agence en question, que le meurtrier de Whitechapel vient de Manchester, de Birmingham ou d'une autre ville des Midlands dans le but de commettre ses crimes. A Willesden et à Euston, plusieurs détectives surveillent donc l'arrivée des trains en provenance des Midlands et du Nord... »

C'est alors que Maybrick a pris conscience d'une réalité terrifiante : il risquait d'être pris.

> Je ne peux pas vivre sans mon médicament. J'ai peur de m'endormir de crainte que mes cauchemars reviennent. Je vois des milliers de gens qui me pourchassent, avec Abberline en tête qui agite une corde.

Partant, il n'est guère surprenant que ses maux de tête aient empiré au mois de novembre et qu'il ait ajouté un autre nom à la liste déjà longue de ses médecins traitants : le Dr J. Drysdale, Écossais d'une soixantaine d'années, avare de ses paroles et toujours tiré à quatre épingles. Maybrick a consulté ce médecin de Liverpool les 19, 22 et 26 novembre, puis les 5 et 10 décembre. Il lui a confié que, depuis trois mois, il souffrait de douleurs d'un côté à l'autre de la tête, toujours précédées d'une douleur sur le côté droit de la tête et par une migraine sourde. Il a ajouté que cette douleur ne le quittait jamais, sauf parfois le matin. S'il fumait ou buvait trop, sa main et sa jambe gauches s'engourdissaient et il n'était pas rare que des rougeurs apparaissent sur la peau de sa main. Il n'a pas mentionné qu'il se droguait.

« Il paraissait souffrir de dyspepsie nerveuse », a diagnostiqué le Dr Drysdale. C'est ce qu'il a répété lors du procès de Florie, ajoutant : « Je dirais qu'il était hypocondriaque. »

Sentant la police londonienne à ses trousses, il semble naturel que Maybrick ait décidé de retourner sur le lieu de son premier crime, Manchester, où vivait son frère Edwin.

Je suis fatigué et j'ai peur que la cité des putains soit devenue trop dangereuse pour que j'y retourne. Noël approche et Thomas m'a invité à lui rendre visite. Je le connais bien. J'ai décidé d'accepter son offre, bien que je sache ce qui se cache derrière, il veut parler affaires un point c'est tout. Thomas ne pense à rien d'autre qu'à l'argent à l'inverse de moi, *ha ha.*
Ma première était à Manchester alors pourquoi pas ma prochaine ? Si je devais faire pareil qu'avec la dernière, ça plongerait les imbéciles dans la panique, surtout cet imbécile d'Abberline. Les enfants me demandent constamment ce que je vais leur acheter pour Noël ils prennent peur quand je leur dis un couteau étincelant pas très différent de celui de Jack l'Éventreur afin que je puisse leur couper la langue pour avoir la paix. Je crois sincèrement que je suis complètement fou. Je n'ai jamais fait de mal aux enfants durant les années depuis qu'ils sont nés. Mais maintenant je prends grand plaisir à leur faire peur de cette façon. Que Dieu me pardonne.

Selon David Forshaw, à l'instar de la plupart des auteurs de crimes en série, Maybrick voue un amour indéfectible à ses enfants. Tout au long du journal, il parle d'eux avec tendresse. Il a essayé, écrit-il, de prendre ses distances, mais sans succès. Cet échec l'accule au suicide.

Peut-être que je devrais me pendre.

Mais le souvenir de Mary Jane Kelly a beau le torturer, ce dernier meurtre ne lui a pas suffi. A preuve la coupure de presse adressée le 5 décembre au Dr William Sedgwick Saunders, l'analyste officiel de la *City*. Ce message avait été griffonné sur la coupure :

Angleterre
Cher Patron. Ouvrez l'œil le 7 courant. En train de m'essayer à la désarticulation, et si j'y arrive vous enverrai un doigt. Bien à vous Jack l'Éventreur.
M. Saunders
Magistrat de police.

Les graphologues n'ont pu absolument confirmer que ce message avait été écrit de la même main que la lettre adressée au « Cher Patron ». Mais les deux écritures se ressemblent. Ces deux missives sont reproduites dans la section iconographique. Il est intéressant de noter que le deuxième message est rédigé sur un article relatant comment trois hommes d'affaires de Liverpool se sont promenés nus en public. Il contient les mots « Liverpool », « fou » et « homme d'affaires ». S'agissait-il d'un autre indice semé par Maybrick ? Selon David Forshaw, Maybrick ne souhaitait pas être pris, mais cette possibilité l'excitait.

Que cette coupure de presse ait été ou non envoyée par Maybrick, il n'en reste pas moins que ce dernier songeait sérieusement à un septième meurtre. Dans son journal, il donnait libre cours à sa hargne en biffant une ligne après l'autre, signe de sa frustration croissante. Les juifs, Michael, Abberline, Lowry, tous sont l'objet de sa colère.

* Sir Jim va,
Suis-je aliéné ?
canne, gain
* Sir Jim avec sa drôle de canne
* Va encore frapper bientôt [...]

* Sir Jim il les découpe d'abord
bon sang

* Abberline dit qu'il est maintenant stupéfait,
* Sir Jim n'en a pas frappé une autre
* Il attend patiemment

> * pour voir rapidement
>
> * Noël sauve le bonnet de taupe des putains
> * damnées soient les garces damné soit Michael
> * Donnez son dû à Sir Jim
> * Il déteste tous les Juifs
> * Car parmi les hommes il n'a pas de favori
> * Quand il se hâte vers son abri.

Mais malgré ses efforts, Maybrick ne parvient pas à retrouver la maîtrise de soi qui lui fait défaut, et il perd confiance.

> si Dieu le veut ma prochaine sera de loin la pire, ma tête me fait mal, mais je continuerai maudit soit Michael d'être si malin l'art de la poésie est loin d'être simple. Je le maudis tellement. Abberline Abberline, je finirai par démolir cet imbécile, si Dieu le veut.

Dans l'édition de poche de l'ouvrage de Paul Beggs, *The Mystery of Jack the Ripper* (le Mystère de Jack l'Éventreur), parue en 1962, figure un curieux poème que Beggs attribue aux *Chronicles of Crime* (Chroniques du crime) de Thomas Dutton. Les chroniques en question, qui se présentent sous la forme de trois livres de réflexions manuscrites, ont été découvertes en 1932 par Donald McCormick, auteur d'ouvrages sur le crime. On ne sait pas où elles se trouvent aujourd'hui, et bien qu'aucun autre expert n'ait vu ces livres, McCormick ne paraissait avoir aucune raison de les fabriquer.

Dutton, leur auteur, était un médecin qui vivait à Whitechapel à l'époque des meurtres : il a réalisé des microphotographies de cent vingt-huit spécimens de messages signés Jack l'Éventreur et en a conclu qu'au moins trente-quatre d'entre eux étaient de la même main. L'un de ces messages était une lettre contenant ce poème :

Huit petites putains le paradis n'espèrent pas
Si Gladstone [1] en sauve une, sept il en restera
Sept petites putains mendient deux, trois pennies
L'une reste à Heneage Court, et il y a une tuerie

Six petites putains, heureuses d'être en vie.
L'une se glisse vers Jack, et il en reste cinq.
Quatre rime avec fille légère
Tout comme trois avec moi,
Je mettrai la ville en feu
Il n'y en aura plus que deux.

Deux petites putains, tremblantes d'épouvante,
Cherchent dans la nuit noire une porte accueillante
Le couteau de Jack brille, et il n'en reste qu'une,
La dernière, la plus mûre, voilà comme Jack s'amuse.

Ce poème trouve des échos dans le journal. Lorsque Maybrick menace de mettre le feu à l'église St. James et dit de Mary Jane Kelly :

Elle s'est fendue comme une pêche mûre.

On y trouve également le thème de la lettre citée par Beggs : « Huit petites putains le paradis n'espèrent pas ».

* Une putain au paradis
* deux putains côte à côte
* trois putains sont toutes mortes
* quatre

Maybrick est pris de panique. Il est déprimé et se plaint constamment de la fatigue. Il a perdu confiance et ne parvient même plus à terminer ses poèmes. Il biffe une ligne

1. Premier ministre de l'époque. (*N.d.T.*)

après l'autre, à l'exception significative de « Suis-je aliéné ? », et finit par abandonner, au comble de la frustration.

bon sang bon sang bon sang

Toutefois, il lui faut poursuivre.

J'ai froid maudit soit ce salaud de Lowry qui m'a poussé à éventrer. Je n'arrête pas de voir des flots de sang jaillir de ces garces. Les cauchemars sont abominables. Je ne peux pas m'empêcher de vouloir en manger encore. Que Dieu me vienne en aide, va au diable. Non personne ne m'arrêtera. Que Dieu aille au diable.

Réfléchis réfléchis réfléchis écris dis-leur à tous prouve-leur que tu es qui tu dis que tu es fais-les croire que c'est la vérité que je dis.

Tous les mois de novembre, un bal avait lieu à Battlecrease House. Cette année-là, Alfred Brierley comptait au nombre des invités, de même que le collègue et ami de longue date de Maybrick, Charles Ratcliff. Quelques jours après, Ratcliff a écrit à Charles Aunspaugh, qui se trouvait alors en Amérique. A la fin de la lettre se trouvait le commentaire suivant : « Je crois qu'Alf est en train de gagner l'affection de Mme James. »

C'est à ce moment-là que l'inspecteur Walter Andrews et une équipe de collègues, qui enquêtaient à Montréal sur une autre affaire, ont été dépêchés à New York pour suivre une nouvelle piste. D'après la *Pall Mall Gazette*, le tueur avait quitté l'Angleterre pour l'Amérique trois semaines plus tôt.

A l'approche de Noël, les souffrances éprouvées par Maybrick n'ont fait que s'accentuer. Comme toujours, l'ami fidèle, George Davidson, se trouvait à ses côtés.

Je ne peux pas me résoudre à me relire, tout ce que j'ai écrit m'effraie tellement. George m'a rendu visite aujourd'hui. Je crois qu'il sait ce que j'endure, bien qu'il ne dise rien. Je le vois dans ses yeux. Pauvre George, c'est un si bon ami. [...]
Je suis fatigué, très fatigué. J'aspire à la paix, mais je sais bien au fond que je continuerai. Je serai à Manchester d'ici quelques jours. Je crois que je me sentirai beaucoup mieux quand j'aurai répété ma dernière prestation. Je me demande si je peux apporter des améliorations à mes actes diaboliques. [...] Le jour tire à sa fin, Lowry était de bonne humeur. Je suis satisfait. Je regrette, car j'ai montré ma colère avec mes amis juifs. A Noël je ferai amende honorable.

Mais à Noël, Maybrick n'avait aucune raison de se réjouir.

Les enfants se sont bien amusés à Noël. Pas moi. Mon humeur n'est plus noire, bien que j'aie mal à la tête. Je ne m'habituerai jamais à la douleur. Je maudis l'hiver. J'attends avec impatience mon mois favori, ça me ferait tant plaisir de voir les fleurs tout épanouies. C'est de chaleur que j'ai besoin, je tremble tant. Maudit soit ce temps et cette putain de garce.

Cette chaleur, il ne pouvait plus l'obtenir de la part de Florie. Dans ce passage rédigé quelques jours après Noël, il décrit son septième meurtre – qui a eu lieu à Manchester, comme prévu. Mais il ne se sent plus « malin ».

Je n'ai pas pu découper comme ma dernière, je n'arrêtais pas de la revoir en frappant. J'ai essayé de réprimer toutes pensées d'amour. Je l'ai laissée pour morte, ça je le sais. Ça ne m'a pas amusé.

On trouve là une réminiscence de son premier meurtre, commis à Manchester lui aussi.

> Je n'ai pas eu de plaisir à serrer.

Il écrit qu'il l'a laissée pour morte. La même expression est utilisée plus tard dans le journal, lorsque Maybrick menace toutes les prostituées de :

> enlever les yeux
> enlever la tête
> les laisser toutes pour mortes

Mais il ne se sent plus aussi puissant, et ses pensées le ramènent à Florie, et l'empêchent de laisser libre cours à sa passion. Seul un acte de mutilation symbolique lui permet d'assouvir son appétit de vengeance. Plein de rage et de frustration, il retourne à Battlecrease House et frappe sa femme.

> J'ai déchaîné ma fureur sur la garce. J'ai frappé encore et encore. Je ne sais pas comment je me suis arrêté. Je l'ai laissée sans un sou, je n'ai pas de regrets.

Dans une lettre écrite à sa mère le dernier jour de 1888, Florie mentionne l'incident, mais pas les coups. « Dans sa fureur, il a déchiré son testament ce matin, car il m'avait nommée légataire universelle et m'avait confié l'administration des biens des enfants. Maintenant, il a l'intention de léguer tout ce qu'il peut aux enfants, en ne m'accordant que le tiers légal. Mais cela m'importe peu tant que les enfants ont tout ce qu'il faut. Mes propres revenus me suffiront. Agréable façon de commencer la Nouvelle Année. »

Voici ce que David Forshaw dit de l'état d'esprit de Maybrick durant cette période : « Bien que nous en sachions encore fort peu sur les parents de Maybrick, les études portant sur d'autres auteurs de crimes en série révèlent que sous le masque de l'amour filial se cache un profond ressentiment. Le père et la mère de Maybrick dépensaient sans compter pour le talentueux Michael, objet de toute leur attention, ce qui a fait naître la jalousie que révèle le journal de Maybrick à l'égard de son frère.

« A ce moment de sa vie, le sentiment d'inadéquation enraciné chez lui, celui-là même qui inspirait ses confessions moqueuses et fanfaronnes, mais aussi les meurtres, émerge avec une violence incontrôlable. Mary Jane Kelly, avec ses cheveux roux, a pris la place de Florie " la mère putain " et, peut-être, de toutes les mères. »

Le temps était à l'unisson de l'état d'esprit de Maybrick. Le brouillard épais qui recouvrait Liverpool début 1888 était revenu le jour de la Saint-Sylvestre et le journal local, le *Liverpool Echo*, prédisait : « Aucun changement de temps n'est à espérer, et il est probable que nous allons connaître une période de brume, de pluie et de temps gris. »

C'était un mauvais présage pour 1889.

Chapitre 10

Si Florie, ou l'un quelconque des autres membres de la famille, soupçonnait que James Maybrick était l'homme le plus craint et le plus méprisé de Grande-Bretagne, ils ne l'ont jamais admis. Son secret serait enterré avec lui dans le cimetière d'Anfield. Mais sa mort détruirait à jamais la vie de sa jeune épouse américaine. Seul survivrait le mystère entourant les dernières années du marchand de coton. Et les interrogations ne manquent pas. Pourquoi la famille Maybrick et les domestiques de Battlecrease House ont-ils conspiré contre Florie ? Pourquoi les médecins ne se sont-ils pas accordés sur les causes de la mort de Maybrick ? Pourquoi certaines lettres de la famille ont-elles été détruites et les ordonnances de Maybrick déchirées ? Mais plus étrange encore, pourquoi Edwin et Michael ont-ils dissimulé le passé de leur frère et ne sont-ils pas intervenus pour défendre sa veuve ?

Voici ce qu'on sait.

En janvier, au dire de la cuisinière, Elizabeth Humphreys, les visites d'Alfred Brierley se multiplient. En outre, il accompagne régulièrement les Maybrick aux courses. James n'est que trop conscient du penchant éprouvé par sa femme pour son rival. Pourtant, il continue d'inviter Brierley. Ce point ne surprend pas David Forshaw. Selon lui, Maybrick éprouve un plaisir pervers à observer le couple, qui ne se doute de rien. Cela fait partie de l' « exercice du pouvoir ». (Son goût du voyeurisme est flagrant dans sa description de l'éventration de Polly Nichols.)

> La putain vu son maquereau aujourd'hui ça ne m'a pas dérangé. J'ai imaginé que j'étais avec eux, cette seule pensée m'excite. Je me demande si la putain a jamais eu de telles pensées ? Je crois que oui...

Mais à mesure que l'hiver avance, Maybrick devient de plus en plus agité.

> Il ne se passera pas longtemps avant que je frappe de nouveau. J'en prends plus que jamais. La garce peut en prendre deux, Sir Jim en prendra quatre, un double double événement *ha ha.* Si j'étais dans la cité des putains j'accomplirais mes actes diaboliques séance tenante. Au nom de Dieu je le ferais.

> Je me maudis d'avoir été si bête, je n'aurai plus de regrets, qu'ils aillent tous au diable. Attention M. Abberline je reviendrai me venger pour de bon. Une fois de plus, on ne parlera que de moi en Angleterre. Mes pensées me donnent tant de plaisir. [...]

> Quand j'aurai terminé mes actes diaboliques, le diable lui-même me félicitera. Mais il lui faudra attendre longtemps pour que je lui serre la main. J'ai des travaux à faire beaucoup de travaux *ha ha* du rognon pour le dîner.

A ce moment-là, Maybrick a découvert une autre source où s'approvisionner en « médicament ». Blake, membre d'une équipe qui travaille pour William Bryer Nation, fabrique de produits pharmaceutiques, envisage de remplacer le coton par la ramie. En janvier 1889, Blake se rend à Liverpool pour rencontrer Maybrick. En effet, il a besoin d'aide pour lancer ce nouveau produit. Au cours de la conversation, Maybrick lui demande de lui décrire les produits chimiques utilisés dans la fabrication du textile en question. « Je ne cherche pas à obtenir vos secrets de fabrication, précise-t-il d'un ton rassurant. C'est une question de prix, et les produits chimiques peuvent être obtenus plus facilement à Liverpool. »

L'une des substances employées n'est autre que l'arsenic. La conversation s'oriente ensuite vers les paysans autrichiens, consommateurs d'arsenic, et vers Thomas de Quincey, auteur de *Confessions of an Opium Eater (Confessions d'un mangeur d'opium)*. Blake s'étonne que « de Quincey puisse avoir absorbé jusqu'à 900 gouttes de laudanum par jour ».

Maybrick sourit. « Ce qui tue l'un guérit l'autre, répond-il. Et il existe un soi-disant poison qui me guérit mieux que tous les médicaments lorsque je me sens faible et déprimé; il me rend plus fort de corps et d'esprit. Je n'en parle pas à tout le monde, et je ne vous en aurais pas parlé si vous n'aviez pas mentionné l'arsenic. Car c'est de l'arsenic qu'il s'agit. J'en prends quand je peux en avoir mais les médecins ne veulent pas en mettre dans mon remède, ou juste une larme de temps en temps, histoire de me faire souffrir le supplice de Tantale. »

Blake ne dit rien. Maybrick poursuit : « Puisque vous vous servez d'arsenic, pourriez-vous m'en donner un peu ? J'ai des difficultés pour en obtenir ici. »

Plus tard, dans une déclaration écrite, Blake mentionnera l'incident : « J'ai répondu que j'en avais et que, puisque je ne m'en servais que pour mes expériences, terminées à ce moment-là, je n'en avais plus l'utilité et qu'il pouvait avoir tout ce qui restait. Il m'a ensuite demandé pour combien il y en avait et a offert de payer d'avance. J'ai répondu que je n'étais pas habilité à vendre des médicaments et j'ai suggéré que nous fassions échange de bons procédés. M. Maybrick ferait de son mieux pour vendre mon produit à base de ramie et je lui ferais cadeau de l'arsenic. »

Lorsqu'ils se rencontrent de nouveau en février, Blake donne à Maybrick environ trois cents grains d'arsenic dans trois paquets différents. « Je lui ai dit de faire attention, car il en avait presque assez pour empoisonner un régiment. »

> J'en prends plus que jamais.

Le fait que Maybrick absorbe de plus en plus d'arsenic est visible dans la texture même du journal : son écriture devient plus irrégulière, ses menaces de plus en plus effrayantes.

Finalement, il va décider de frapper une fois de plus dans la « cité des putains ». Mais de la même façon que lors du meurtre d'Elizabeth Stride, il va être interrompu. D'après la description qu'il donne de l'incident, il n'a pas eu le temps de tuer sa victime.

> Bon sang bon sang bon sang ce salaud m'a presque attrapé, qu'il soit maudit qu'il aille au diable, la prochaine fois je le découperai en morceaux, je le jure devant Dieu. Quelques minutes et je l'aurais fait, *salaud*. Je m'en vais le dénicher, lui donner une leçon. Personne ne m'arrêtera. Que son âme noire soit maudite. Je me maudis d'avoir frappé trop tôt, j'aurais dû attendre que tout soit vraiment calme je le jure devant Dieu la prochaine fois j'emporterai tout et je le *mangerai*. Ne laisserai *rien* pas même la tête. Je la ferai bouillir et je la mangerai avec des carottes nouvelles.

Si une agression réalisée à la manière de l'Éventreur avait été perpétrée à Londres, la presse n'aurait pas manqué de s'en faire l'écho. On peut donc supposer que la victime s'en est tirée sans blessures graves.

En mars, les deux enfants de Maybrick contractent la

coqueluche et le Dr Humphreys est appelé à leur chevet. Il pose des questions à Florie au sujet de la santé de James. Elle lui répète ce qu'elle avait confié au Dr Hopper l'été précédent. Elle ajoute que son mari prend désormais de la poudre blanche, qu'elle pense être de la strychnine, et demande au médecin quels peuvent être les effets de cette drogue. Le Dr Humphreys lui répond que la strychnine peut tuer Maybrick et, avec une prescience étrange, il affirme : « S'il venait à mourir subitement, appelez-moi et je pourrai confirmer que nous en avons discuté. »

Toutefois, lorsque le moment viendra pour le Dr Humphreys d'offrir l'aide promise, il abandonnera Florie. Comme tous les autres, ou presque.

Ce même mois, Maybrick se rend chez le Dr Drysdale. Bien que ses maux de tête ne cessent jamais, explique-t-il, il se sent mieux depuis sa dernière visite en décembre. Toutefois, sa langue est chargée et il souffre toujours d'un engourdissement du bras et de la main gauches.

Florie écrit à Michael, qui se trouve à Londres, pour lui faire part de ses inquiétudes au sujet de la poudre blanche. Elle affirme que son mari est très irritable et se plaint de douleurs à la tête. D'après elle, il ne sait pas qu'elle a découvert sa toxicomanie, ni qu'elle a écrit à Michael.

Ce dernier détruira cette lettre, non sans avoir au préalable posé des questions à son frère. Il obtient de lui une réponse courroucée, ce qu'il mentionnera lors du procès de Florie.

> La garce a tout révélé
> ce soir elle va tomber
>
> Je le jure devant Dieu je vais découper cette garce et la servir aux enfants. Comment cette putain ose-t-elle écrire à Michael, cette maudite garce n'avait aucun droit de l'informer de mon médicament.

Durant l'hiver, les Maybrick se font de nouveaux amis : Charles Samuelson, courtier en tabacs, et sa jeune épouse, Christina. Pendant quelques jours les deux couples séjournent à l'hôtel Palace de Birkdale, près de Southport. Alfred Brierley est présent, lui aussi.

Le dernier soir, une partie de whist se termine par un éclat de Christina Samuelson, qui part se coucher en criant à son mari « Je te déteste ». Émue par les larmes de sa nouvelle amie, Florie tente d'apaiser le couple. « Ne prenez pas cela au sérieux, conseille-t-elle à Charles. Moi-même, je dis souvent à Jim que je le déteste. »

Quelques mois plus tard, lors de l'enquête criminelle consécutive au décès de Maybrick, Christina donnera une version différente de cette confession : « J'ai eu une conversation avec Mme Maybrick, et elle m'a dit qu'elle détestait son mari. »

Aux alentours du 15 mars, Maybrick se rend à Londres pour séjourner chez son frère. Si l'on en croit Bernard Ryan, l'auteur de *The Poisoned Life of Mrs. Maybrick*, Florie et Brierley ont fomenté un complot en son absence. Et de fait, au retour de son mari, Florie lui annonce qu'elle souhaite se rendre à Londres elle-même, pour tenir compagnie à une tante malade.

> J'achèterai quelque chose à la putain pour sa visite. Donnerai à cette garce l'impression que je considère qu'il est de son devoir d'aller rendre visite à sa tante. [...] Ha, quelle farce, laisser la garce croire que je n'ai pas connaissance de ses petites affaires de putain.

Le 16 mars, Florie envoie un télégramme au directeur de l'hôtel Flatman, dans Henrietta Street à Londres. Elle réserve une suite pour une semaine, au nom de « M. et Mme Thomas Maybrick de Manchester ». Mais l'hôtel ne confirme pas la réservation. Elle écrit donc une lettre, et demande spécifiquement que le menu suivant leur soit servi à leur arrivée : soupe, sole, caneton et petits pois, pommes de terre nouvelles, fromage, céleri et dessert. Le choix de l'hôtel est provocateur : c'est en effet celui où se rencontrent les marchands de coton de Liverpool. Elle arrivera la première, et son mari le lendemain, annonce-t-elle au directeur de l'hôtel. Celui-ci met donc la chambre 9 et le salon 16, contigus, à la disposition des Maybrick à partir du 21 mars.

Au même moment, Florie écrit à son ami d'enfance, John Baillie Knight, domicilié à Holland Park, à Londres, pour lui dire qu'elle se trouvera à Londres le 21 et qu'elle souhaiterait le rencontrer pour dîner. Elle lui confie avoir de graves problèmes, mais sans donner d'explication.

Le 21, Florie arrive à l'hôtel Flatman vers 13 heures. A 18 h 30, John Baillie Knight frappe à sa porte. Ils s'assoient dans le salon et elle lui annonce qu'elle est venue à Londres parce qu'elle désire se séparer de son mari. Elle ne peut plus supporter qu'il entretienne une autre femme. Elle ajoute qu'il est cruel et la bat.

Baillie Knight estime qu'une séparation apparaît effectivement comme la meilleure solution et lui suggère un cabinet d'avocats, Markby, Stewart et Compagnie. Il ajoute que le mieux, ensuite, sera que Florie se rende chez sa mère à Paris. Ce soir-là, John et Florie dînent au Grand Hôtel et se rendent au théâtre. Ils sont de retour vers 23 h 30.

C'est le lendemain que Brierley arrive et s'installe dans la suite de Florie. Tous deux y restent jusqu'à 13 heures le dimanche, heure à laquelle ils règlent la note.

« Il a piqué ma vanité et résisté à mes efforts pour lui plaire, commentera Florie. Avant que nous ne nous séparions, il m'a fait comprendre qu'il s'intéressait à quelqu'un d'autre, qu'il ne pouvait pas m'épouser, et qu'il préférerait se tirer une balle dans la tête que de voir notre liaison exposée au grand jour. J'ai alors éprouvé une telle répulsion que j'ai déclaré que nous devions y mettre un terme sur-le-champ. »

Après le procès, voici ce que Brierley déclarera pour sa part au *New York Herald* : « Nous nous sommes quittés à

Londres comme si nous ne devions jamais nous revoir [...]. Il était clair de part et d'autre que nous ne devions pas correspondre. »

Mais tous deux vont renoncer très vite à cet accord tacite.

Avant de quitter Londres, Florie se rend chez l'avocat Markby et tous deux rédigent une lettre adressée à James. Florie y demande la séparation et suggère qu'elle demeure à Battlecrease House, nantie d'une rente annuelle. On ne sait pas si cette lettre a été reçue, ni même si elle a été postée.

Le mercredi, Florie dîne avec Michael et le lendemain, elle rentre à Liverpool.

Les rumeurs vont bon train à la bourse du coton. On va même jusqu'à murmurer que, si Maybrick avait vent de la liaison entre sa femme et Brierley, ce dernier recevrait « une volée de plombs ».

D'après ses amis, Florie adorait faire des scènes lorsqu'elle était enfant. Elle trouvait parfois difficile d'établir la frontière entre fantasme et réalité. L'épisode qui suit montre que cette inclination survit chez la femme adulte.

Le 29 mars a lieu le Grand National, dont c'est la 50e édition. Il s'agit d'une manifestation splendide, à laquelle assiste le prince de Galles. Mais un autre invité est présent, lui aussi : Brierley.

Une fois encore, Maybrick joue les voyeurs.

> la garce m'a donné le plus grand plaisir possible. La putain n'a-t-elle pas vu son maquereau devant tout le monde, certes la course était la plus rapide que j'ai vue, mais l'excitation de voir la putain avec le salaud m'a plus excité que de savoir que son Altesse Royale était à peine à quelques mètres de votre humble serviteur ha ha quelle farce, si ce salaud trop gourmand aurait su qu'il était à moins de quelques mètres du nom dont toute l'Angleterre parlait il serait mort sur le coup.

Regrette de n'avoir pas pu le dire à ce stupide imbécile.
Au diable la souveraineté, au diable toutes les putains,
au diable la garce qui règne.

En dépit de leur promesse mutuelle de ne jamais se revoir, c'est bras dessus bras dessous que Florie et Brierley assistent aux fastes royaux. Mais cette fois, ils sont allés trop loin, et Maybrick se met dans une colère noire.

Victoria, Victoria
Qui est leur reine à tous
Au sujet de Sir Jack
Elle ne sait rien du tout [...]
qui sait,
peut-être un jour
Je lui rendrai visite [...]
Je lui montrerai mon couteau
et elle m'honorera pour la vie [...]
Levez-vous Sir Jack dira-t-elle
et maintenant vous pouvez partir,
je vous le perMAY ha ha ha
ha ha ha ha

Furieuse de l'éclat provoqué par son mari, Florie quitte le champ de courses en se vantant auprès de Christina Samuelson qu'une fois de retour à la maison, elle « lui sonnera les cloches ».

Mais ce soir-là, c'est Maybrick que les domestiques entendront crier : « Dès demain, toute la ville sera au courant d'un tel scandale. »

De quel scandale veut-il parler ? De l'écart de conduite de Florie aux courses ? De la lettre de l'avocat concernant leur séparation ?

Une scène terrible s'ensuit : « Ça a commencé dans la chambre, a raconté Mary Cadwallader. M. Maybrick a dit à la bonne, Bessie, de renvoyer sa femme. Elle est descendue dans le hall et s'est dirigée vers la voiture. Il l'a suivie en hurlant et en tapant du pied comme un fou – et il agitait son mouchoir de poche au-dessus de sa tête. Les boutonnières de la robe de Mme Maybrick étaient toutes déchirées tellement il l'avait malmenée. Elle portait aussi une cape de fourrure : il lui a dit de l'enlever, parce qu'il n'était pas question qu'elle s'en aille avec. Il la lui avait achetée pour qu'elle aille à Londres avec.

« Je suis allée voir le maître et je lui ai dit : " Oh, maître, je vous en supplie ne continuez pas ainsi, les voisins vont vous entendre. " Il m'a répondu : " Laisse-moi tranquille, tu ne sais rien de tout ça. " J'ai dit : " Ne renvoyez pas la maîtresse ce soir. Où peut-elle aller ? Laissez-la rester jusqu'au matin. " Alors il a crié : " Au nom du ciel, Florie, si tu franchis cette porte, tu ne remettras plus jamais les pieds ici. " Il était si épuisé qu'il s'est laissé tomber sur un banc et il est devenu tout raide. Je ne savais pas s'il était soûl ou s'il avait une crise. J'ai renvoyé la voiture et nous avons fait monter Mme Maybrick au premier et M. Maybrick a passé toute la nuit dans la salle à manger. »

Il ne manifestera pas le moindre repentir.

> Je l'ai frappée plusieurs fois œil pour œil, *ha ha* trop de serviteurs qui se mêlent de ce qui ne les regarde pas, au diable les garces. Hopper va bientôt sentir le tranchant de mon couteau étincelant, au diable l'intrigant ébahi, qu'ils aillent tous au diable.

Le lendemain matin, Florie a un œil poché. Elle se rend aussitôt chez Matilda Briggs pour lui demander conseil, mais aussi de l'aide. Ensemble, elles vont chez le Dr Hopper. Florie lui confie qu'elle n'a pas dormi de la nuit, que son mari l'a battue et qu'elle se rend de ce pas chez un avocat. Elle lui confesse également qu'elle ne supporte plus que son mari s'approche d'elle.

En bon médecin de famille, le Dr Hopper décide

d'essayer d'arranger les choses et prend la direction de Battlecrease House un peu plus tard dans la journée. Il s'y entretient avec Maybrick et avec Florie, qui paraissent plus calmes et prêts à résoudre leurs différends. Florie répète toutefois qu'elle ne peut pas supporter de dormir avec son mari et qu'elle ne veut plus d'enfants. En dépit de cet aveu, Maybrick accepte d'éponger les dettes de son épouse. Et comme ils semblent disposés à se pardonner et à oublier, le Dr Hopper les quitte, sincèrement persuadé, non sans naïveté, d'être parvenu à les réconcilier complètement.

Le lendemain, Matilda Briggs rend visite au couple et une autre terrible dispute a lieu. Les domestiques entendent Florie crier à Maybrick qu'elle n'a jamais invité personne sans le consulter au préalable. Pourquoi n'en fait-il pas autant ?

A 18 heures, lorsque Mary Cadwallader porte une tasse de thé à Florie, elle trouve cette dernière évanouie sur le sofa. La domestique se précipite au rez-de-chaussée pour prévenir Maybrick et Mme Briggs, et tous trois montent au premier. C'est alors que Maybrick change du tout au tout. Il s'agenouille devant sa femme et lui chuchote : « Bunny, Bunny, c'est ton petit mari. »

Il n'y a pas de réponse. L'espace d'un instant, la domestique croit que Florie est morte.

La nuit qui suit est agitée, elle aussi. Cette fois, c'est le Dr Humphreys qui est appelé au chevet de Florie. Il le sera à cinq autres reprises durant la nuit.

Florie passera une semaine alitée durant laquelle elle confiera à la cuisinière, Elizabeth Humphreys, qu'elle et Maybrick ont des problèmes d'argent.

Quant à Maybrick, il ordonne à Mary Cadwallader de ne monter aucune lettre à Mme Maybrick avant qu'il ne l'ait lue. « Votre maîtresse voit tout mon courrier, explique-t-il. Il n'y a pas de raison que je ne voie pas le sien. »

Une fois rétablie, Florie rencontre de nouveau Brierley. A Liverpool, le 6 avril. Elle lui révèle que Maybrick l'a battue et l'a traînée sur le sol de sa chambre à coucher.

Dans les jours qui suivent, elle écrit deux lettres à Brierley, apparemment à l'instigation du Dr Hopper, pour lui annoncer qu'elle est réconciliée avec son mari. Abasourdi, Brierley déchire les lettres.

Le samedi 13 avril, Maybrick se rend à Londres. Selon le journal, il désire régler les dettes de Florie. Mais le souvenir de son dernier meurtre avorté le hante. Il est prêt à frapper de nouveau.

> Une fois de plus la garce a des dettes, mon Dieu je vais la découper. [...] Je me rendrai dans la cité des putains je paierai ce qu'elle doit et je réclamerai mon dû, au nom de Dieu je le ferai. Je m'en vais éventrer éventrer éventrer. Je dénicherai peut-être le salaud qui a interrompu mes drôles de petits jeux et je l'éventrerai lui aussi. J'ai dit qu'il paierait. Et bon sang il va payer, je ferai ce qu'il faut pour.

Mais la visite de Maybrick à Londres avait un autre motif. Il désirait voir le Dr Fuller, qui l'examine chez Michael pendant une heure ce dimanche-là. Maybrick se plaint de douleurs dans la tête et d'engourdissement. Il craint la paralysie. Le Dr Fuller estime que Maybrick exagère et ne lui prescrit en conséquence qu'un tonique pour les nerfs et des comprimés pour le foie.

Le samedi suivant, Maybrick retourne à Londres. Il se rend chez le Dr Fuller et reconnaît qu'il se sent beaucoup mieux. A l'évidence, le Dr Fuller a exercé une influence très positive sur son patient. L'écriture, dans le journal, est beaucoup plus maîtrisée. Son auteur semble plus calme et abandonne toute idée de meurtre. Il se livre maintenant à un exercice d'introspection qui l'amène à envisager sa propre mort.

> Fuller croit que je n'ai pas vraiment de problème. Étrange, les pensées qu'il a placées dans mon esprit. Je

n'ai pas pu frapper, je crois que je suis fou, complètement fou. J'essaie de combattre mes pensées je parcours les rues jusqu'à l'aube. Je n'ai pas eu le cœur de frapper, des visions de ma chère Bunny m'accablent. Je l'aime encore, mais comme je la hais. Elle a tout détruit et pourtant mon cœur souffre pour elle, oh comme mon cœur souffre. Je ne sais pas quelle souffrance est la pire mon corps ou mon esprit.

Il songe même à se débarrasser de son couteau. La Mersey se trouve à quelques centaines de mètres de Battlecrease House.

Quand je rentrerai à Battlecrease, je saurai que je ne peux plus continuer ma campagne. C'est l'amour qui m'a éconduit, et c'est l'amour qui y mettra un terme.

Le dimanche, coup de théâtre : Florie envoie une lettre à Maybrick, où elle fait montre d'un changement d'attitude pour le moins surprenant.

« Mon cher petit mari à moi !

[...] J'ai passé une nuit terrible – et j'ai beau essayer d'être brave et courageuse parce que Jim pense que je peux quand même lui apporter du réconfort ainsi qu'aux enfants ma faiblesse physique l'emporte sur ce qui me reste de résistance morale. Je n'ai plus assez d'amour-propre pour remonter du gouffre de disgrâce dans lequel je suis tombée, car maintenant que je suis au plus bas je suis mieux à même de juger combien les autres sont au-dessus de moi moralement. Je n'ai guère d'espoir de retrouver ce statut même si je peux regagner ta confiance en menant une existence vouée à l'expiation de mes péchés, seulement pour toi et pour les enfants. Rien de ce que tu peux dire ne me porte à considérer mes actes autrement que sous le jour le plus dégradant et plus tu me fais sentir l'énormité de mes crimes, moins je nourris d'espoir de regagner ma position. J'ai l'impression que désormais je suis vouée [...] à te rappeler constamment [...] les problèmes que je t'ai causés et que rien ne peut effacer le passé dans ta mémoire [...].

« Je t'en prie chéri délivre-moi de ma souffrance dès que tu le pourras. Je t'ai trompé et presque ruiné mais puisque tu veux que je vive, dis-moi le pire tout de suite – et n'en parlons plus [...]. Chéri, essaie d'être aussi indulgent que tu le peux envers moi car en dépit de toute ta gentillesse, de ta générosité, de ta tendresse et de ton affection mon fardeau est presque trop lourd pour moi, mes remords et le mépris que j'éprouve à mon endroit me rongent le cœur et si je ne pensais pas que mon amour pour toi et mon obéissance pouvaient en partie racheter le passé j'abandonnerais mon combat et je perdrais courage ! Pardonne-moi si tu peux chéri et pense moins de mal de

Ta petite femme aimante
Bunny

Les enfants vont bien. Je ne suis allée nulle part et je n'ai vu personne. »

Cette lettre a été écrite par une femme qui vient de confier à son médecin qu'elle ne supporte plus de dormir avec son mari, et qui adressera dix jours plus tard une lettre à son autre « chéri » : Alfred Brierley. Désirait-elle sincèrement faire pénitence ou avait-elle décidé que, pour sa sécurité, il valait mieux jouer les épouses soumises ?

Durant les semaines suivantes, les événements se précipitent. Aux alentours du 24 avril, Florie se rend chez Wokes, la pharmacie située au coin d'Aigburth Road et de Beechwood Road, pour acheter une dizaine de bandes de papier tue-mouches. Elle prétend que la cuisine est envahie de ces insectes et demande au garçon de course de les lui livrer. En réalité, elle a acheté le papier tue-mouches afin d'en extraire l'arsenic, comme on le lui a enseigné dans sa jeunesse. A l'époque, en effet, toutes les jeunes filles d'Allemagne et d'Amérique utilisaient de l'arsenic pour rendre leur teint plus éclatant.

Mais lorsque la bonne, Bessie, aperçoit le lavabo recouvert d'une serviette, en soulève un coin et voit les bandes de papier tue-mouches, elle les jette dans la corbeille à papier, sans rien dire à personne.

Le 24 avril, Maybrick se rend chez Clay et Abraham's avec l'ordonnance du Dr Fuller. Sa santé se détériore rapidement.

C'est le lendemain qu'Edwin revient d'Amérique.

Mon cher frère Edwin est revenu. J'aimerais pouvoir tout lui raconter.

Le 25 avril, quatre mois après avoir détruit son testament, James en a rédigé un autre. Les experts doutent toutefois de l'authenticité de ce deuxième testament.

Celui qui a été préservé a été rédigé sur du papier bleu très fin, d'une main énergique. Il comporte deux pages. La première est reproduite dans ce livre. Deux témoins y ont apposé leur signature : le comptable de Maybrick, George Smith, et son ami George Davidson.

Ce testament pose davantage de questions qu'il n'apporte de réponses.

On sait, d'après la lettre adressée par Florie à sa mère, qu'en décembre 1888 Maybrick avait déchiré son testament et en avait rédigé un nouveau. Comment se fait-il, dès lors, que le testament écrit sur papier bleu commence de cette façon : « Si je venais à mourir avant d'avoir rédigé un testament en bonne et due forme, je souhaite que ceci soit considéré comme mes dernières volontés et comme mon dernier testament [...] » ? Se pourrait-il que ce document plutôt décousu et imprécis, qui se trouve à Somerset House, n'ait pas été écrit par lui mais par quelqu'un d'autre ?

Le testament continue ainsi : « Je lègue tous mes biens quels qu'ils soient, meubles, tableaux, vins, linge, assiettes, polices d'assurance sur la vie, argent liquide, actions, biens immobiliers, en fait tout ce que je possède à mes deux enfants James Chandler Maybrick et Gladys Eveleyn Maybrick. Ces biens seront administrés en fidéicommis par mes frères Michael Maybrick et Thomas Maybrick. Je désire que les meubles demeurent intacts et qu'ils soient utilisés pour meubler un foyer qui peut être partagé par ma veuve et par mes enfants mais les meubles seront la propriété des enfants. »

« Je désire en outre que les sommes au nom des fiduciaires susnommés (Michael et Thomas Maybrick) et les revenus qu'elles produiront soient utilisés au profit des enfants et de leur éducation, et que cette éducation soit laissée à l'appréciation desdits fiduciaires.

« La portion de ma succession afférente à ma veuve sera la suivante : les polices sur ma vie, c'est-à-dire les 500 livres du Scottish Widows Fund et les 2 000 livres du Mutual Reserve Fund Life Association of New York, ces deux polices ayant été souscrites à son bénéfice. Les intérêts qu'elle percevra sur ces 2 500 livres et les 125 livres par an que lui rapportent ses propriétés à New York lui fourniront 125 livres par an, somme qui, pour être peu importante, lui permettra tout de même d'avoir un niveau de vie respectable.

« Je désire également que ma veuve réside sous le même toit que les enfants, aussi longtemps qu'elle demeurera ma veuve.

« Si c'est possible d'un point de vue juridique, je souhaite que les 2 500 livres d'assurance-vie sur ma vie au bénéfice de ma femme soient investies au nom desdits fiduciaires mais qu'elle soit seule bénéficiaire des intérêts perçus sur cette somme durant toute sa vie, mais qu'à son décès le capital revienne à mesdits enfants James Chandler et Gladys Eveleyn Maybrick.

« Devant témoins et scellé ce vingt-cinquième jour d'avril 1889.

« signé James Maybrick.

« signé par le Testateur en notre présence, qui sur sa demande et en présence l'un de l'autre avons apposé notre nom en tant que témoins George R. Davidson et George Smith. »

Même à l'époque, ce testament a soulevé de nombreuses interrogations. Il a été mentionné pendant l'enquête judiciaire, bien que Michael ait demandé qu'il ne fût pas lu.

Voici l'avis d'Alexander MacDougall, qui a écrit un livre sur l'affaire Florie Maybrick en 1891 : alors que Maybrick était mourant, « les employés Thomas Lowry et George Smith sont venus chez lui avec certains documents. Michael et Edwin Maybrick étaient présents et les ont montés à James Maybrick. Au bout d'un moment, James Maybrick s'est mis à crier sur ses frères d'une voix si forte qu'on pouvait l'entendre dans toute la maison : " Oh, Seigneur, si je dois mourir, pourquoi dois-je être inquiété de cette façon ? Laissez-moi mourir en paix. " Il a été très violent ».

D'après MacDougall, les domestiques ont pensé que les frères n'avaient pas trouvé de testament et qu'ils essayaient de lui en faire signer un nouveau. Et MacDougall estime « absolument inconcevable que James Maybrick ait été en possession de toutes ses facultés quand il a signé ce testament ». Voici son témoignage :

> « Ce testament place tout ce que James Maybrick possédait [...] sans exception [...] sous le contrôle absolu de Michael Maybrick et de Thomas Maybrick. Non seulement cela, mais il place les enfants, âgés de sept et trois ans, sous leur responsabilité, afin qu'ils les traitent selon

leur bon plaisir [...]. S'ils le voulaient, ils auraient pu faire du garçon un ramoneur et de la fille une couturière ! Et Maybrick est mort en remettant toutes ses possessions entre les mains de Michael et de Thomas, qui disposaient du pouvoir absolu d'investir le capital selon leur bon plaisir, et d'employer les revenus qui en découleraient comme ils le désiraient ! Ce testament ne contient aucune clause stipulant qu'une part quelconque de ces biens devrait revenir à l'un ou l'autre de ces enfants à leur majorité, ou même après ! [...]

« Mme Maybrick n'a droit ni à un lit ni à une couverture mais il “ désire ” qu'elle vive “ sous le même toit ”, dans le “ foyer ” que Michael et Thomas devront meubler, et ses deux enfants devront être élevés et éduqués par Michael et Thomas Maybrick comme bon leur semblera ! Mais ce n'est pas tout ! James Maybrick va dans ce testament jusqu'à tenter de faire bénéficier les fiduciaires de polices d'assurance qui appartiennent à Mme Maybrick [...]. Il s'agit là d'un testament qu'aucun tribunal siégeant dans un pays civilisé n'aurait pu considérer comme l'œuvre d'un mari et d'un père en pleine possession de ses moyens. »

Quoi qu'il en soit, ce testament n'a pas fourni à Florie de mobile financier pour le meurtre de son mari. Et il ne reflète pas les souhaits de Maybrick, tels que Florie les rapportait à sa mère dans sa lettre du 31 décembre 1888, ou tels que Maybrick les exprime dans son journal.

J'ai rétabli l'équilibre dans mon testament. Bunny et les enfants auront ce qu'il leur faut et je fais confiance à Michael et à Thomas pour exécuter mes souhaits.

Deux détails de ce testament paraissent suspects : les chiffres sont faux et Maybrick épelle de façon incorrecte (« Eveleyn ») le prénom de sa fille. Il est tout aussi surprenant de constater qu'il existe plusieurs différences entre le testament de Somerset House et celui que MacDougall a vu et recopié. Par exemple, les mots « lègue » et « souscrites » sont absents de la version de MacDougall, ainsi que « en sa présence ».

Si le testament de Somerset House n'était pas celui que Maybrick avait rédigé, ou à tout le moins souhaité, qui l'a fabriqué et pourquoi ? Ce document a-t-il été rédigé sous la contrainte des frères et antidaté ? Michael et Edwin l'ont-ils écrit avant de forcer James à le signer quand il était au seuil de la mort ? Ou faut-il comprendre que non seulement le contenu, mais aussi les signatures, sont des faux ?

La photocopie des deux pages signées du testament de Somerset House et celle du certificat de mariage de Maybrick ont été examinées par un éminent spécialiste, Reed Hayes, de Kailua, à Hawaii. M. Hayes appartient à l'*American Board of Forensic Handwriting Analysts*, c'est-à-dire l'association américaine des graphologues légaux.

Il a examiné les trois signatures, s'attachant à déterminer les similitudes et les différences entre les pleins et les déliés de chacune des lettres. Il a noté, par exemple, que sur le certificat de mariage, la boucle de la majuscule « J » de James rejoint le plein pour former un cercle fermé. Sur la première page du testament, la boucle commence depuis la droite du plein, de sorte que ce dernier vient croiser le début de la boucle. Mais sur la deuxième page, la boucle commence à gauche du plein et forme un cercle ouvert. Ces trois lettres sont différentes.

Reed Hayes a découvert dix similitudes entre le certificat de mariage et la première page du testament, et six entre le certificat et la deuxième page. Toutefois, il a établi quinze différences entre le certificat de mariage et la première page du testament, et treize entre le certificat et la deuxième page. Il a également observé des similitudes entre la signature d'Edwin et celle de James sur le testament de Somerset House. « D'une manière générale, la formation des lettres est différente selon qu'il s'agit de la signature connue [sur le certificat de mariage] ou de celles qui sont en doute [sur le testament]. Le rythme distinctif dont ces dernières sont dotées est absent de la signature connue.

« A mon avis, il est fortement probable que les signatures mises en doute n'ont pas été apposées par la main qui a formé la signature connue de James Maybrick. »

Détail intéressant, Sue Ironmonger note une similitude entre la signature de Michael et celle de James : « Même en tenant compte de leur scolarité commune, je ne m'attendais pas à trouver de telles similitudes entre le style et le poids des pleins et des déliés. »

Michael et ses frères utiliseraient ensuite le testament pour obtenir le contrôle total de la succession de Maybrick. On le voit, ils avaient tout à gagner dans cette affaire.

Et Florie tout à perdre.

Chapitre 11

Le 26 avril 1889, à 8 h 30, un colis en provenance de Londres est livré à Battlecrease House. C'est Mary Cadwallader qui le reçoit et qui le monte directement à son maître. Il s'agit du médicament que Maybrick attend depuis plusieurs jours.

Le lendemain, il est malade. Il dit à Mary qu'il a vomi et que ses jambes sont engourdies. Il ajoute qu'il doit avoir pris une dose excessive de la substance livrée le jour précédent. Mais en dépit de son état physique et du mauvais temps, il est décidé à se rendre plus tard dans la journée aux courses de Wirral, événement mondain de la plus haute importance.

Il va à son bureau vers 10 h 30 et en repart vers 13 h 00. Il rentre alors chez lui pour chercher son cheval.

Lorsqu'il parvient au champ de courses, il est trempé jusqu'aux os et tremble de tous ses membres. Son ami William Thomson remarque qu'il éprouve des difficultés à rester en selle. Maybrick lui explique qu'il a pris une double dose de « médicament » le matin.

Mme Morden Rigg, l'épouse d'un vieil ami de Maybrick originaire d'Amérique, s'étonne elle aussi de le voir en pareil état. Il lui fournit la même explication, mais précise que le « médicament » en question est en fait de la strychnine.

Bien que ses vêtements soient trempés, Maybrick décide

de dîner avec les Hobson, un couple de ses amis. Mais il est alors si mal en point qu'il ne parvient même pas à tenir son verre. Après avoir renversé du vin par deux fois, il s'éclipse, embarrassé à l'idée que ses amis l'ont cru ivre.

Le lendemain matin, son état a encore empiré. Florie demande à la cuisinière de préparer un mélange d'eau et de moutarde. « Le maître a pris une autre dose de cet horrible médicament », commente cette dernière.

Le Dr Humphreys est appelé d'urgence. Lorsqu'il arrive à Battlecrease House, Florie lui confie que, selon elle, l'indisposition de son mari est imputable au mauvais cognac qu'il a bu aux courses. Pour sa part, Maybrick affirme que les symptômes se sont aggravés après qu'il a bu une tasse de thé bien fort, mais ajoute aussitôt qu'il souffre de maux de tête depuis plus d'un an.

Le médecin demande à Maybrick quel effet produisent sur lui la strychnine et la *nux vomica*. En contradiction totale avec ce qu'il a dit la veille à Mme Rigg, le patient répond alors : « Je crois que j'en connais un rayon en médecine. Et je ne peux supporter ni la strychnine ni la *nux vomica.* »

Le Dr Humphreys recommande à Maybrick de ne manger de la viande qu'une fois par jour, et d'emporter à son bureau du bouillon épaissi de Revalenta Du Barry. Ce remède très populaire à l'époque victorienne était censé guérir « l'indigestion, les flatulences, la dyspepsie, la pituite, la constipation, tous les troubles d'ordre nerveux et biliaire, les problèmes de foie, la dysenterie, la diarrhée, l'acidité, les palpitations, les brûlures d'estomac, les hémorroïdes, les maux de tête, l'asthénie, la mélancolie, les crampes, les spasmes, les nausées, les accès d'abattement, la toux, l'asthme et la bronchite, la phtisie et les troubles de l'enfant ». En d'autres termes, le remède idéal pour un hypocondriaque.

Ce jour-là, Edwin vient déjeuner, et Maybrick écrit ensuite à Michael une lettre d'une franchise surprenante, où il lui donne une version encore différente des événements récents. Il y laisse entendre qu'il se sait condamné. L'original de cette lettre a disparu, mais le greffier présent lors du procès de Florie en a effectué une copie qui existe encore. Le nom de Michael a été biffé et remplacé par « Blucher », sans raison apparente, par l'avocat William Swift, qui représentait les plaignants lors du procès de Florie. Une note en marge rédigée de la même main explique que Blucher est le surnom que Maybrick avait donné à son frère. Blucher est un général prussien qui a combattu Napoléon à Waterloo. Or, Michael était connu pour ses positions anti-allemandes, aussi s'agit-il sans doute là d'une des « petites plaisanteries » de Maybrick.

> Liverpool, 29 avril
> Mon cher Michael [biffé] Blucher,
> Je suis vraiment mal fichu en ce moment. Samedi matin je me suis rendu compte que mes jambes devenaient raides et inutiles mais grâce à un sursaut de volonté j'ai chassé ce sentiment de mon esprit et je suis allé à cheval aux courses de Wirral où j'ai dîné avec les Hobson. Hier matin je me sentais plus mort que vivant à tel point que Florie a appelé un autre médecin qui a dit qu'il s'agissait d'une grave indigestion et m'a donné quelque chose pour soulager ces symptômes alarmants, alors ensuite tout est bien allé jusque vers 20 heures quand je suis retourné au lit et que je suis resté allongé tout seul à lire. J'ai bien senti plusieurs contractions mais n'y ai guère prêté attention pensant qu'elles passeraient mais au lieu de passer elles ont empiré et quand j'ai essayé de me retourner pour actionner la sonnette je me suis rendu compte que je n'y arrivais pas mais j'y suis finalement parvenu mais le temps que Florie et Edwin arrivent en haut j'étais raide et pendant deux heures mortelles mes jambes sont restées comme deux barres de fer étirées à fond mais rigides comme de

l'acier. Le médecin a fini par revenir mais n'a pas pu me faire le coup de l'indigestion cette fois et la conclusion à laquelle il est parvenu c'est que la *nux vomica* que j'avais prise sur les instructions du Dr Fuller m'avait empoisonné, du fait que tous les symptômes justifiaient cette conclusion je sais qu'aujourd'hui je souffre de la tête aux pieds et que je suis complètement vidé.

Aucun des médecins n'a encore été capable de déterminer de quoi je souffre et je suppose qu'ils n'y parviendront que quand je serai étendu et froid et alors les générations futures en profiteront peut-être s'ils font une autopsie que je suis tout à fait d'accord qu'ils devraient faire.

Je ne pense pas venir à Londres cette semaine car je ne me sens pas en état de voyager et je ne peux pas continuer avec le médicament de Fuller encore un peu mais je viendrai le voir de nouveau bientôt. Edwin ne vient pas encore chez toi mais il t'écrira lui-même. Je suppose que tu vas dans ta maison de campagne mercredi...

Jim ton frère affectionné

Pour sa part, Florie écrit à sa mère comme si de rien n'était.

« On nous invite à un bal masqué, mais vu qu'il a lieu à Liverpool et que les gens y seront des provinciaux, je doute que ce soit un succès. Une certaine dose de " diablerie ", d'esprit et de vie est toujours requise dans les soirées de ce genre : et comme il s'agira d'une innovation plutôt nouvelle les gens ne sauront pas vraiment ce qu'on attend d'eux. Toutefois, on nous demande de venir " en domino et avec un masque ", et j'aimerais bien savoir de quoi est fait un domino et si l'on ne peut pas se procurer un masque en gaze plutôt qu'en " papier mâché ".

Comme il se doit, Florie veut paraître sous son meilleur jour au bal masqué. C'est pourquoi elle s'est rendue la veille – c'est-à-dire le 28 avril – à la pharmacie tenue par M. Hanson pour y acheter de la teinture cosmétique à base de benjoin et de fleur de sureau. Elle a également acheté un autre article, ce qu'elle regrettera jusqu'à la fin de ses jours : un second lot de bandes de papier tue-mouches.

Le lendemain, 30 avril, Maybrick se sent un peu mieux et retourne travailler. La cuisinière lui prépare un peu de Ravalanta, et comme Edwin séjourne à Battlecrease House, Florie lui demande de porter le médicament au bureau, à temps pour le déjeuner de Maybrick. C'est Thomas Lowry, l'employé, qui va acheter une casserole pour y réchauffer la mixture.

Et ce soir-là, c'est Edwin qui escorte Florie au bal, sans doute parce que Maybrick ne s'en sent pas capable. Le lendemain, 1er mai, le capitaine Irving de la White Star Line rencontre Edwin et Maybrick dans le bureau de ce dernier. Pendant qu'ils discutent – Irving le confirmera plus tard dans une déclaration écrite sous serment –, Maybrick sort un petit paquet dont il vide le contenu dans un verre d'eau. Le capitaine le verra absorber deux doses en quinze minutes. « Tout le monde savait que Jim prenait toujours un médicament ou un autre », dira Irving. Mais quand ce dernier rentre avec les deux frères à Battlecrease House, Maybrick est incapable de s'asseoir à table.

Lorsque le capitaine rencontrera Edwin en ville, peu de temps après, il lui demandera : " Qu'est-ce qui ne va pas avec Jim ? » « Il se tue avec cette fichue strychnine », répondra Edwin.

Mais quand un journal s'est avisé de publier le compte rendu donné par le capitaine Irving de ces incidents, Edwin a tout nié en bloc. « Déclaration absolument et entièrement fausse à tous égards », a-t-il affirmé dans un télégramme adressé à la presse. « Jamais vu de ma vie mon frère consommer quelque poudre blanche que ce soit dans du vin ou d'une autre façon. » Au procès de Florie, Edwin a prétendu n'avoir aucune connaissance de la toxicomanie alléguée de Maybrick.

Le jeudi 2 mai, Maybrick emporte son déjeuner au bureau, mais revient malade à la maison.

> Je ne prends plus de la substance redoutable de peur de faire du mal à ma chère Bunny, pire encore aux enfants.

Si ce qu'il a écrit était vrai – c'est-à-dire s'il avait effectivement cessé de se droguer du jour au lendemain –, il aurait éprouvé une sensation de manque presque insupportable. En 1885, le *Chambers Journal of Popular Literature, Science and Art* a publié un compte rendu d'une conférence consacrée entre autres à la consommation d'arsenic. En voici un extrait : « Quand un homme a commencé d'en absorber, il doit continuer de le faire. On peut dire que c'est la dernière dose qui le tue. En vérité, le consommateur d'arsenic doit non seulement continuer de s'autoriser sa faiblesse, mais aussi accroître la quantité de drogue qu'il absorbe, c'est pourquoi il est extraordinairement difficile de mettre un terme à cette habitude ; car, si l'arrêt soudain provoque la mort, l'arrêt progressif ronge le cœur d'une manière si douloureuse qu'on peut probablement affirmer que jamais un véritable consommateur d'arsenic n'a cessé d'en manger tant qu'il était en vie. »

Les pages du journal qui précèdent la mort de Maybrick donnent à penser qu'il devait souffrir le martyre. Il y exprime ses remords et supplie que cesse la torture d'être en vie.

> Je n'ai pas le courage de me supprimer. Je prie chaque soir pour trouver la force de le faire, mais le courage

m'échappe. Je prie constamment pour que tous pardonnent. Je regrette profondément de l'avoir frappée, j'ai trouvé dans mon cœur la force de lui pardonner pour ses amants.

Je crois que je vais tout lui raconter, lui demander de me pardonner comme je lui ai pardonné. Je prie Dieu pour qu'elle comprenne ce qu'elle m'a fait.

Le 3 mai, Maybrick voit le Dr Humphreys et se plaint : le médicament ne lui fait pas de bien. D'un ton aigre, Florie observe qu'il en vient toujours à la même conclusion au bout de deux ou trois jours, quel que soit le médicament. Après la visite du médecin, Maybrick se rend à son bureau pour la dernière fois. C'est ce jour-là qu'il rédige les dernières lignes du journal. Dans l'après-midi, il se rend aux bains turcs avec l'aval du médecin.

Le soir venu, Maybrick se sent très mal. Il éprouve « une douleur tenaillante depuis les hanches jusqu'aux genoux ». A minuit, le Dr Humphreys prend à nouveau le chemin de Battlecrease House. Une fois sur place, il décide que les douleurs sont le résultat de frictions trop vigoureuses aux bains turcs et, sans tenir compte du fait que Maybrick a vomi par deux fois, il lui administre un suppositoire de morphine.

Le lendemain matin, l'état physique de Maybrick a empiré. Il est pris de vomissements violents.

Le Dr Humphreys vient de bonne heure et ordonne que le patient ne boive absolument rien. Pour apaiser sa soif, il n'aura qu'à se rincer la bouche avec de l'eau, ou encore sucer de la glace ou un linge mouillé.

Un peu plus tard, le pharmacien livre un médicament que Mary Cadwallader monte directement à Maybrick, au grand désarroi de Florie. « Rien ne doit être monté à sa chambre sans que je le voie d'abord », ordonne-t-elle. Elle récupère le médicament en question et vide le contenu du flacon dans l'évier. Elle expliquera ensuite à Cadwallader que la moindre dose supplémentaire aurait tué son mari. A-t-elle pressenti le risque qu'elle encourait à défier les ordres du médecin ?

Dans la matinée, Florie envoie Mary Cadwallader chez Wokes pour y chercher certain médicament prescrit par ordonnance. M. Wokes refuse de le lui remettre. Il veut que le médecin vienne le chercher lui-même. Cette décision du pharmacien ne fait qu'alimenter les rumeurs émanant du sous-sol de Battlecrease House. Ainsi, James Grant, le jardinier, raconte à Nurse Yapp qu'il a été informé par Wokes de la nature du médicament requis par Florie : il s'agit d'un poison mortel. C'est la raison pour laquelle le pharmacien a refusé de le remettre à Mary.

Le dimanche 5 mai, Elizabeth Humphreys monte voir son maître, qui la supplie de lui donner de la limonade avec un peu de sucre : « Je vous demande de le faire, comme vous le feriez pour n'importe quel pauvre mourant de soif. » Florie, qui se trouve dans la pièce, répond : « Tu ne peux pas en avoir, sauf pour te faire un gargarisme. » Elle suit en cela les instructions du Dr Humphreys : Maybrick ne doit rien boire.

Mais dans l'après-midi, Edwin rend visite à son frère et, désobéissant aux ordres du médecin, lui donne un verre de cognac avec du soda, que Maybrick s'empresse de vomir.

Le lundi 6 mai au matin, le médecin vient voir son patient vers 8 h 30. Il rappelle à Maybrick qu'il ne doit pas prendre son jus de viande Valentine ni son acide prussique comme à l'accoutumée, car ces deux boissons le font vomir. Il prescrit de la Solution de Fowler, qui contient de l'arsenic.

Pendant que Florie va faire les courses, Nurse Yapp surveille Maybrick. Il gémit sans arrêt, il a trop chaud. Elle lui frotte les mains, il affirme une fois encore qu'elles sont engourdies. Lorsque Florie revient, Yapp lui suggère d'appeler le médecin. Mais Florie refuse, arguant que de toute façon, son mari ne suivra pas les conseils du médecin.

Toutefois, en début d'après-midi, elle envoie un télégramme au bureau d'Edwin, à Liverpool, dans lequel elle lui demande de trouver un autre médecin. Elle désire une seconde opinion.

Battlecrease House est maintenant envahie par la famille, les amis et le personnel. Tout le monde s'agite, échange des murmures, s'observe du coin de l'œil. Bien sûr, Florie est le centre de l'attention, et l'atmosphère de méfiance qui règne à Battlecrease House transforme ses moindres actions en gestes suspects. Ainsi, lorsque Alice Yapp aperçoit Florie en train de transférer le contenu d'une bouteille de médicament dans une autre, elle devient soupçonneuse. En effet, elle a gardé en mémoire ce que lui a raconté Bessie à propos de ces bandes de papier tue-mouches qui trempaient dans le lavabo.

Or, c'est à ce moment précis que Florie reçoit une lettre de Brierley : il craint que leur secret ne soit sur le point d'éclater au grand jour et il s'en va pour se mettre à l'abri du danger.

En fin d'après-midi, le Dr Humphreys passe de nouveau et applique un cataplasme sur le ventre de Maybrick, dans l'espoir d'apaiser la douleur. A 5 h 30, le Dr William Carter, sollicité par Edwin, se joint à lui. Le Dr Carter se décrit lui-même comme « un médecin d'une expérience considérable qui dans certains cas administre de trop fortes doses d'arsenic à titre médical ».

Tous deux examinent le patient, très agité. Il se plaint maintenant d'avoir « un cheveu » dans la gorge.

Les médecins décident qu'il souffre de dyspepsie et lui prescrivent des doses minimes d'antipyrine pour soulager sa gorge douloureuse, et de la teinture de jaborandi accompagnée de chlorodyne diluée pour le débarrasser du mauvais goût dans sa bouche. Son régime alimentaire se compose désormais uniquement de bouillon de poulet et de lait.

Les médecins déclarent à Florie que son mari n'a rien de grave et qu'il ira bientôt mieux. Mais cette nuit-là, Maybrick vomit continuellement et se plaint encore de son « cheveu » dans la gorge.

Le mercredi 8 mai, il est incapable de se lever et confie au Dr Humphreys qu'il pense être sur le point de mourir. Lorsque Edwin passe voir son frère avant d'aller travailler, Maybrick lui suggère d'engager une infirmière pour aider Florie, qui est épuisée. Cette dernière envoie un télégramme à sa mère, qui se trouve à Paris. Cette fois, le message est laconique, et le ton bien différent de celui de la lettre envoyée une semaine plus tôt : « Jim très malade de nouveau ».

Ce jour-là, Mme Briggs et Mme Hughes arrivent en visite à Battlecrease House. C'est Nurse Yapp qui les aperçoit la première, depuis une fenêtre du haut. Elle se précipite dans la cour et leur tient ce langage : « Dieu merci, vous êtes venues. Heureusement, car la maîtresse est en train d'empoisonner le maître. » Et de leur faire part de toutes les rumeurs et de tous les soupçons qui pèsent sur Florie, avant de les conduire tout droit à la chambre de Maybrick.

Lorsqu'elle découvre que les deux sœurs se trouvent déjà dans la chambre de son mari, Florie, très contrariée, les fait appeler dans le salon. C'est à ce moment-là qu'elle se décide à engager une infirmière. Mme Briggs et Mme Hughes repartent vers midi et envoient sur-le-champ un télégramme à Michael : « Venez de suite. Il se passe ici des choses étranges. » Le même jour, Michael reçoit un autre télégramme de mauvais augure. Ce dernier est signé d'Edwin : lui aussi insiste pour que son frère vienne à Battlecrease House.

Vers 14 h 15, une infirmière répondant au nom de Gore arrive chez les Maybrick. Elle a été envoyée par la *Nurses Institution* de Liverpool.

Maintenant qu'elle a un peu de temps libre, Florie en profite pour répondre à Brierley. C'est une erreur fatale, bientôt suivie d'une seconde : elle demande à Alice Yapp de poster cette lettre. La nurse part aussitôt avec Gladys, afin d'arriver à temps pour la levée de 15 h 45, et elle remet la missive entre les mains de la fillette. Sur le chemin, racontera-t-elle lors du procès de Florie, Gladys fait tomber la lettre dans la boue.

« Je suis allée à la poste et j'ai demandé une enveloppe propre pour recopier l'adresse. Je l'ai ouverte au moment où j'entrais dans le bureau de poste. »

Mais ce qu'Alice Yapp a lu l'a choquée à un point tel qu'elle a caché la lettre dans sa poche et ne l'a jamais postée.

Chéri

[...] Je ne peux pas répondre à ta lettre, mon chéri, mais tranquillise-toi, n'aie aucune *crainte d'être découvert*, que ce soit maintenant ou dans le futur. M. délire depuis dimanche, et je sais maintenant qu'il est *parfaitement ignorant* de tout, même *du nom de la rue*, et aussi *qu'il n'a pas cherché à obtenir quelques renseignements que ce soit!* Ce qu'il m'a raconté était pure fabrication, dans le seul but de me faire peur pour que je lui dise la vérité. En fait, *il croit* ce que je lui ai dit, même s'il ne veut pas *l'admettre*. Tu n'as donc pas besoin de partir à l'étranger pour cette raison, chéri; mais, quoi que tu décides, s'il te plaît ne *quitte pas l'Angleterre avant que je ne t'aie revu une fois encore!* Tu dois sentir que mes deux lettres ont été écrites dans des circonstances qui doivent même excuser l'injustice que tu leur prêtes. Tu crois vraiment que je pourrais agir comme je le fais si je ressentais vraiment ce que j'ai laissé entendre? Si tu souhaites m'écrire pour une raison ou pour une autre fais-le *maintenant*, car à présent toutes les lettres passent entre mes mains. Excuse-moi d'avoir griffonné ce mot à la hâte, mon chéri à moi, mais je n'ose pas quitter la chambre ne serait-ce qu'un moment, et je ne sais pas quand j'aurai la possibilité de t'écrire de nouveau. En hâte, à toi pour toujours,

Florie

Lorsque Edwin est de retour, vers 17 heures, Nurse Yapp se trouve à son poste de vigie habituel, et elle l'intercepte avant qu'il ne pénètre dans la maison. Ils vont s'asseoir dans le jardin et elle lui fait part de ce qu'elle a découvert. Pour l'heure, ils décident de ne rien faire.

C'est un peu avant 21 heures que Michael arrive à la gare d'Edge Hill. Son frère est venu l'attendre dans une voiture à cheval. Quand Edwin lui fait part des derniers événements, Michael prend la situation en main. De retour à la maison, les deux hommes lisent la lettre adressée à Brierley. Et une fois que Michael a vu l'état de semi-inconscience dans lequel se trouve son frère James, il remontre ses torts à Florie. Il ne lui révèle pas qu'il a lu sa lettre, mais la critique pour n'avoir pas engagé une infirmière professionnelle et un second médecin plus tôt. Puis il se rend au domicile du Dr Humphreys, où il arrive à 22 h 30.

Le médecin reconnaît qu'il n'est pas satisfait de l'état physique de Maybrick, et Michael l'informe des soupçons de Nurse Yapp. Mais le médecin ne fera rien. Il se contente de répondre : « Votre frère m'a dit qu'il allait mourir. »

Tout le monde passe une nuit agitée. L'infirmière a reçu pour instructions de veiller à ce qu'elle seule donne à Maybrick nourriture et médicaments. Une nouvelle bouteille de jus de viande Valentine est fournie par Edwin. On la donne à une seconde infirmière, qui a remplacé la première, épuisée.

Le lendemain après-midi, le Dr Carter revient à Battlecrease House. Il persiste à diagnostiquer une « dyspepsie aiguë ». Michael, extrêmement agité, a une autre explication. Depuis le mois d'avril, prétend-il, son frère est malade lorsqu'il se trouve à la maison et en parfaite santé quand il est en voyage. Il ajoute que le désaccord entre Maybrick et sa femme présente un caractère sérieux et que Florie achète régulièrement du papier tue-mouches.

Maintenant que les soupçons portant sur Florie ont été abordés avec le médecin, Michael décide de multiplier les précautions en vue d'assurer la protection du patient.

Florie se voit quasiment dépossédée de toute prérogative dans sa propre maison. Elle erre de pièce en pièce et va de crise de larmes en crise de larmes. Le soir, elle monte à la nursery de nuit, où Nurse Yapp s'occupe des enfants, et elle lui confie : « Vous savez qu'on me blâme pour ce qui se passe ? »

Non sans fourberie, Nurse Yapp lui demande : « Pour quoi ? » Florie répond : « Pour la maladie de M. Maybrick. »

Tous les éléments sont contre elle. Elle sait que le Dr Humphreys n'était pas favorable à la convocation d'un second médecin. Quant au Dr Carter, il ne voyait pas la nécessité d'engager une infirmière. Florie a pris la décision d'appeler l'un et l'autre, mais voilà que Michael l'accuse de n'avoir pas agi assez tôt. Elle est désorientée et contrariée.

Florie ne compte que deux amis loyaux dans la maisonnée : Mary Cadwallader, qui a trouvé du vieux papier tue-mouches dans l'office et l'a brûlé ; et la cuisinière, Elizabeth Humphreys, à qui Florie vient se confier, en larmes. Depuis l'arrivée de Michael, raconte-t-elle, on lui a refusé l'entrée de la chambre de Maybrick. « Ma position ne vaut rien dans cette maison. » Michael la hait, ajoute-t-elle, et si James se rétablit, elle n'autorisera jamais Michael à remettre les pieds dans la maison.

Ce soir-là, Maybrick est trop mal en point pour être examiné. En guise de sédatif, les médecins lui donnent une double dose de bismuth avec un peu de cognac. Pour la première fois, ils prélèvent de l'urine et des selles que le Dr Carter va analyser.

On soupçonne Florie d'avoir altéré le contenu de deux petites bouteilles de Neaves Food : aussitôt, Michael les remet entre les mains du médecin pour analyse, ainsi qu'une bouteille de cognac et une autre d'extrait de viande, qu'il trouve également suspectes. Le résultat de tous ces tests est négatif, fait qui ne sera jamais mentionné pendant le procès de Florie.

Durant la soirée du 9 mai, l'état de santé de Maybrick empire encore. Contre les instructions du médecin, l'infirmière prend la bouteille de jus de viande Valentine qu'Edwin vient de sortir du tiroir de la table située sur le palier, et elle en donne à Maybrick deux cuillerées dans de l'eau. Florie, qui est présente, proteste en vain : les médecins ont dit à Maybrick de ne plus prendre de ce jus, car il le rend toujours malade.

Juste après minuit, l'infirmière donne à Maybrick un peu de champagne, peut-être pour calmer la douleur, et elle remarque que Florie emporte la bouteille de jus de viande dans le vestiaire attenant. Au dire de l'infirmière, Florie serait revenue deux minutes plus tard et aurait replacé « subrepticement » la bouteille sur la table de chevet.

Selon une troisième infirmière, du nom de Callery, qui veillait également sur Maybrick, Michael a ensuite repris la bouteille : on n'avait pas donné de jus de viande au patient depuis que Florie l'avait replacée. Plus tard, il l'a remise au Dr Carter pour analyse. Il s'est avéré qu'elle contenait un demi-grain d'arsenic en solution. Cette substance a été utilisée comme preuve lors du procès de Florie, mais selon MacDougall, il ne s'agissait pas de la bouteille que Florie avait emportée dans le vestiaire. L'auteur de *Treatise on the Maybrick Case* soupçonne que Florie a été victime d'un coup monté.

Le vendredi, Maybrick est au plus mal.

Une quatrième infirmière, répondant au nom de Wilson, racontera qu'elle a entendu Maybrick dire plusieurs fois à Florie : « Oh, Bunny, Bunny, comment as-tu pu faire ça ? Je n'aurais pas cru ça de toi. » Florie aurait répondu : « Ne sois pas bête, chéri, ne t'encombre pas la tête avec ces choses. »

Plus tard, Thomas Lowry et George Smith, qui ont apporté certains documents à Battlecrease House, entendent Maybrick crier à Michael et à Edwin qu'il veut mourir en paix.

Le samedi 11 mai à 4 heures, Florie envoie Mary Cadwallader chercher Mme Briggs et Mme Hughes. On conduit les enfants dans la chambre de leur père, pour qu'ils le voient une dernière fois.

Dans la matinée, on transporte Florie de la chambre du malade à la chambre d'amis, où elle restera en proie à un mystérieux évanouissement pendant plus de vingt-quatre heures, tout à fait inconsciente de ce qui se passe.

Le Dr Carter arrive et annonce à Michael qu'il a trouvé de l'arsenic dans une seconde bouteille de jus de viande. Lui et son collègue Humphreys ne pourront donc pas certifier que la cause du décès est « naturelle ».

A 8 h 40 – entre les bras de son « ami le plus intime », George Davidson –, Maybrick s'éteint.

Le lendemain, Florie, toujours inconsciente, ne sait rien de ce qui s'est passé.

Huit jours plus tôt, le vendredi 3 mai, jour où le Dr Carter suspecte que la dose « fatale » a été administrée, Maybrick a rédigé les dernières lignes de son journal. A-t-il vraiment confié à sa femme et à son meilleur ami qu'il se droguait ? A-t-il révélé son identité secrète ? A-t-il raconté toute l'histoire à sa femme et à son meilleur ami ?

> La douleur est insupportable. Ma chère Bunny sait tout. Je ne sais pas si elle a la force de me tuer. Je prie Dieu pour qu'elle la trouve. Ce serait simple, elle connaît mon médicament, et avec une dose ou deux de plus tout serait fini. Personne ne saura que j'y ai moi-même pourvu. George connaît mon habitude et je ne doute pas que Michael en ait bientôt vent. En vérité, je crois qu'il est au courant. Michael saura

> comment agir c'est lui le plus raisonnable de nous tous. Je ne crois pas que je verrai le mois de juin, de tous les mois mon favori. Ai supplié Bunny d'agir bientôt, je me maudis d'être si lâche.

En termes on ne peut plus clairs, Maybrick révèle qu'il a demandé à Florie de lui administrer une dose mortelle. Mais lui a-t-elle obéi ?

Mais où se trouvait le journal ?

Maybrick l'avait-il caché dans son bureau avant de partir ? A-t-il été trouvé par quelqu'un d'autre – dans le bureau ou à Battlecrease House – qui l'aurait ensuite dissimulé ? D'aucuns avaient intérêt à ce que personne ne découvre que James Maybrick était Jack l'Éventreur. George Davidson, par exemple. S'il était informé des meurtres, sa loyauté aurait peut-être suffi à le dissuader de révéler la terrible vérité.

Ou bien le journal a-t-il été découvert par Michael et Edwin, qui auraient eu à cœur de protéger la réputation de la famille ?

Se trouvait-il dans le coffre contenant les possessions de Florie, celui qui a disparu ?

Ou bien est-il tout simplement resté caché pendant un siècle à Battlecrease House ?

Quoi qu'il en soit, le souhait ultime de Maybrick a fini par se réaliser :

> Je place maintenant ceci dans un endroit où on le trouvera. Je prie pour que quiconque lira ces pages ait le cœur de me pardonner. Rappelez à tous, qui que vous soyez, que j'étais autrefois un gentleman.

Le journal a été retrouvé, mais on ne sait toujours pas avec précision quand, ni par qui. On sait seulement que cette découverte a eu lieu avant mai 1991, date à laquelle Mike Barrett l'a reçu.

Maybrick ne l'a pas légué à un membre de sa famille. Au lieu de cela, il l'a dissimulé dans l'espoir qu'il serait un jour découvert, et que « quiconque » le trouverait « rappellerait à tous » comment ce père de famille prospère était devenu un tueur dépravé, au terme d'une longue descente aux Enfers.

C'est le but du présent ouvrage que d'exaucer ce souhait.

Chapitre 12

Le 13 mai, deux jours après la mort de Maybrick, les Drs Humphreys, Carter et Barron ont pratiqué son autopsie en présence du *Superintendent* Bryning. La police avait ouvert une enquête pour déterminer les circonstances de la mort de Maybrick puisque les deux premiers médecins avaient refusé de signer un certificat de décès et en avaient référé au coroner.

Michael s'est occupé de tout après la mort de son frère. Y compris de Florie. La veuve, souffrante, a été placée sous la garde d'une infirmière inconnue. Elle révélerait ensuite avoir entendu Michael dire à cette dernière : « Mme Maybrick n'est plus la maîtresse de cette maison. En qualité d'exécuteur testamentaire, je vous interdis de la laisser sortir de cette pièce. »

Florie se trouvait donc en prison avant même d'avoir été reconnue coupable.

Bien qu'on soupçonnât depuis plusieurs jours un empoisonnement à l'arsenic, la maison n'avait pas été fouillée. Mais maintenant que Florie était sous clé, la voie était libre. Michael, Edwin, Mme Briggs, Mme Hughes et les domestiques ont donc entrepris de passer Battlecrease House au peigne fin. Lors du procès, ils affirmeraient avoir trouvé dans le coffre à linge du palier une bouteille de morphine, un flacon d'essence de vanille et un paquet de poudre jaune inoffensive.

Bessie, la domestique en charge de ce coffre, n'avait jamais auparavant remarqué la présence de ces objets.

Mais une découverte encore plus grave fut faite par les adversaires de Florie. Il s'agissait d'un paquet sur lequel on avait écrit à l'encre rouge : « Arsenic. Poison pour les chats. » Au verso se trouvait une étiquette imprimée : « Poison. » Le paquet contenait un mélange d'arsenic et de charbon de bois. Michael a enveloppé le paquet dans du papier, avant d'y apposer le sceau familial.

Florie aimait beaucoup les chats, et l'écriture sur le paquet n'était pas la sienne. D'après les défenseurs de sa cause, il se serait agi d'une mauvaise plaisanterie de Nurse Yapp et de son amie Alice Grant, la femme du jardinier.

Tous les médicaments récupérés dans la maison ont été remis à la police. Leur liste confiée plus tard au chimiste chargé de les analyser est réellement étonnante par sa diversité et révélatrice d'un homme esclave des médicaments. Mais ce qui défie l'entendement, c'est que parmi toutes les personnes qui vivaient à Battlecrease House et avaient accès à ces dizaines de médicaments, ce soit Florie qui ait été accusée, et sur la base de simples commérages.

Le chimiste, Edward Davies, a déclaré au procès qu'il avait trouvé assez d'arsenic pour « tuer deux ou trois personnes ». Mais son témoignage revêtait un caractère tellement technique que ni les témoins, ni le jury, ni même le juge ne l'ont trouvé intelligible.

On pouvait toutefois conclure que seuls six articles contenaient de l'arsenic, et sous une forme qui n'aurait pas convenu pour un meurtre. Par exemple, l'arsenic retrouvé dans la poche de la robe de chambre de Florie aurait très bien pu provenir du mouchoir avec lequel elle s'essuyait le visage après avoir utilisé des produits de beauté arséniés. Mais personne n'a avancé cette explication pendant le procès.

Alexander MacDougall critique avec virulence le manque de fiabilité des méthodes utilisées par Davies et l'imprécision des résultats obtenus. Selon lui, la totalité de l'arsenic retrouvé « aurait pu être avalée d'un coup, car il n'y en aurait pas eu assez pour tuer qui que ce soit ».

Des années plus tard, Florie Maybrick publierait un livre, *My Fifteen Lost Years* (Mes quinze années perdues), dans lequel elle décrirait les jours qui ont suivi la mort de son mari. « Lentement, j'ai repris conscience. J'ai ouvert les yeux. La chambre était plongée dans l'obscurité. Tout était calme. Soudain, le silence a été brisé par le claquement d'une porte qui m'a fait émerger de ma stupeur. Où étais-je ? Pourquoi étais-je seule ? Que s'était-il passé de si terrible ? Tout d'un coup, je me suis souvenue. Mon mari était mort. Puis j'ai dérivé de nouveau au-delà des frontières du conscient. C'est alors qu'une voix, si lointaine, a parlé. Une sensation de douleur et de détresse a parcouru mon corps. J'ai ouvert les yeux avec terreur. J'étais allongée sur mon lit et mon beau-frère, Edwin Maybrick, était penché sur moi. Il maintenait fermement mes bras et me secouait violemment. “ Je veux tes clés. Tu entends. Où sont tes clés ? ” s'est-il exclamé d'un ton dur. J'ai essayé de former une réponse mais les mots sont restés au fond de ma gorge et une fois de plus j'ai perdu conscience. »

Le lendemain de la mort de Maybrick, Florie a dit à son infirmière-geôlière qu'elle voulait voir ses enfants.

« Vous ne pouvez pas voir monsieur James ni mademoiselle Gladys, a répondu l'infirmière d'une voix froide et insensible. Monsieur Michael Maybrick a ordonné qu'ils quittent la maison sans vous voir. »

Florie écrit : « Je suis retombée sur mon oreiller, stupéfaite et accablée, faible, sans recours, impuissante. Pourquoi me traitait-on de la sorte ? [...] Mon âme a imploré Dieu de me laisser mourir [...] le désir de voir mes petits enfants devenait insupportable. »

Bobo et Gladys avaient été envoyés chez des amis. En

l'espace de quelques jours, ils avaient perdu leur père et leur mère, ainsi que le confort familier de la nursery. Leur mère, l'ancienne Belle du Sud qui était tombée amoureuse à dix-huit ans et avait échangé une vie aisée et cosmopolite en Amérique contre la claustrophobie sécrétée par la petite bourgeoisie de Liverpool, était maintenant prisonnière dans sa propre maison, soupçonnée par le personnel et par les membres de sa belle-famille d'avoir assassiné son mari.

Le 14 mai, les rumeurs ont cédé la place à des allégations officielles. Voici ce qu'écrit Florie : « Soudain, la porte s'est ouverte et le Dr Humphreys est entré. Il s'est approché de mon lit en silence, a pris mon pouls et a quitté la pièce sans un mot. Quelques minutes plus tard, j'ai entendu le bruit des pas de plusieurs personnes dans l'escalier. Les pas se sont arrêtés devant la porte. L'infirmière a ouvert et un groupe d'hommes est entré. L'un d'entre eux s'est avancé jusqu'au pied du lit et m'a dit : « Madame Maybrick, je suis le commissaire de police et je vais vous dire quelque chose. Une fois que j'aurai dit ce que je m'apprête à dire, prenez garde à ce que vous répondrez car tout ce que vous direz pourra être retenu contre vous. Madame Maybrick, vous êtes accusée du meurtre de feu votre mari, James Maybrick, le onze courant, et vous êtes donc en état d'arrestation. " »

Un peu plus tôt ce jour-là, le coroner avait décidé que du « poison avait été trouvé dans les viscères du défunt en quantité suffisante pour justifier des poursuites ».

Un policier a été affecté à la chambre de Florie, bien qu'elle n'eût guère de chance de s'échapper. Le jour de l'enterrement de Maybrick, le jeudi 16 mai, des voix étouffées et des pas précipités ont réveillé Florie. L'infirmière lui a annoncé sèchement : « La cérémonie commence dans une demi-heure. »

Tout d'abord, Florie s'est vu interdire l'accès de la chambre où le cercueil de son mari, couvert de fleurs blanches, avait déjà été refermé.

« Je me suis adressée au policier et à l'infirmière, écrit

Florie dans son autobiographie. Laissez-moi seule avec le défunt. Ils ont refusé. Je me suis agenouillée à côté du lit et j'ai enfin pu faire couler les larmes que de nombreuses journées de souffrance n'avaient pas libérées [...]. Une fois calmée, je suis retournée dans ma chambre et je me suis assise près de la fenêtre, toujours en larmes.

« Soudain, la voix sèche de l'infirmière est parvenue à mes oreilles. " Si vous voulez voir le mari que vous avez assassiné partir vers sa dernière demeure, vous feriez mieux de vous lever. " Je me suis mise debout à grand-peine et j'ai agrippé le rebord de la fenêtre, et je suis restée là, rigide et l'œil sec, jusqu'à ce que le corbillard ait disparu. Puis je me suis évanouie. »

Le lendemain, la baronne a fait irruption à Battlecrease House, alertée par un télégramme envoyé à contrecœur par Michael. « Florie malade et dans une situation terrible », disait la missive, sans prendre la peine de mentionner le décès de Maybrick.

« Edwin m'a accueillie dans le vestibule et m'a emmenée dans le petit salon, écrirait-elle plus tard. Il était très agité [...]. Puis il m'a annoncé en balbutiant que Michael avait soupçonné quelque chose d'anormal, que le médecin pensait de même [...] et que d'après l'infirmière, Florie avait versé quelque chose dans le jus de viande. »

La baronne s'est aussitôt rendue au premier étage et a tenté de parler à Florie en français. Lorsque cette dernière eut dit à sa mère qu'elle était soupçonnée d'avoir empoisonné Maybrick, la baronne a répondu : « S'il est empoisonné, il ne peut s'en prendre qu'à lui-même. Il avait tout d'une pharmacie ambulante. »

Le samedi 18 mai au matin, la baronne a consulté les avocats de Florie, les frères Arnold et William Cleaver, de Cleaver, Holden, Garnett & Cleaver. Pendant qu'elle se trouvait dans leur cabinet, un télégramme est arrivé : il annonçait que Florie était sur le point d'être emmenée par les autorités.

Treize juristes et médecins étaient arrivés par le train et s'étaient assemblés autour du lit de la veuve, dont Arnold et William Cleaver, parvenus sur place avant la baronne. Ils s'étaient préalablement consultés dehors, sous les yeux d'une foule de journalistes et de badauds. A l'issue de cette conversation, les Cleaver avaient accepté de ne pas s'opposer à la détention préventive.

La baronne est arrivée au moment où Florie allait être emmenée. « Je suis montée dans ma chambre qui donnait sur l'entrée de la propriété, pour essayer de voir son visage au moment où ils faisaient monter mon enfant dans la voiture, et ils ont tourné la clé dans la serrure et m'ont enfermée [...]. Ils l'ont emmenée en hâte d'une façon si inconvenante que même son sac à main et ses objets de toilette ont été oubliés [...]. L'infirmière a saisi ma cape et mon chapeau et les a placés sur elle, ils l'ont installée dans un fauteuil, car elle était trop faible pour se tenir debout, et elle a été transportée jusqu'à la voiture. »

Quelques semaines après la mort de James, Charles Ratcliff, l'ami des Maybrick, a écrit une longue lettre à John Aunspaugh, qui se trouvait à Atlanta, en Georgie. Trevor Christie la mentionne dans son livre *Etched in Arsenic*, et elle faisait partie de la collection de souvenirs personnels de Florence Aunspaugh.

Elle donne des informations très importantes sur les événements qui ont conduit à la mort de Maybrick. En effet, Ratcliff était un ami de longue date et un témoin digne de confiance. C'est une description brute, mais fort probablement exacte, du piège tendu à Florie.

« Cela m'a causé un grand choc. Je m'attendais à une tragédie au sein de cette famille, mais je pensais que l'autre partie en serait à l'origine. James avait eu vent de la liaison de l'hôtel Flatman et je m'attendais à ce qu'il flingue Brierley d'un jour à l'autre. »

Ratcliff explique ensuite qu'à son retour des courses de

Wirral, le 27 avril, Maybrick s'est bourré de médicaments, « comme d'habitude ». Ratcliff parle aussi de « serpents femelles ». Il rapporte à tort que Mme Briggs a montré la lettre de Brierley à Edwin, alors qu'il s'agissait en fait de Nurse Yapp. Ratcliff ajoute ensuite qu'Edwin, « LUI-MÊME DANS LE BOURBIER JUSQU'AU COU », n'y a pas prêté attention.

« Ce bon vieux Dr Humphreys s'est couvert de ridicule, poursuit Ratcliff. Après la mort de James, lui et le Dr Carter pensaient écrire sur le certificat de décès que la cause de la mort était une inflammation aiguë du ventre. Mais après avoir discuté avec Michael, il a refusé d'apposer sa signature à un tel certificat et il a dit qu'il existait des symptômes d'empoisonnement à l'arsenic [...]. Ça te la coupe, non ? Un compositeur qui donne son diagnostic à un médecin.

« Michael, ce fils de pute, devrait avoir la gorge tranchée. Mme Maybrick était au lit, malade, quand James est mort. Il était mort depuis quelques heures à peine quand Michael [...] s'est mis à fouiller dans toute la maison et dans sa chambre [celle de Florie] ils ont prétendu avoir trouvé des quantités d'arsenic, treize lettres d'amour d'Edwin, sept de Brierley et cinq de Williams. »

Et Ratcliff de conclure : « J'ai toujours pensé que madame était gourde, mais je dois admettre franchement que je ne la pensais pas assez gourde pour laisser traîner de pareils indices à la portée de n'importe qui... »

De leur côté, les journaux de Liverpool ont entamé leur propre procès, multipliant les articles vengeurs dans lesquels ils présentaient des preuves et prononçaient des jugements avant même que Florie n'ait été officiellement accusée. Le *Liverpool Echo* a ouvert une chronique intitulée « Maybrick-mania ». Quant au *Liverpool Review*, il avouait avec une franchise louable : « L'affaire Maybrick est un coup de chance pour les journaux. »

Le 28 mai, avocats, témoins, spectateurs et une meute de journalistes se sont entassés dans le vieux tribunal de simple police de Wellington Road. L'acoustique était très mauvaise et pendant douze heures, a rapporté le *Liverpool Echo*, les journalistes ont pris des notes « debout entre les rangs serrés de policiers, sur leurs genoux, parfois sur le dos d'éminents avocats et dans d'autres positions tout aussi inconfortables, car il leur était impossible d'entendre quoi que ce soit depuis les tables qui leur avaient été assignées ».

Ils s'étaient rassemblés pour l'enquête du coroner, mais ce n'étaient là que les préliminaires d'un procès à sensation, et il se révélerait impossible de trier le vrai du faux dans le déluge de témoignages contradictoires, de mensonges et d'erreurs qui allait suivre. En Grande-Bretagne, l'enquête du coroner n'est pas le procès proprement dit : son objectif est d'établir la cause du décès. Mais en 1889, elle permettait aussi de répartir les torts, et dans le cas de l'affaire Maybrick, beaucoup attendaient son verdict avec impatience.

Le président du jury, M. Dalgleish, ami du défunt, a reconnu que, le jour du Grand National, Maybrick lui avait confié qu'il prenait de la strychnine. On l'a immédiatement congédié et son témoignage sur la toxicomanie de Maybrick a été oublié.

Florie était encore trop mal pour assister à l'enquête, aussi n'a-t-elle pas entendu chaque témoin répéter les rumeurs répandues à mi-voix par ses domestiques. Le papier tue-mouches, le jus de viande, le « poison pour les chats » et, surtout, la lettre de Brierley étaient autant de pièces à conviction. En guise de mobile, on a choisi l'infidélité. Aux yeux des Victoriens, en effet, il n'était pire crime que l'adultère commis par une femme.

La recherche de la cause exacte du décès de Maybrick est passée au second plan. Peut-être parce que, en dépit de ce que le coroner avait affirmé tout de suite après l'autopsie, aucune dose d'arsenic mesurable n'avait été trouvée dans son corps. Ledit coroner a néanmoins insisté pour que l'enquête soit ajournée, afin que « le ventre et son contenu puissent être analysés chimiquement ». En conséquence, le

30 mai, le cadavre de James Maybrick a été exhumé au cimetière d'Anfield.

C'est le 5 juin que Florie est apparue pour la première fois au tribunal. Comme elle était sifflée par les femmes, deux fois plus nombreuses que les hommes, on l'a fait asseoir dans l'antichambre pendant que les derniers témoins s'exprimaient. Brierley se trouvait au fond de la salle du tribunal, mais lui et Florie ne se sont pas rencontrés, et il ne lui a pas été demandé de témoigner.

Les médecins ont fait part de leurs conclusions, les uns après les autres. S'est ensuite exprimé M. Flatman, le propriétaire de l'hôtel de Covent Garden dans lequel Florie et Brierley avaient séjourné. Puis Alfred Schweisso, serveur dans le même hôtel, a identifié Florie et Brierley. Mais il devait se rétracter dans une lettre adressée à MacDougall le 18 janvier 1890 : « En ce qui concerne M. Brierley. Bien sûr, je n'aurais pas dû le reconnaître mais c'est ce que la police m'avait demandé; j'étais témoin à charge et j'ai suivi leurs ordres, ce que je regrette maintenant car ils ont agi d'une façon tout à fait honteuse [...]. Je n'ai pas pu le reconnaître quand il est entré; mais un policier s'est approché de moi et m'a montré où se trouvait M. Brierley [...]. C'était un coup monté. »

Le témoin suivant était Thomas Lowry, l'employé qu'on avait envoyé acheter une casserole, un bol et une cuiller pour que Maybrick puisse prendre son Revalenta. Puis on a entendu la femme de ménage qui avait lavé ces ustensiles, et Mme Briggs, qui avait dirigé la fouille de Battlecrease House.

Le lendemain, le jury a entendu Edwin, Frederick Tozer – le vendeur de Clay and Abrahams, l'une des pharmacies qui avaient fourni des médicaments à James – et la police.

Edward Davies a déclaré que l'exhumation avait permis de retrouver une quantité d'arsenic impossible à estimer dans les intestins de Maybrick, environ un millième de grain dans ses reins, environ un huitième de grain dans son foie, mais rien ailleurs.

Il faut se souvenir que, même si le XIXe siècle a vu se matérialiser des progrès techniques considérables, la médecine demeurait relativement peu sophistiquée. Et à l'époque, on était obsédé par l'arsenic, à tel point qu'on n'a pas cherché à déterminer la présence de strychnine, dont Maybrick abusait également, et ce d'autant moins qu'on en ignorait les effets à long terme.

Lorsque j'ai sollicité l'opinion du Dr Glyn Volans, du Guy's Hospital de Londres, à ce sujet, voici ce qu'il m'a répondu : « Si un homme avait absorbé de l'arsenic et de la strychnine pendant des années, personne n'aurait pu, à l'époque, déterminer avec précision en quelle quantité car on ne disposait pas des techniques appropriées. On comprend donc bien pourquoi si peu d'arsenic a été trouvé dans le corps de Maybrick. La cause exacte de la mort n'a pas été déterminée : il s'agissait sans doute d'une insuffisance rénale due à l'abus prolongé de substances toxiques. »

Enfin, Mme Hughes est venue identifier la lettre de Florie à Brierley.

En dépit du manque de preuves convaincantes, le jury – dont la plupart des membres avaient été reçus chez les Maybrick à un moment ou à un autre – a décidé que « James Maybrick est mort des effets d'un poison irritant qui lui a été administré par Florence Elizabeth Maybrick, et que ladite Florence Elizabeth Maybrick a tué et assassiné ledit James Maybrick avec préméditation, criminellement, et avec intention délictueuse ».

Le trajet de retour à Walton Jail, aux abords de la ville, aurait peut-être été trop long pour Florie, aussi les autorités l'ont-elles dirigée vers la prison de Lark Lane. On l'y a traitée avec gentillesse et on lui a servi des plats en provenance d'un hôtel voisin. Un journaliste du *Liverpool Post*, qui lui avait rendu visite, a écrit : « Elle dispose d'une petite table placée près de l'entrée de sa cellule. On l'autorise à prendre autant d'exercice qu'elle le souhaite dans le couloir et, lorsqu'elle est fatiguée, elle s'assied à la table, qui est recouverte d'un linge blanc comme neige. Il y avait deux livres dessus : la reliure de l'un était pourpre, l'autre dans des teintes moins voyantes. Elle iit les comptes rendus relatifs à son procès avec l'intérêt le plus vif et se laisse aller de temps à autre à des commentaires sarcastiques à propos de ce qui lui déplaît. Elle a un comportement quelque peu fantasque. »

L'étincelle de vie n'avait pas disparu.

Le 13 juin, Florie, en grand deuil, a été conduite au tribunal d'Islington pour l'enquête des magistrats. Pour la première fois, elle allait entendre les témoins à charge : ses domestiques, ses beaux-frères et les médecins.

Même à ce moment, ils n'étaient pas tombés d'accord sur la cause du décès et ils ont reconnu ne pas comprendre suffisamment bien ce dont Maybrick avait souffert. En outre, certains détails essentiels ont été omis. En particulier, personne n'a fait observer qu'aucune trace d'arsenic n'avait été trouvée dans les urines ni dans les selles prélevées quelques jours avant la mort de James. En vérité, au terme de cette enquête, le seul élément qui n'était pas disputé, c'était que Florie et Alfred Brierley avaient passé deux nuits à l'hôtel Flatman en mars. Et il s'agissait apparemment là d'un crime capital.

Florie a été officiellement mise en accusation et la date de son procès fixée au 26 juillet. Lorsque la voiture qui l'emmenait à Walton Jail a quitté Islington, elle a été huée par la foule.

Les photographes locaux n'ont pas tardé à exploiter cette affaire. Dans les vitrines des magasins on apercevait des photos du couple Maybrick, et même un cliché sensationnel de Florie et de Brierley ensemble au Grand National. Battlecrease House est devenue une attraction pour les touristes.

Le 8 juillet, moins de sept semaines après l'arrestation de Florie, Michael a passé outre de manière flagrante aux instructions contenues dans le testament de son frère et a vendu tout son mobilier aux enchères. Il semblait convaincu que Florie ne reviendrait jamais.

Mais qu'est-il advenu du produit de cette vente ? Michael a d'abord prétendu qu'il en avait dépensé la moitié pour contribuer à payer l'avocat de Florie. Mais plus tard, arguant qu'il devait témoigner contre elle, il a déclaré qu'il ne financerait pas la défense de sa belle-sœur. Une contradiction de plus.

Heureusement pour Florie, la Mutual Reserve Fund Life Association de New York lui a versé 1 000 livres avant le délai réglementaire de trois mois après le décès du souscripteur. En outre, sa mère a vendu des terres appartenant à la famille dans le Kentucky. Florie avait besoin de tout l'argent qu'elle pouvait obtenir. En effet, les termes du nouveau testament de Maybrick étaient impitoyables à son égard.

Par ailleurs, Florie souhaitait vivement que le procès n'ait pas lieu à Liverpool. Voici ce qu'elle a écrit à sa mère à ce propos :

« J'espère sincèrement que les Cleaver vont s'arranger pour que mon " procès " ait lieu à Londres. Là-bas, je bénéficierai d'un verdict impartial, que je ne peux pas attendre d'un jury de Liverpool qui est déjà parvenu à une " condamnation morale ", en attendant [1], qui ne manquera pas d'influencer leur décision jusqu'à un certain point. Les cancans des domestiques, du public, des amis et des ennemis, et de mille autres personnages secondaires, outre leurs sentiments personnels envers Jim, ne manqueront pas de laisser des traces et d'entretenir des préjugés dans leur esprit, quelle que soit la défense. »

Mais elle n'obtiendrait pas satisfaction. Les conseillers de Florie ont estimé qu'elle aurait davantage de chances si

1. En français dans le texte. (*N.d.T.*)

elle tenait bon et livrait bataille à Liverpool. Elle a accepté leurs recommandations.

Arnold Cleaver est parti pour l'Amérique, dans l'espoir de rallier soutien et témoins à décharge. Aux États-Unis, les journaux prenaient la défense de cette Américaine expatriée, abandonnée, sans amis, mariée à un étranger débauché dans une contrée lointaine. Florie y bénéficierait d'un soutien massif.

Mais à Londres, Madame Tussaud, le célèbre musée de cire, préparait déjà une statue de Mme Maybrick. Elle y serait exposée dans la Chambre des Horreurs.

Chapitre 13

St. George's Hall, impressionnante bâtisse aux pierres noircies par la fumée, trônait au centre de Liverpool. Les habitants de la ville la considéraient avec affection comme leur salle des fêtes, et s'y réunissaient à l'occasion de concerts, de festivals, ou de cérémonies. Mais c'est aussi là que siège encore aujourd'hui la *Crown Court* (équivalent britannique d'une cour d'assises). Le procès de Florie aurait un énorme retentissement à Liverpool.

« Je me sens si seule, a écrit Florie à une amie, comme si le sort s'acharnait contre moi. Penser que je dois être dévoilée devant des yeux si peu charitables [...]. Je dois maintenant endurer les jours les plus sombres de mon existence. Mais j'ai confiance en la justice de Dieu, quel que soit le regard que portent sur moi les hommes. »

Après l'enquête du coroner et l'instruction des magistrats, qui avaient déterminé que Florie serait jugée pour meurtre, il lui restait une autre étape à franchir avant de s'asseoir au banc des accusés : l'inquisition du *Grand Jury*.

La fonction du *Grand Jury* (jury d'accusation) consistait à déterminer si une personne mise en accusation par les magistrats devait ou non être jugée. Si le *Grand Jury* ne donnait pas son accord, en déclarant fondés les chefs d'accusation, il ne pouvait y avoir de procès. C'est donc lui qui avait le dernier mot. Ses membres n'étaient pas choisis au hasard, mais en fonction de leur rang et de leur intelligence. On admettait qu'ils étaient en dehors de toutes influences locales et libres de toute contrainte imposée par les magistrats. Les membres du *Grand Jury* représentaient le peuple, et le juge représentait la Couronne.

Le juge au procès de Florie, *Mr. Justice* James Fitzjames Stephen (plus connu sous le sobriquet de Monsieur Injustice), était arrivé au terme d'une carrière distinguée. Le *Liverpool Review* le décrivait comme un « homme imposant, impressionnant et intelligent » et précisait : « Son cerveau est semblable à une de ces machines merveilleusement exactes qu'on peut voir dans les quartiers industriels. Elles font leur travail avec une précision remarquable et une rigueur laborieuse et infatigable, mais si elles ne sont pas surveillées de près et remises de temps en temps sur le droit chemin par le préposé à leur bon fonctionnement, elles risquent de s'enrayer. »

Au moment du procès Maybrick, il est très clair que *Mr. Justice* Stephen s'était déjà « enrayé ». Sa raison déclinait et le grand homme semblait désormais incapable de se concentrer. Dans une correspondance adressée à Lord Lytton en 1889, il avait d'ailleurs révélé : « Je continue de temps à autre à fumer une pipe d'opium. En effet, mon nez en requiert une occasionnellement car elle lui fait grand bien. »

Le 26 juillet, le jour où le *Grand Jury* devait siéger, plusieurs milliers de personnes se sont bousculées pour apercevoir la prisonnière à son arrivée au tribunal.

Mr. Justice Stephen a présenté au *Grand Jury* les détails de l'affaire N° 24, parsemant son discours de sous-entendus et d'erreurs factuelles. Entre autres commentaires scandaleux, il a décrit James Maybrick comme un homme « qui avait le malheur d'avoir une femme infidèle ».

« Si la prisonnière est coupable du crime dont elle est accusée, a-t-il poursuivi, il s'agit là du meurtre le plus cruel et le plus horrible qui se puisse commettre. »

Ses paroles ont été rapportées dans les moindres détails,

de sorte que, dès avant le procès, le monde entier connaissait l'opinion du juge quant à l'adultère. Et malheureusement pour Florie, Stephens réservait ses critiques aux femmes. Jamais la question des activités extra-maritales de James Maybrick n'a été abordée.

Deux questions essentielles étaient au cœur du procès intenté contre Florie : l'arsenic avait-il causé la mort ? Et le cas échéant, l'arsenic avait-il été administré par Mme Maybrick avec intention délictueuse ?

La Cour était libre d'ajouter d'autres chefs d'accusation, et il était fréquent qu'elle use de cette prérogative. Toutefois, dans le cas de Florie, le seul chef d'accusation retenu serait celui de meurtre, en dépit du fait que rien ne permettait d'établir un lien entre l'accusée et l'arsenic trouvé à Battlecrease House (à l'exception de celui contenu dans le papier tue-mouches). Les délibérations du *Grand Jury* terminées, l'ouverture du procès de Florie a été fixée au 31 juillet.

L'avocat de Florie, Sir Charles Russell, était conseiller de la Couronne. Tout le monde estimait que Florie avait beaucoup de chance d'être défendue par un homme si célèbre.

Cependant ce choix était mal inspiré. Les années précédentes, en effet, Sir Charles avait essuyé de cuisants échecs.

Le 31 juillet, date à laquelle le procès devait débuter, l'avocat était épuisé.

A 10 heures, au son d'une fanfare de trompettes, tout le monde s'est levé et *Mr. Justice* Stephen est apparu, le visage grave sous une perruque carrée. Après les préliminaires d'usage, le greffier a lancé : « Faites avancer Florence Elizabeth Maybrick. »

Florie portait une veste de crêpe par-dessus sa robe noire, et un chapeau de crêpe avec un voile noir très fin. C'est d'une voix claire et d'un ton ferme qu'elle a répondu : « Non coupable » aux accusations portées contre elle.

Plus tard, pendant l'heure du déjeuner, certains spectateurs ont protesté en apercevant des membres du jury en compagnie de journalistes et de témoins. Mais aucun juré n'a été congédié.

L'ouvrage exhaustif qu'Alexander MacDougall a consacré à l'affaire établit la liste des erreurs et des incohérences qui ont émaillé le procès. Les dix médecins qui ont témoigné se sont accordés à attribuer la cause du décès de James Maybrick à une gastro-entérite. Mais quant à la cause de la gastro-entérite elle-même, les avis divergeaient : s'agissait-il de nourriture avariée ou de poison ? Et dans ce dernier cas, le poison en question était-il oui ou non de l'arsenic ?

Le Dr Richard Humphreys, qui avait traité Maybrick le premier durant sa maladie, fait partie de ceux qui ont attribué la mort à l'arsenic. Mais lors de l'enquête des magistrats, il a reconnu n'avoir aucune expérience réelle sur ce diagnostic.

Quant au Dr William Carter, il avait rendu visite à Maybrick seulement quatre fois. En outre, lors d'un contre-interrogatoire, il a avoué, lui aussi, n'avoir aucune connaissance particulière sur les décès par arsenic.

Le 7 mai, il avait émis le diagnostic suivant : dyspepsie due à l' « ingestion imprudente de certaine nourriture ou boisson ». Mais deux jours plus tard, à la suite d'une conversation au cours de laquelle Michael lui avait fait part de ses soupçons, Carter avait changé d'opinion. Et lors du procès, il était du même avis que le Dr Humphreys.

Le Dr Alexander Barron, professeur de pathologie à l'University College de Liverpool, était présent lors de l'autopsie de Maybrick et lors de l'exhumation, mais il ne l'avait jamais traité. Il a conclu que le décès était dû à « une inflammation aiguë du ventre, probablement causée par quelque poison irritant ».

Lors d'un contre-interrogatoire mené par Sir Charles, la question suivante a été posée au Dr Barron : « Est-il possible de faire la différence entre les symptômes de l'empoisonnement par arsenic et ceux de l'empoisonnement par nourriture avariée ? »

« Je ne serais moi-même pas capable de le faire », a répondu le médecin.

Pour sa part, le Dr Charles Meymott Tidy, qui avait travaillé pendant vingt ans pour le ministère de l'Intérieur en qualité d'expert médico-légal du London Hospital, et qui était spécialiste des poisons depuis 1862, déclara : « Les symptômes révélés lors de l'autopsie écartent nettement l'hypothèse de l'arsenic. »

Le Dr Charles Fuller, qui jouissait d'une expérience de trente ans en matière de médecine et d'homéopathie, a affirmé que rien ne permettait de penser que Maybrick prenait de l'arsenic. Les symptômes qui accompagnent la consommation habituelle de ce produit n'étaient pas présents dans ce cas précis.

Le Dr Rawden Macnamara, chargé de cours au Royal College of Surgeons d'Irlande et docteur en médecine de l'université de Londres, avait administré de l'arsenic « à un très grand nombre de patients ». Lorsqu'il lui a été demandé si Maybrick était mort des suites d'un empoisonnement par arsenic, il a répondu : « Certainement pas. »

Le Dr Frank Thomas Paul, pathologiste avec quelque trois mille autopsies à son actif et professeur de médecine légale au University College de Liverpool, a émis ce verdict : les symptômes décrits dans cette affaire « sont ceux d'une gastro-entérite pure et simple. [...] Je présume qu'il est mort de l'épuisement causé par ladite gastro-entérite ».

Le Dr Thomas Stevenson, analyste du ministère de l'Intérieur qui enseignait la médecine légale au Guy's Hospital de Londres, a lui aussi examiné les viscères de Maybrick. Au terme d'un contre-interrogatoire prolongé, il a affirmé n'avoir « aucun doute » : la mort était bien due à un empoisonnement par arsenic.

Le Dr Arthur Hopper, médecin de la famille Maybrick

depuis 1881, a confirmé que Maybrick se droguait, mais on ne lui a pas demandé son opinion quant à la maladie fatale qui avait emporté son patient.

Le Dr Glyn Volans, du Guy's Hospital de Londres, a lu sur notre demande le « Rapport toxicologique » portant sur l'affaire Maybrick et s'est déclaré « pas du tout convaincu » que James soit mort d'un empoisonnement par arsenic à forte dose. « La plus petite dose mortelle jamais enregistrée s'élève à deux grains. Pourtant, on n'a retrouvé qu'un dixième de grain dans le corps de James Maybrick. La vérité, c'est qu'on ne dispose d'aucune preuve permettant d'affirmer que Florence Maybrick a administré du poison. Il est plus probable qu'il est mort des effets cumulés de la toxicomanie et des substances que lui ont fait ingérer les médecins durant ses dernières semaines. Il faut ajouter qu'il n'avait plus accès à ses poisons et se trouvait donc en manque. L'insuffisance rénale est une cause de décès plus probable. »

Si les jurés n'ont pas été perturbés par la confusion des avis médicaux, c'est sans doute parce qu'ils disposaient d'un témoignage bien plus convaincant.

Au terme de la première semaine du procès, Florie avait entendu les témoins rapporter chaque détail de sa vie avec Maybrick et particulièrement les événements situés entre 1888 et 1889. C'est alors que la question du jus de viande a été abordée. Contre les ordres du Dr Carter, Edwin avait donné la bouteille à l'infirmière Gore, et elle était posée, encore inutilisée, à côté du lit de Maybrick le soir du 9 mai. Or, l'infirmière savait que des soupçons pesaient sur Florie. Elle savait aussi que le médecin avait interdit à son patient de prendre de ce jus de viande. Elle a vu Florie emporter la bouteille dans la pièce d'à côté et la rapporter quelques secondes plus tard. Lorsque Maybrick s'est réveillé, elle a également noté que Florie avait posé cette bouteille sur la coiffeuse, hors de portée de son mari. Ce dernier n'a donc pas bu de jus de viande.

La bouteille a ensuite été remise à Michael par l'infirmière, et au Dr Carter par Michael. Edward Davies, qui en a analysé le contenu, a ensuite déclaré qu'un demi-grain d'arsenic dilué se trouvait dedans, découverte qui a renforcé la position de l'accusation.

Quand Florie a raconté son histoire pour la première fois à son avocat, avant l'enquête, elle a admis librement, mais sans doute de façon maladroite, qu'elle avait versé un peu de poudre dans l'extrait de viande, à la demande de son mari. A la fin du procès, voici ce qu'elle a déclaré à la cour :

« Le jeudi 9 mai au soir, après que l'infirmière Gore eut donné du bouillon à mon mari, je suis allée m'asseoir sur le lit à côté de lui. Il s'est plaint d'être très malade et très déprimé, et il m'a de nouveau implorée de lui donner de cette poudre dont il avait parlé en début de soirée et que j'avais refusé de lui donner. J'étais à bout, terriblement anxieuse, on ne peut plus malheureuse, et sa détresse évidente m'a été insupportable. Il m'avait assurée que la poudre en question ne lui ferait pas de mal et que je pouvais la verser dans sa nourriture. J'ai alors consenti. Mon Dieu, je n'avais pas un seul ami véritable ou honnête dans la maison. Je ne pouvais consulter personne, personne n'était là pour me conseiller. On m'a destituée de ma position de maîtresse de ma propre maison et on m'a empêchée de veiller sur mon mari, bien qu'il soit si malade. Quelles que soient les déclarations des infirmières et des domestiques, permettez-moi de dire qu'il souhaitait m'avoir près de lui; je lui manquais chaque fois que je n'étais pas auprès de lui; chaque fois que je sortais de la chambre, il demandait après moi, mais pendant les quatre jours qui ont précédé sa mort, je n'ai pas été autorisée à lui donner ne fût-ce qu'un morceau de glace sans qu'on le retire de ma main. Quand j'ai trouvé la poudre, je l'ai emportée dans le vestiaire avec le jus de bœuf, et en poussant la porte j'ai incliné la bouteille, alors pour remplacer la quantité de fluide que j'avais renversée, j'ai rajouté une quantité d'eau considérable. En retournant dans la chambre, j'ai trouvé mon mari endormi, et j'ai placé la bouteille sur la table près de la fenêtre. Quand il s'est réveillé, il a eu la sensation d'étouffer puis s'est mis à vomir; ensuite, il a eu l'air d'aller un peu mieux, et comme il ne m'a pas redemandé de la poudre et que je n'étais pas particulièrement désireuse de lui en donner, j'ai retiré la bouteille de la petite table, où elle risquait d'attirer l'attention, et je l'ai placée sur le dessus du lavabo, où il ne pouvait pas l'apercevoir. Et je l'ai laissée là, mon Dieu, jusqu'à ce que Michael Maybrick, je crois, en prenne possession. Jusqu'au mardi 14 mai, quelques minutes avant que M. Bryning ne porte cette accusation terrible contre moi, personne dans cette maison ne m'avait informée du fait qu'un certificat de décès avait été refusé, ni qu'une autopsie avait eu lieu, ni qu'on avait lieu de supposer que mon mari était mort d'une cause autre que naturelle. C'est seulement quand Mme Briggs a fait allusion à la présence d'arsenic dans le jus de viande que j'ai pris conscience de la nature de la poudre que mon mari m'avait demandé de lui donner... »

Ce dont Florie ne s'était pas rendu compte, c'est que l'arsenic blanc en poudre ne se dissout pas facilement. Or, l'arsenic trouvé dans la bouteille de jus de viande devait se présenter sous forme de solution et n'aurait donc pas pu y être ajouté de la manière décrite par Florie. Alors, quelle était la nature de la poudre que Maybrick l'avait suppliée de lui donner ? Aurait-il pu s'agir de strychnine ? Dix jours auparavant, il avait écrit dans son journal qu'il avait l'intention de demander à Florie de le tuer, et il se demandait si elle en aurait la force. Or, si elle l'avait empoisonné avec de la strychnine, les tests effectués par les experts, conçus pour révéler la présence d'arsenic, auraient été négatifs. Mais de toute façon, les experts ne recherchaient pas de la strychnine.

On a beaucoup exploité l'épisode du papier tue-mouches. Il faut préciser que quatre ans auparavant, à Liverpool, deux sœurs mariées du nom de Flanagan et de

Higgins, avaient été pendues pour avoir empoisonné trois personnes à l'aide d'arsenic extrait de papier tue-mouches. La défense a argué que le papier tue-mouches ne pouvait être responsable de la mort de Maybrick, puisqu'on n'avait retrouvé de fibres de ce papier dans aucune des bouteilles contaminées. Mais Florie a insisté, contre l'avis de son avocat, pour lire une déclaration qu'elle avait remise aux frères Cleaver avant l'enquête et que ces derniers avaient délibérément omis de mentionner. Cette déclaration était quelque peu naïve. La première partie était consacrée au papier tue-mouches.

« J'ai acheté les bandes de papier tue-mouches dans l'intention de m'en servir comme produit de beauté. Depuis bien des années, et même avant mon mariage, j'ai l'habitude d'utiliser un nettoyant pour visage qui m'a été prescrit par le Dr Greggs, de Brooklyn. Il est principalement constitué d'arsenic, de teinture de benjoin, d'eau de fleurs de sureau, et de quelques autres ingrédients. J'ai perdu ou égaré cette ordonnance en avril dernier et, comme je souffrais à ce moment-là de rougeurs légères sur le visage, j'ai pensé que j'aimerais essayer de fabriquer un substitut moi-même. Je voulais absolument me débarrasser de ces rougeurs avant un bal où je devais me rendre le 30 de ce mois. Quand je me trouvais en Allemagne, j'avais vu beaucoup de mes amies se servir d'une solution fabriquée à partir de papier tue-mouches, d'eau de fleurs de sureau, d'eau de lavande, et d'autres ingrédients mélangés. On l'appliquait ensuite sur le visage à l'aide d'un mouchoir bien imbibé de cette solution. J'ai utilisé le papier tue-mouches de la même manière. Mais pour éviter que le parfum ne s'évapore, il était nécessaire qu'il soit le plus possible à l'abri de l'air, c'est pour cette raison que j'ai placé une assiette sur le papier tue-mouches et une serviette pliée par-dessus, puis encore une autre. Ma mère sait depuis de nombreuses années que j'utilise un cosmétique arsénié en solution. »

Cela semblait bien innocent. Mais du fait que cette

déclaration n'avait pas été faite lors de l'enquête des magistrats, le juge Stephen l'a interprétée comme un mensonge, fabriqué pour l'occasion – et il l'a dit.

Plusieurs mois après le procès, la baronne von Roques tournait les pages de la bible familiale – l'un des seuls objets sauvés de la vente aux enchères – lorsqu'elle a retrouvé l'ordonnance égarée, rédigée au verso d'une étiquette de pharmacien et datée de 1878.

Et en 1890, trop tard pour Florie, E. Godwin Clayton, chimiste conseil et membre de la Société des analystes d'État, a effectué une expérience consistant à extraire de l'arsenic de deux bandes de papier tue-mouches. Son verdict : « Il est pratiquement impossible pour une personne sans connaissances ni opportunités en matière de manipulations chimiques de fabriquer ou d'obtenir une infusion aqueuse à partir de papier tue-mouches qui puisse être ajoutée à du jus de viande Valentine en quantité suffisante pour introduire l'équivalent d'un demi-grain d'arsenic. »

Le procès a duré sept jours. Il a fallu au juge douze heures pour effectuer le résumé de l'affaire. « Une personne qui administre délibérément du poison à un pauvre homme malade et sans défense à qui elle a déjà infligé une blessure affreuse – une blessure fatale pour la vie conjugale – la personne capable d'un tel acte doit en vérité être dépourvue de la moindre trace d'humanité. »

A la fin du résumé, la plus grande confusion régnait dans les esprits. (L'un des spectateurs a dit qu' « il n'avait jamais assisté dans un tribunal à démonstration plus pitoyable d'incompétence et d'imprécision ».)

Les journalistes, les spectateurs et les milliers de badauds rassemblés sur la place à l'extérieur de St. George's Hall étaient sûrs que Florie serait acquittée. En effet, l'opinion publique avait pris son parti massivement. Après tout, aucune preuve ne permettait d'établir un lien entre Florie et l'arsenic retrouvé dans la maison. Rien ne prouvait non plus qu'elle avait administré l'arsenic consciemment ni même que l'arsenic était responsable de la mort de James Maybrick.

Mais il n'a fallu au jury que trente-cinq minutes pour rendre un verdict qui continue encore aujourd'hui de déconcerter les experts : coupable.

Nombre de questions relatives à ce procès demeurent toujours sans réponse. Comment justifier le comportement de Michael et d'Edwin durant toute cette période ? Avant même le décès de Maybrick, les frères avaient discuté avec Mme Briggs, Mme Hughes et Nurse Yapp de la possibilité d'un empoisonnement, mais pourtant ils n'ont rien entrepris pour le sauver à temps. C'est seulement après sa mort que la maison a été fouillée de fond en comble.

En outre, des lettres compromettantes découvertes plus tard à Battlecrease et attribuées à Edwin ont disparu.

Edwin avait confié à des amis que Maybrick avait l'habitude de consommer de « cette satanée strychnine », mais il l'a nié durant le procès. Michael le savait aussi, mais il a nié avec autant de vigueur.

Entre le décès de Maybrick et le procès, le Dr Hopper a détruit toutes les ordonnances de Maybrick. Pourquoi ?

Michael a réussi à empêcher que le dernier testament de Maybrick ne soit utilisé comme pièce à conviction : en effet, ce document leur conférait, à lui et à Thomas, des pouvoirs considérables en tant que *fidéicommissaires*. Florie, pour sa part, était dépouillée de tous ses droits. De surcroît, les avocats de Florie n'ont pas empêché Michael de procéder à une vente aux enchères de tout le mobilier de Battlecrease.

On a beaucoup évoqué les dettes de Florie. Pourquoi n'a-t-on pas mentionné celles de son mari ?

L'infidélité de Maybrick, qui durait depuis des années, n'a pas non plus été abordée.

Pourquoi tant de témoins importants n'ont-ils pas été appelés à la barre ? On n'a pas entendu la mère de Florie, les autres frères de Maybrick – Thomas et William –, George Davidson, Alfred Brierley, John Baillie Knight, Mme Christina Samuelson, le jardinier James Grant, ni les Hobson, avec lesquels Maybrick avait dîné aux courses de Wirral.

L'affaire Maybrick devait être la dernière jugée par Stephen. Deux ans plus tard, il serait interné dans un asile d'aliénés privé à Ipswich. Il y est mort en 1894.

Outre son rôle dans le procès de Florie, il a été lié d'une autre manière à l'affaire de l'Éventreur : son fils, J.K. Stephen, était le précepteur et le compagnon du prince Albert, duc de Clarence, lui-même suspecté d'être responsable des crimes commis à Londres.

On érigeait l'échafaud pour la pendre quand Florie Maybrick a bénéficié d'une grâce accordée par le ministre de l'Intérieur, Henry Matthews, qui avait travaillé si dur et avec si peu de succès un an plus tôt dans l'espoir de résoudre le mystère des meurtres de Whitechapel.

Chapitre 14

En 1891, Scotland Yard a déclaré classée l'affaire Jack l'Éventreur. Depuis le meurtre de Mary Jane Kelly, trois ans auparavant, la police avait déployé des effectifs importants dans le quartier de Whitechapel. Ainsi, pendant cette période, l'inspecteur Abberline et son équipe avaient amassé quelque mille six cents documents relatifs à cette affaire.

De temps en temps, certains d'entre eux sont examinés avec une attention particulière et alors les experts élaborent de nouvelles théories.

Quand Mike Barrett est entré dans le bureau de Doreen Montgomery avec le journal, en avril 1992, il était intimement convaincu que ce dernier contenait suffisamment de preuves pour incriminer le véritable tueur de Whitechapel. En tout cas, il s'agissait là de la confession la plus détaillée et la plus convaincante à ce jour. Mais était-elle authentique ?

En effectuant des recherches sur les Maybrick et sur l'Éventreur, c'est-à-dire sur deux des affaires criminelles britanniques les plus déconcertantes, je me suis rendu compte qu'il était très facile de multiplier les théories et de spéculer à l'infini. Pour cette raison, j'ai résisté à la tentation de me lancer dans un débat avec les spécialistes de l'Éventreur et j'ai concentré mon attention sur les faits historiques, sur le journal lui-même. J'ai demandé aux experts de faire de même, sans tenir compte des hypothèses émises par les innombrables livres et articles consacrés à ce sujet.

En étudiant les journaux de 1888 et de 1889, j'ai découvert qu'ils regorgeaient d'informations sur les meurtres de l'Éventreur et sur l'affaire Maybrick. Un faussaire aurait donc disposé d'une quantité impressionnante de documents sur ces deux affaires, à partir desquels fabriquer son journal. Pourtant, ce dernier ne contient aucune date, et ne mentionne presque rien de ce que l'on savait ou supposait à l'époque sur l'Éventreur ou sur Maybrick. Pourquoi un faussaire aurait-il résisté à la tentation de rendre son entreprise plus convaincante en tirant parti de toutes ces informations.

Il faut noter que certains détails mentionnés dans le journal n'ont jamais été révélés au grand public par voie de presse. Tout d'abord, quand le journal débute, probablement vers mars 1888, le futur amant de Florie, Alfred Brierley, connaît déjà Mme Maybrick. De fait, dans une déclaration écrite sous serment, Brierley a plus tard admis qu'il avait fait la connaissance de Florie en 1887. Ainsi, en mentionnant ce rival sans toutefois le nommer, Maybrick suggère une chronologie différente de celle présentée lors du procès, où plusieurs témoins ont déclaré que la liaison de Florie avec Brierley avait débuté aux alentours de Noël 1888.

En deuxième lieu, l'antipathie éprouvée par Maybrick à l'égard de Thomas Lowry, son employé, fait pour ainsi dire figure d'« intrigue secondaire ». En effet, en qualité de témoin, Lowry n'a fait qu'une brève apparition au procès de Florie. Il est donc fort improbable qu'un faussaire ait possédé des informations relatives à Lowry et qu'il ait été au courant de l'hostilité ressentie par le marchand de coton à l'égard de son commis.

En troisième lieu, les références fréquentes et spontanées à George Davidson, dans les bras duquel Maybrick s'est éteint, confirment bien qu'ils étaient amis intimes. Pourtant, Davidson n'a pas été appelé à la barre des témoins. Là encore, la nature de ses relations avec Maybrick n'était pas connue du public.

Enfin, une Mme Ham(m)ersmith apparaît au début du journal. Nous ne savons pas qui elle est, en dépit de la masse d'informations dont nous disposons sur les relations des Maybrick. Elle n'apparaît pas non plus dans le répertoire des rues de Liverpool établi en 1889. Alors pourquoi un faussaire l'aurait-il inventée ?

Par contre, plusieurs personnages essentiels ne sont pas mentionnés dans le journal. A commencer par Mme Briggs, jalouse de Florie et qui a imposé sa présence dans la maisonnée en affirmant sa domination sur Maybrick lui-même. Manque également la nurse trop bavarde, Alice Yapp : Maybrick avait causé un petit scandale en l'engageant. Enfin, pourquoi n'est-il pas fait état de la belle-mère de Maybrick, la baronne von Roques, ce personnage si présent dans la vie du couple Maybrick ?

Par ailleurs, le journal ne rend pas compte des meurtres de Martha Tabram et d'Emma Smith. Les autorités de l'époque les avaient en effet attribués à l'Éventreur, et cette hypothèse n'a été écartée que dans les années 1950.

Pourquoi le faussaire aurait-il pris le risque de jeter un voile de doute sur l'authenticité du journal en mettant à l'actif de l'Éventreur trois meurtres au sujet desquels il n'existe aucune preuve ? Deux d'entre eux ont été commis à Manchester – début 1888 et en décembre – et le troisième à Whitechapel en janvier 1889. Seul le journal les mentionne.

De même, la lettre « M » a été laissée sur le lieu d'un crime de l'Éventreur en trois occasions. Elle apparaissait sur un fragment d'enveloppe abandonné à côté du corps de la deuxième victime, Annie Chapman. Elle avait été inscrite sur chacune des joues de la quatrième victime, Catharine Eddowes – un fait que Mike Barrett a été le premier à remarquer. Enfin, elle avait été gribouillée, peut-être à l'aide de sang, sur le mur de la chambre de Mary Jane Kelly, la dernière des cinq victimes que tout le monde s'accorde à attribuer à l'Éventreur. Plus troublant encore, dans ce dernier cas, la lettre « F » figurait à côté du « M ». Or, Maybrick parle dans son journal d'« une initiale ici et [d'] une initiale là ». Si l'on estime que le « M » signifie Maybrick, il est raisonnable d'en déduire que « F » et « M » sont les initiales de sa femme.

L'expertise légale du journal a été menée par le Dr Nicholas Eastaugh, qui a assorti son rapport de la mise en garde suivante : « Dans le cas célèbre des " carnets d'Hitler ", ce sont les matériaux mêmes dont les documents étaient faits – le papier et l'encre – qui ont permis de révéler le faux. Aussi, quand un document d'une importance potentielle aussi grande que le journal de " Jack l'Éventreur " est soudain mis au jour, une grande prudence s'impose et la première des précautions consiste à examiner la composition physique du document en question à l'aide d'expériences pratiquées par les experts légaux.

« Il n'existe encore aucune expérience qui puisse déterminer clairement, précisément et sans ambiguïté l'âge de documents écrits tels que le journal. La seule technique de datation qui aurait pu être utilisée de façon concevable sur le journal – à savoir la datation du papier au radiocarbone – n'est pas applicable du fait de sa précision plus adaptée à l'étude des documents postérieurs à l'an 1500. Certaines évaluations approximatives de l'âge de l'encre sont possibles, mais seulement dans le but de déterminer si des pages ont été ajoutées ou interverties, ce qui ne présente que peu d'intérêt dans le cas présent.

« En outre, même si nous pouvions déterminer avec efficacité l'âge de l'encre et du papier, ce serait insuffisant pour " authentifier " le document car nous ne saurions toujours pas à quel moment cette encre et ce papier ont été combinés. En fait, ce sont précisément des documents tels que le journal qui mettent en lumière le fait que les scientifiques et les historiens ne sont pas en mesure de les dater avec précision. On peut cependant se fonder sur la composition des divers éléments constitutifs du document, la période durant laquelle ces derniers étaient accessibles, et la fréquence de leur utilisation. On peut également parvenir à certaines déductions d'ordre général à partir de l'apparence du document (par exemple, nous pourrions avoir des soupçons si l'écriture recouvrait des endroits du papier à l'évidence récemment endommagés). Cette situation n'est pas rare et il se trouve simplement que l'examen de documents historiques est un domaine encore nouveau, qui a été relativement peu étudié.

« Pour “ dater ” l'encre et le papier, nous devons comparer leurs éléments constitutifs à ce que nous savons de la composition de l'encre et du papier durant les cent dernières années. Par exemple plusieurs types de teintures colorées utilisées dans les encres n'ont été inventées qu'après le décès de Jack l'Éventreur, et si l'encre contenait l'une d'entre elles, nous saurions qu'il s'agit d'un faux. En pratique (et pour simplifier), cela signifie que nous devons effectuer une série de tests de plus en plus détaillés pour rechercher les défauts. Plus le document subit de tests avec succès, plus il est probable que nous avons affaire soit à un faux très sophistiqué, soit à l'authentique. Voici comment pourrait s'établir la chronologie de nos recherches :

« Historiquement, un changement essentiel a eu lieu dans le domaine des encres depuis le XIXe siècle et l'apparition des becs de plumes en acier. Vers le début des années 1830, ces plumes étaient fabriquées industriellement en grande quantité. Mais on a découvert que les encres acides traditionnelles à base de fer et de noix de galle les corrodaient rapidement. En conséquence, de nouvelles encres ont dû être élaborées. A cette époque (1834), on voit donc des compagnies telles que Stephens construire de nouvelles usines pour produire des encres à base de teintures, de fer et de noix de galle soigneusement contrôlées. Ces nouvelles encres n'attaquent pas l'acier. Mais les innovations n'allaient pas s'arrêter là ; les besoins spécifiques des stylos à plume (et) l'apparition de teintures synthétiques durant la seconde moitié du siècle ont conduit à l'élaboration d'encres, qui n'ont pas subi de modifications notables jusqu'à ce jour.

« Avant que les teintures synthétiques soient découvertes, diverses teintures naturelles telles que l'indigo, la teinture de garance et l'extrait de campêche étaient utilisées. Dans la seconde moitié du XIXe siècle, des teintures synthétiques telles que la nigrosine (brevetée en 1867) ont été de plus en plus largement employées. Ensuite, d'autres matières tinctoriales synthétiques y ont été substituées par économie; ou parce qu'elles étaient plus appropriées. Il est aussi intéressant de noter que les stylos billes et les feutres, si répandus aujourd'hui, sont des inventions du XXe siècle qui ont elles aussi conduit à l'élaboration de nouveaux types d'encres.

« Il existe en fait deux types d'encre pour stylo du XIXe siècle. La première est issue des anciennes compositions à base de fer et de noix de galle, alors que la seconde contient surtout des teintures (de type synthétique) qui se dissolvent dans l'eau. La composante principale des encres du premier type est incolore jusqu'à ce qu'elle s'oxyde pour laisser de façon permanente une couleur noire sur le papier; c'est pourquoi on y ajoute en général une teinture pour lui donner une couleur immédiate. Il s'agit là des encres bleu-noir, et leur composition n'a pratiquement pas changé, à part quelques variations de détail. Quant aux encres à base de teintures synthétiques, elles possèdent une couleur vive et produisent une écriture agréable à l'œil. Toutefois, elles ont tendance à passer et sont sensibles à l'eau. Certaines versions récentes de ce type d'encre contiennent des pigments modernes stables (tels que les composés d'acide phtalique et de cyan) pour ajouter un degré de permanence.

« Il a été procédé à l'analyse de l'encre du journal selon les méthodes d'examen légal conventionnelles, bien que pour diverses raisons pratiques nous ayons choisi certaines formes d'analyse plutôt que d'autres. L'encre est de type bleu-noir permanent, et aurait pu être utilisée depuis l'époque victorienne jusqu'à nos jours.

« Pour obtenir une “ empreinte digitale ” de cette encre, nous avons cherché à savoir quels éléments nous pourrions détecter à l'aide d'un microscope électronique à balayage – équipé de façon à permettre une spectrométrie de fluorescence X – et d'un instrument appelé microsonde à protons. Ces deux machines sont capables de mesurer la présence d'une large variété d'éléments chimiques : le premier système peut donner des mesures à 0,5 pour cent près, et la microsonde à protons à quelques particules près par millions. En évaluant à l'aide de ces instruments quels éléments sont présents et en quelle quantité, nous pouvons alors déterminer un profil caractéristique pour l'encre du journal et la comparer aux références en notre possession.

« Pour les besoins de notre propre recherche, nous avons étudié un certain nombre d'encres modernes “ bleu-noir permanentes ” telles que celles de marques Quink, Stephens et Waterman, ainsi que des échantillons d'écrit datant de la fin du XIXe siècle. Les résultats des analyses par spectrométrie ont montré qu'il existait des similitudes importantes et des différences mineures. Exemple de différence, nous avons trouvé que la Quink contient relativement peu de fer, alors que celle du journal en contient une quantité significative.

« Les résultats préliminaires de l'analyse par microsonde à protons correspondaient à ceux de l'analyse par spectrométrie et dans certains cas les ont affinés. Toutefois, si l'on veut disposer des données nécessaires pour une interprétation précise, il est essentiel d'examiner un nombre d'échantillons beaucoup plus grand à l'aide de cette technique.

« Pour compléter l'analyse de la composition des encres, une étude des teintures a été effectuée, qui nous a permis d'en apprendre davantage sur les colorants utilisés. La méthode que nous avons employée est connue sous le nom de chromatographie. Elle est fondée sur le fait que les différents composés contenus dans les teintures ne se comportent pas tous de la même façon chimiquement. En pratique, la chromatographie consiste à séparer les teintures de façon qu'elles produisent des motifs caractéristiques sur un papier buvard renforcé de solvants organiques; les motifs obtenus peuvent être comparés à ceux de teintures connues et on peut ainsi procéder à une indentification. L'utilisation de cette technique nous a permis de découvrir des différences très nettes entre les encres modernes examinées et celle du journal.

« Néanmoins, aucun composant n'a jusqu'ici été détecté qui exclue l'époque victorienne.

« Tout comme dans le cas de l'encre, des changements sont intervenus dans la fabrication du papier. Le papier est fait de fibres traitées de façon à se fendre et à s'effilocher. Ces fibres peuvent ensuite être " feutrées " pour former des feuilles auxquelles on ajoute d'autres matériaux afin d'obtenir différentes qualités de papier. L'analyse des fibres du papier du journal a révélé la présence de fibres de coton et de pâte de bois, utilisées à la fin de l'ère victorienne. Aucune fibre moderne ni aucun agent éclaircissant fluorescent n'ont été détectés.

« En résumé, les résultats des diverses analyses de l'encre et du papier réalisées jusqu'ici ne sont pas en contradiction avec l'époque victorienne. Si le journal est une contrefaçon moderne, il a subi avec succès toute une série de tests qui auraient révélé la présence de nombreux éléments entrant aujourd'hui dans la fabrication de l'encre et du papier.

Le Dr Eastaugh a conclu son rapport par ces mots : « Ma réponse professionnelle est entièrement neutre. Je ne peux pas préjuger de l'authenticité du document et de ce qu'il prétend ou ne prétend pas être autrement qu'en lui assignant une date hypothétique. Le fait qu'il émane ou non de Jack l'Éventreur n'entre pas en ligne de compte dans l'analyse de l'encre et du papier. Ce projet soulève cependant un certain nombre de questions importantes et met en lumière le fait que l'analyse de documents historiques est un domaine où il reste beaucoup de travail à effectuer. »

Selon le Dr Eastaugh, il est possible que la poudre noire découverte dans les petits fonds du journal soit du charbon animal purifié. Si l'on en croit le *Squires Companion to the British Pharmacopeia* (1886), cette substance « a la propriété de neutraliser les effets toxiques de la morphine, de la strychnine et de l'aconit [...]. Ces alcaloïdes peuvent être avalés en toute impunité s'ils sont mélangés en proportion suffisante avec du charbon animal purifié ».

Or, nous savons que Maybrick était dépendant de l'arsenic et de la strychnine. Il a donc pu employer le charbon animal trouvé dans le journal pour contrebalancer les effets néfastes de la drogue.

J'ai également interrogé une équipe de médecins spécialisés dans les symptômes de la toxicomanie. Les médecins du *Poisons Unit* de Guy's Hospital et ceux de l'*Alcool and Addiction Unit* de Maudsley Hospital m'ont appris que le journal révélait une maîtrise de la psychopathologie et de la physiologie du consommateur d'arsenic qui aurait été bien difficile à obtenir à l'époque, étant donné le manque de documentation disponible. Par ailleurs, un faussaire aurait été bien en peine d'assimiler les connaissances nécessaires à la fabrication d'une telle personnalité. A moins, bien sûr, que l'auteur n'ait lui-même fait l'expérience de cette drogue.

L'arsenic, si l'on en consomme pendant plusieurs années, conduit à une accumulation de pyruvate dans le sang. Cette substance est importante pour le métabolisme des coenzymes-A, composante essentielle des glucides. En cas d'empoisonnement aigu par arsenic, on note l'apparition des symptômes gastro-intestinaux dont Maybrick souffrait. Au siècle dernier, on pensait que ces difficultés gastriques signalaient l'empoisonnement chronique. Aujourd'hui, cependant, on reconnaît que ce sont surtout les symptômes neurologiques qui permettent d'établir un diagnostic.

A cet égard, on pensait à tort, à la fin de l'ère victorienne, que la consommation chronique d'arsenic pendant vingt ou trente ans pouvait entraîner la paralysie. L'auteur du journal révèle cette crainte.

Le Dr David Forshaw, en sa qualité de consultant à l'*Alcool and Addiction Unit* du Maudsley Hospital, a observé dans son rapport écrit que Maybrick aimait l'alcool et utilisait également de l'arsenic. Or, ces deux substances peuvent produire un désordre chronique des nerfs situés dans les membres, ainsi que des problèmes gastrointestinaux. Il explique : « Si la thyroïde, cette glande située dans le cou qui aide à réguler le niveau général d'activité métabolique dans le corps, n'est pas assez active, cela peut engendrer un désordre qui se manifeste par des symptômes similaires à ceux décrits par l'auteur du journal : fatigue, léthargie, intolérance du froid, muscles douloureux. Surdité et hallucinations peuvent survenir [...], le visage paraît sans expression, large et bouffi, la mémoire est mauvaise et il arrive que le patient soit déprimé. La présence de cette maladie, connue sous le nom d'hypothyroïde, peut seulement être confirmée par une analyse de sang, pratique qui n'existait pas à l'époque de Maybrick. »

Pour examiner l'écriture et la comparer à d'autres documents attribués à Maybrick et à l'Éventreur, j'ai fait appel à deux spécialistes de l'examen légal de documents, Sue Ironmonger et Anna Koren. Cette dernière est aussi graphologue.

Formée à Chicago et au Royaume-Uni, Sue Ironmonger appartient à l'Association mondiale des experts en matière d'examen de documents. C'est également une psychothérapeute spécialisée dans la personnalité des psychopathes. En 1993, elle a présenté à l'Association dont elle est membre un document consacré aux lettres de Jack l'Éventreur.

Sue est enfin experte en matière de chèques frauduleux, de comparaison de signatures et d'identification de messages anonymes. « L'écriture est tout autant révélatrice que les empreintes digitales, explique-t-elle. Il importe peu que la personne soit jeune ou vieille, ou qu'un droitier se soit mis à écrire de la main gauche après un accident. Le style donne l'impression d'avoir changé, mais en fait les composantes de l'écriture de chaque individu demeurent intactes. »

Anna Koren est directrice du Centre de graphologie – qui possède des locaux à Haïfa, à Tel Aviv, à Londres et à Sydney. Elle est membre de l'Association américaine des graphologues et experte légale en matière d'examen de documents pour le ministère de la Justice et les services de Sécurité sociale israéliens.

Les deux expertes ont été confrontées d'emblée à une grande difficulté : excepté une signature sur le certificat de mariage de Maybrick et sur le testament suspect, elles ne disposaient pas d'échantillons de l'écriture de James Maybrick avec lesquels comparer le journal. En effet, aucun autre n'avait pu être retrouvé !

A l'aide d'un appareil photo et d'un microscope, Sue a examiné le journal en étudiant la forme de chaque lettre. Pour sa part, Anna a étudié le profil psychologique révélé par le journal et a étudié la masse impressionnante de microfilms et de documents conservés au Public Record Office de Kew, à Londres. Elle a fouillé dans les archives de la police et du ministère de l'Intérieur, en quête d'un document qui permettrait d'établir une correspondance entre l'écriture de Jack l'Éventreur et celle du journal.

Elle nous a ensuite fourni un rapport détaillé sur la personnalité de l'auteur du journal, telle qu'elle l'avait comprise à partir de son écriture. Voici des extraits de ce rapport :

« Le journal révèle une personnalité instable. Des conflits intérieurs, un manque d'adaptabilité sociale et une tendance à la schizophrénie caractérisent l'écriture.

« Un sentiment d'infériorité, un refoulement émotionnel et un manque de confiance en soi peuvent lui faire perdre la maîtrise de lui-même à tout moment.

« Des tendances au despotisme, à l'irascibilité et la brutalité sont clairement discernables. Il est affecté par des instincts inconscients et l'agressivité accompagne constamment ses ambitions.

« Il souffre de changements d'humeur extrêmes, qui résultent d'un conflit entre son ambition élevée et son défaut d'amour-propre.

« Une tendance à l'hypcondrie ainsi que la consommation de drogue ou d'alcool sont évidentes.

« Toute activité impulsive est menée en secret, et il donne libre cours à l'esprit de vengeance et à l'agressivité qu'il a héritées de son combat contre une figure hostile et autoritaire dans son enfance.

« Une affection psychotique le rend incapable de distinguer entre le bien et le mal, l'interdit et le permissible, et peut le conduire à une activité criminelle.

« Son comportement est exceptionnellement bizarre. Son mode de pensée troublé le conduit à entretenir des idées étranges, des soupçons paranoïaques et des croyances magiques. Son mode de pensée est circulaire, embrouillé, stéréotypé et métaphorique. Selon toute probabilité, on peut qualifier sa maladie de chronique et persistante, avec une tendance à l'aggravation.

« Il fait montre d'un désordre de l'identité. Confus quant à son identité sexuelle, il a une image déformée de sa masculinité, et on note une absence de système de valeurs stable. On relève des faiblesses très nettes dans le sur-moi, ainsi qu'une incapacité de persévérer dans les domaines qui impliquent le choix d'une carrière, la fixation de cibles à long terme, la consolidation d'une amitié, la loyauté.

« Derrière les sautes d'humeur violentes se cache un sentiment profond de solitude, de vide et d'insécurité, qui conduisent à la dépression et à un repli partiel du sujet, qui évite le contact avec la réalité. On note une tendance à l'égocentrisme, à la vanité, à l'exhibitionnisme, aux enfantillages, à la dramatisation, ainsi qu'une recherche constante de l'attention et un manque de considération pour les autres, cette dernière étant sacrifiée au profit des intérêts propres du sujet.

« Sa perception de la sexualité et de l'union est déformée à un point tel qu'apparaît une tendance au sadisme. Son manque de confiance en les autres et le sentiment paranoïaque d'être tourmenté sont apparents. Il est incapable d'avoir des relations d'égal à égal avec autrui.

« Il souffre de désordres psychologiques qui produisent un comportement illogique, obsessif, destructif et agressif. »

Sue Ironmonger ne voit pas de correspondance entre l'écriture du journal et celle de la lettre adressée au « Cher Patron » ou du « testament » de Maybrick. « Si nous comparons la majuscule " I " dans le journal et dans la lettre adressée au " Cher Patron ", on note que la forme de ce " I " évoque celle d'un " g " minuscule. Dans la lettre au " Cher Patron ", elle comporte une boucle initiale étroite qui démarre approximativement à mi-chemin de la hampe. Dans la lettre, la queue se termine par un gros point alors que dans le journal, elle a la forme d'une petite boucle circulaire. En outre, la ponctuation des deux documents est totalement différente et, d'une manière générale, ces différences l'emportent nettement sur toute similitude de détail. Deux de ces similitudes sont la marge de gauche et le poids (l'épaisseur du trait) de certaines lettres. »

Sue pense que l'écriture d'un individu contient toujours des caractéristiques inconscientes qui peuvent être identifiées par un expert. Anna Koren n'est pas de cet avis. Pour nous montrer qu'une seule et même personne peut écrire dans plusieurs styles très différents, elle nous a adressé des échantillons de l'écriture de schizophrènes, mais aussi de l'écriture d'une femme affectée d'un désordre multiple de la personnalité. Selon Anna, l'analyse par un expert de styles si divergents ne peut pas nécessairement permettre de les identifier comme issus d'une seule et même main. Les variations entre les échantillons d'écriture de cette femme, qui possède plus de quatre-vingt-dix personnalités, apparaissent nettement : on distingue jusqu'à seize écritures distinctes.

Le Dr Forshaw souligne quant à lui que le style d'écriture d'une personne tout au long d'un journal rédigé sans contrainte sera très distinct de celui qu'emploiera le même individu pour une correspondance officielle ou un court message dans lequel il désire déguiser son identité. Un auteur de crimes en série aussi intelligent que Maybrick se serait donné beaucoup de mal pour préserver son anonymat dans les lettres qu'il aurait rédigées en vue d'une publication ou qu'il aurait adressées à la police.

Si l'on en vient maintenant au vocabulaire lui-même, on constate que le journal contient trois expressions qui semblent plus modernes que victoriennes. Cependant, mes recherches dans les dictionnaires ont révélé que les expressions « *topped* » et « *gathering momentum* [1] » étaient utilisées avant la fin de l'ère victorienne.

Mais l'expression « *one off* [2] » nécessitait des recherches plus approfondies. Selon l'*Oxford English Dictionary*, elle aurait été utilisée pour la première fois en 1934. En Amérique, le *Webster's Dictionary* fait remonter la première attestation à 1925.

J'ai donc sollicité l'aide de John Simpson, l'un des éditeurs de l'*Oxford English Dictionary*, qui m'a adressé la réponse suivante : « *L'Oxford English Dictionary* s'efforce de donner des indications relatives à l'histoire et à l'évolution du vocabulaire de l'anglais depuis le début du Moyen

1. *To top oneself* : se suicider; *To gather momentum* : prendre de la vitesse (*N.d.T.*)
2. *One off* : unique, exceptionnel. (*N.d.T.*

Age jusqu'à nos jours. Son analyse repose sur la lecture d'une palette de textes aussi vaste que possible, desquels sont extraits des exemples d'usage de la langue que nous intégrons ensuite à nos dossiers de citations. La première attestation d'un mot représente le premier emploi trouvé dans les ouvrages auxquels les éditeurs du Dictionnaire avaient accès au moment où ils ont rédigé un article donné.

« J'espère que le Dictionnaire représente un guide utile quant à l'apparition dans la langue de termes donnés, mais des attestations antérieures (qui précèdent parfois de beaucoup la date que nous fournissons) sont continuellement portées à notre attention. La langue est parlée avant d'être écrite, et dans certains domaines (comme l'argot dialectal et l'artisanat local), il peut s'écouler bien des années entre le moment où le terme est employé pour la première fois et son apparition sur le papier.

« Dans le cas de " *one off* " je serais surpris, mais pas sidéré, s'il s'avérait que la première apparition de ce terme avait précédé d'un demi-siècle la première attestation enregistrée par le Dictionnaire. Si l'on obtenait confirmation de cette hypothèse, je présume que les recherches à venir dans le domaine de la littérature technique révéleraient des exemples de son utilisation. »

J'ai également parlé à Mark Agnes, membre de l'équipe éditoriale du *Webster's New World Dictionnary*, qui s'est déclaré du même avis que John Simpson. « Même aujourd'hui, il existe des expressions que nous connaissons et utilisons tous, mais qu'on ne peut trouver dans aucun dictionnaire. Il peut s'écouler très longtemps, surtout dans les domaines techniques, avant que la tradition orale ne soit perpétuée par l'écrit. »

J'ai moi-même découvert des utilisations orales de cette expression à la fin de l'ère victorienne, qui n'apparaissent pas dans les dictionnaires. Au XIXe siècle, il était employé dans les prisons : on écrivait en effet à la craie sur des ardoises les noms des prisonniers de corvée ou de repos (« *one-on* » ou « *one-off duty* »). Un « *one-off* » était également un type de brique décorative utilisée dans les canaux victoriens. Et en construction mécanique (voire peut-être dans d'autres domaines), ce terme désignait un exemple unique ou un prototype.

C'est précisément dans ce sens que l'emploie Maybrick dans son journal.

Chapitre 15

James Maybrick était un hôte très cordial, affectueux avec les enfants et toujours prêt à plaisanter. Il se souciait beaucoup de son apparence et avait à cœur d'améliorer sa position sociale. D'après William Stead, « ses amis disaient de James Maybrick que c'était un homme très bien ».

Comment a-t-il donc pu se transformer en drogué doublé d'un assassin, et terroriser toute l'Angleterre ?

Le Dr David Forshaw s'intéresse de très près à la psychologie des auteurs de crimes en série. Sa curiosité a donc été éveillée quand je lui ai révélé la découverte du journal. Il a offert de l'étudier et de me remettre un rapport sur l'état d'esprit de son auteur.

Forshaw s'est fixé deux objectifs :

1) Expliquer les processus pathologiques de la vie psychique des auteurs de crimes en série ;

2) Déterminer dans quelle mesure ces processus affectaient le profil psychique de l'auteur du journal.

« Dans son journal, explique David Forshaw, Jack l'Éventreur rend compte de ses pensées et de ses sentiments. Pour être plus précis, il exprime et analyse le trouble émotionnel et intellectuel qu'il éprouve ; le journal fait donc partie intégrante de son profil psychopathologique.

« Bien sûr, les meurtres de Whitechapel ne sont pas les premiers crimes en série qui aient jamais été perpétrés. De tels crimes ont eu lieu de toute éternité. Certains exemples remontent à l'Antiquité. Dans leur livre intitulé *Perverse Crimes in History* (Les Crimes pervers dans l'Histoire), Masters et Lea décrivent la vague d'éventrations et d'assassinats au poignard qui a atteint son point culminant dans les années 1880 et 1890. Jack l'Éventreur, pour monstrueux qu'il fût, n'était pas un cas isolé. Et s'il ne s'était pas affublé d'un surnom si bien choisi, il n'aurait sans doute pas accédé à la célébrité.

« Souvent, les auteurs de crimes en série, comme James Maybrick, donnent l'impression d'être des hommes tranquilles – des hommes qui ont une famille, qui vont travailler chaque jour et s'occupent du jardin pendant le week-end. »

David Forshaw cite l'exemple d'Andrei Chikatilo, qui vivait dans la ville minière de Shakty, dans l'ex-Union soviétique. C'était un homme de quarante-deux ans, membre du parti communiste, qui avait une femme, deux enfants et travaillait comme professeur dans une école pour mineurs. Mais un jour de 1978, il a entraîné une enfant de neuf ans, Lena Zakotnova, dans une cabane délabrée aux abords de la ville. Là, il l'a étranglée avant de la poignarder et de lacérer son corps. Il en a tiré un plaisir immense et a découvert qu'il avait le goût du sang. Désormais, il ne pourrait plus s'arrêter. C'est ainsi que, sur une période d'une douzaine d'années, il a massacré cinquante-trois enfants, arrachant leurs entrailles de ses propres mains. Tout comme Maybrick, il laissait sur le lieu de ses crimes des indices moqueurs pour narguer la police.

On a dit de Chikatilo qu'il n'avait jamais levé la main sur ses propres enfants. En outre, il avait gravi les échelons sociaux, depuis ses origines paysannes jusqu'à l'intelligentsia. Mais il aurait voulu être un soldat courageux et un amant romantique. Il aspirait à un respect qui aurait commandé aux écoliers de se lever quand il entrait en classe. Et selon lui, le vrai Chikatilo n'était pas à la hauteur ; il avait échoué dans la vie.

Lorsqu'il a enfin été capturé en 1991, voici ce qu'il a écrit à sa femme : « Pourquoi Dieu m'a-t-il envoyé sur cette Terre ? Moi, une personne si affectueuse, si tendre et si prévenante, mais si totalement sans défense contre ma propre faiblesse. »

Les mots de Chikatilo reflètent ce sentiment d'inadaptation socio-affective présent dans le journal de Maybrick. Ils évoquent aussi l'image d'un homme qui peut à la fois se montrer doux et d'une violence extrême.

> Le gentleman aux gentilles pensées va bientôt frapper de nouveau.

Forshaw a également établi une comparaison avec Peter Krten, le meurtrier de Düsseldorf pendu en 1937 pour avoir massacré neuf personnes et tenté d'en tuer sept autres. Le fait de se livrer à ses activités criminelles ne l'a jamais empêché de vivre avec sa femme ni de dormir chaque nuit à son côté. Il en va de même avec Peter Sutcliffe, l' « Éventreur du Yorkshire ». Sa mission, à l'instar de Maybrick, consistait de son propre aveu à « débarrasser les rues des prostituées ». Sur une période de cinq ans, il a tué treize femmes et tenté d'en assassiner sept autres.

Tout comme Andrei Chikatilo, Peter Krten et Peter Sutcliffe, Maybrick était un monsieur Tout-le-Monde, voisin ordinaire et quelconque.

A bien d'autres égards, il présentait les caractéristiques des auteurs de crimes en série. « Ces individus, explique Forshaw, sont presque toujours des hommes, souvent sujets à des obsessions, et hypocondriaques.

« Ils ont en général des manières douces et trahissent rarement leur agressivité, bien qu'une colère sourde les ronge intérieurement. Ils mènent des vies fantasmatiques très riches, qu'ils trouvent préférables à la réalité. Ils rêvent d'occuper une position de pouvoir et sont préoccupés par leur masculinité et leur puissance sexuelle. »

En 1965, Revitch a étudié plusieurs rapports consacrés à des attaques perpétrées sans provocation par des hommes contre des femmes. Il a classé les agresseurs en deux catégories, selon qu'ils étaient âgés de plus ou moins de dix-huit ans, et il a découvert que l'hostilité dirigée contre les femmes était davantage le fait des hommes plus âgés. Chez les jeunes gens, la préoccupation majeure était plutôt le comportement sexuel. Plus l'attaquant était âgé, plus le motif principal de l'agression reflétait la colère ou la haine.

« La nature répugnante des meurtres commis par l'Éventreur appelle la conclusion suivante, explique David Forshaw : ils reflétaient une profonde hostilité plutôt qu'un besoin de satisfaction sexuelle. Il ne s'agissait probablement donc pas d'un homme jeune. »

Maybrick avait célébré son cinquantième anniversaire le 24 octobre – peu de temps avant le meurtre de Mary Jane Kelly.

« La présence de sperme n'est pas mentionnée dans les rapports d'autopsie, aussi ignore-t-on si l'assaillant avait eu des rapports sexuels avec sa victime, ou s'il s'était masturbé sur le lieu du crime, poursuit le Dr Forshaw. Cela paraît improbable, étant donné que ses crimes semblent avoir été motivés par la haine, et non par le sexe. De toute façon, d'après ce que l'on sait, le tueur ne disposait pas du temps suffisant pour se livrer à ce genre d'activité. Il se peut donc que l'Éventreur ait sélectionné ses victimes parce qu'elles représentaient à ses yeux des antisymboles sexuels, choix qui écartait la tentation potentielle du rapport physique. Mais il se peut tout aussi bien que leur dépravation même ait séduit cet homme pervers. »

Il ne fait aucun doute que les cibles choisies par l'Éventreur – les prostituées – présentaient plusieurs avantages pratiques. Puisqu'il n'existait aucun lien entre elles et leur client et qu'elles travaillaient dans des endroits isolés, elles constituaient des victimes faciles pour les agresseurs potentiels. En outre, un auteur de crimes en série qui vise les prostituées le fait souvent parce qu'il est persuadé de rendre service à la société.

> Je suis convaincu que Dieu m'a placé ici-bas pour tuer toutes les putains

Mais les victimes de Whitechapel étaient aussi l'incarnation d'un être précieux entre tous pour Maybrick : sa femme adultère. « Pour l'attaquant, qu'il en soit conscient ou non, les prostituées représentent les êtres aimés infidèles, donc méprisés. Ces derniers sont eux-mêmes relativement à l'abri d'une attaque », ajoute David Forshaw.

Selon toute probabilité, seul le fait de tuer, puis de sentir ou de voir sa victime mourir – ou de la mutiler – donnait satisfaction à l'Éventreur. Il n'en éprouvait aucune à la soumettre à des souffrances prolongées.

Mais Forshaw détecte un autre mobile : « David Berkowitz, le tueur surnommé " Fils de Sam ", qui a terrorisé New York pendant un an, au milieu des années 1970, a parlé du " désir de le faire, de tuer ", qui, a-t-il précisé, " atteignait en moi des proportions explosives et me causait un tel trouble que, lorsqu'il se libérait, on aurait dit un volcan en éruption et la pression retombait, tout du moins pendant un moment. " Le psychiatre américain David Abrahamsen, spécialiste de Jack l'Éventreur, affirme que le tueur de Whitechapel ressentait probablement la même tension intérieure. »

Voici ce qu'écrit Maybrick :

> J'ai besoin de plus d'excitation, ne peux pas vivre sans mes frissons. Je continuerai, je continuerai, rien ne m'arrêtera rien.

Maybrick avait une maîtresse, qu'il mentionne dans son journal comme « la mienne ». Il se tournait vers elle quand ses pensées meurtrières devenaient trop intenses.

Les yeux de la prochaine seront arrachés. Je les enfoncerai dans la bouche de la putain. Ça me donnera certainement du plaisir, j'en ai rien qu'à l'écrire. Ce soir je vais voir la mienne, elle sera contente parce que je serai gentil avec elle comme en vérité je le suis toujours.

Jack l'Éventreur, comme Maybrick, goûtait l'excitation de la poursuite. La perspective d'être capturé lui donnait le frisson, encore plus que le fait d'éventrer ses victimes.

Je crois que l'excitation d'être pris m'a excité encore plus que le fait de découper la putain elle-même.

« Les auteurs de crimes en série, dit Forshaw, se sentent généralement inférieurs aux autres, sauf quand ils pensent à leurs crimes ou en font le compte rendu écrit. C'est la raison pour laquelle l'Éventreur a rédigé son journal. » Il peut y exprimer en effet sa conception exagérée de sa propre importance, et se décerne les titres « Sir Jim » et « Sir Jack ». Le journal lui permet aussi de se réfugier dans des rêveries agréables, pour mieux chasser de sa conscience des idées et des sentiments pénibles.

Je vais me forcer à penser à quelque chose de plus agréable.

« Dans le journal, il utilise assez souvent cette méthode pour manipuler ses pensées, comme s'il plaçait un écran entre lui-même et le monde, explique Forshaw. Cela lui permet de demeurer en apparence calme et maître de lui-même. Mais il tient du même coup la réalité à distance. »

Maybrick avait aussi recours au sexe pour chasser la réalité de son esprit. Après son premier meurtre, voici ce qu'il écrit :

Je prendrai la garce ce soir. J'ai besoin d'oublier un moment les événements de la nuit.

Dès le début du journal, le fait de savoir sa femme en compagnie de son amant donne à Maybrick un plaisir morbide ou pervers.

L'idée du maquereau en train de la prendre commence à m'exciter.

Ces confessions suggèrent qu'il était stimulé sexuellement et tirait de l'écriture du journal une espèce de satisfaction sadomasochiste.

L'un des aspects les plus frappants du journal est l'évolution de l'écriture. A l'évidence, il est l'œuvre d'une seule personne, aussi la transformation d'une écriture scolaire en gribouillage frénétique reflète-t-elle la détérioration croissante de la santé mentale de l'auteur.

David Forshaw a sélectionné quelques échantillons d'écriture et les a examinés dans l'ordre chronologique. Voici ses conclusions : « Au début du journal, aucun meurtre n'a encore eu lieu et l'écriture est nette, régulière, contenue. Mais à mesure que progresse ce qu'il appelle sa " campagne " d'assassinats, les lettres deviennent plus grosses, l'écriture plus irrégulière, moins maîtrisée, et elle reflète une confiance en soi accrue. Elle est chargée de tout un substrat émotionnel. Puis, lorsque l'excitation atteint son comble, vers la fin du journal, l'écriture redevient soudain calme, maîtrisée. Ce revirement intervient juste après que Maybrick a rendu visite au Dr Fuller à Londres. »

Fuller croit que je n'ai pas vraiment de problème.
Étrange, les pensées qu'il a placées dans mon esprit.

De quelles pensées s'agissait-il, on l'ignore. Mais à partir de ce moment, Maybrick cherche à échapper à la torture morale qu'il endure et parle même de suicide.

En ce qui concerne le comportement cannibale de l'Éventreur, Forshaw donne également une explication : « Il se peut que Maybrick ait gardé certaines parties de ses cadavres en souvenir. La Hongroise Elizabeth Bathory, qui est morte en 1654 à l'âge de cinquante-quatre ans, avait l'habitude de se baigner dans le sang de ses victimes pour rester jeune et séduisante. Quant à Christie, qui a été pendu en 1953, il prélevait des poils pubiens sur ses victimes. L'Éventreur était peut-être persuadé qu'en mangeant un utérus il accéderait à l'éternelle jeunesse. »

Les exemples de semblable comportement ne manquent pas. Le criminel américain Ed Kemper, qui a sévi en 1972, collectionnait les organes internes, voire la tête de ses victimes, et il les conservait dans sa penderie. Dennis Mielsen, actif de 1978 à 1983, entreposait les restes de ses victimes démembrées dans des placards et sous le plancher des maisons qu'il possédait dans le nord de Londres.

Le Dr Forshaw conclut en ces termes : « Si l'on ne dispose que d'informations limitées quant au passé ou à la santé mentale d'un auteur de crimes en série, il est difficile de déterminer s'il tue par sadisme ou parce qu'il souffre d'une maladie mentale telle que la schizophrénie. »

Je comprends maintenant pourquoi Mike Barrett aime à se rendre au cimetière d'Anfield et pourquoi il lui arrive de passer un moment devant la grille de Battlecrease House. Je partage en effet la fascination que lui inspire le journal.

James Maybrick n'avait rien d'un vagabond démoniaque venu hanter les ruelles mal éclairées de l'East End. Non, c'était un homme bien habillé, de belle prestance, un bon père de famille. Certes, il avait son jardin secret et menait une double vie, dans la meilleure tradition victorienne! Mais comme le souligne David Forshaw, c'est précisément ce vernis de normalité et de moralité qui le rend encore aujourd'hui si effrayant. L'Éventreur, c'est monsieur Tout-le-Monde.

Et c'est la raison pour laquelle tant de personnes sensées ont ressenti la puissance étrange qu'exerce le journal sur ses lecteurs. Les experts qui nous ont offert leur compétence et leur sagesse ont eux-mêmes passé des nuits blanches à l'étudier. Et ce n'est pas l'argent qui les a motivés. En effet, durant les recherches, l'écriture et la production de ce livre, seule une rémunération modeste a été versée aux intéressés.

Quant aux spécialistes de Jack l'Éventreur, un temps sceptiques, voire cyniques, ils n'ont été en mesure d'avancer aucune preuve indiscutable qui permette de discréditer le journal. Ils admettent aujourd'hui être déroutés.

Le journal a démasqué le véritable James Maybrick – tout comme il l'avait prévu lui-même.

> Je place maintenant ceci dans un endroit où on le trouvera.

Mais le mythe de Jack l'Éventreur n'est en rien diminué par cette découverte, bien au contraire.

Chapitre 16

Même après sa mort, l'ombre maléfique de « James l'Éventreur » continuerait de planer sur sa famille. En particulier sur sa veuve.

Mais Florie Maybrick appartenait à la race des vivants. Elle a enduré sans fléchir les moments les plus difficiles de sa vie en prison – punition de cellule, travaux forcés et maladie. Elle n'avait pourtant aucun espoir de bénéficier d'une libération anticipée, en dépit des efforts déployés par ses nombreux défenseurs.

Sa mère venait de France lui rendre visite tous les deux mois, « parcourant cent soixante kilomètres pour trente minutes » passées avec sa fille. Voici ce que Florie raconterait plus tard : « Durant ces visites, elle me décrivait du mieux qu'elle pouvait les efforts nobles et infatigables de mes compatriotes au service de ma cause ; la compassion et le soutien manifestés par mon gouvernement ; les efforts déployés pour moi par divers ambassadeurs américains [...]. Le fait de savoir qu'ils croyaient en mon innocence et éprouvaient une telle compassion à mon égard me réconfortait, me remontait le moral et me donnait la force de parcourir avec courage cette route semée d'épines : ma vie quotidienne. »

Mais ces visites en prison, ces demi-heures volées un mois sur deux, affectaient la baronne von Roques. Comment s'en étonner ? « Avant même que nous n'ayons le temps de nous calmer, raconte Florie, la geôlière nous adressait un signe silencieux depuis sa chaise : les trente minutes avaient passé. " Au revoir ", disions-nous sans nous quitter des yeux, puis nous nous tournions le dos [...]. Personne ne saura jamais combien ma mère a pu souffrir. »

La baronne a dépensé une fortune pour essayer de réhabiliter Florie et d'obtenir une libération anticipée.

Lord Russell, l'avocat de Florie, a toujours exprimé la conviction que sa cliente était innocente, et il n'a jamais perdu confiance : un jour, elle serait libérée. Mais il est mort en 1900, avant que Florie ne voie sa prédiction se réaliser.

Pendant ses quinze années de prison, la campagne internationale menée pour son bénéfice, et dont l'objectif était de l'innocenter, n'a jamais faibli. Trois présidents américains ont déposé des demandes de grâce. Le cardinal Gibbons, le ministre des Affaires étrangères James G. Blaine et l'ambassadeur en Grande-Bretagne, Robert Lincoln, ont eux aussi plaidé pour Florie.

C'est seulement en 1904 qu'elle a retrouvé la liberté. Le 5 juillet, à l'âge de quarante-deux ans, elle a été libérée sur parole. Mais n'ayant pas bénéficié d'une grâce, elle n'a jamais réussi à se libérer de son passé.

« Un jour viendra où le monde reconnaîtra que le verdict rendu contre moi est absolument injustifié, a-t-elle écrit dans *My Fifteen Lost Years*. Mais qui me rendra les années que j'ai passées à l'intérieur d'une prison; les amis qui m'ont oubliée; les enfants aux yeux desquels je suis morte; les rayons du soleil; les vents du ciel; ma vie de femme, et tout ce que j'ai perdu à cause de cette terrible injustice ? »

Les appels interjetés à plusieurs reprises par Florie n'ont peut-être pas permis d'obtenir sa libération anticipée, mais ils ont contribué à l'établissement d'une Cour d'appel en 1907. Afin que les futurs prisonniers bénéficient d'un système judiciaire plus équitable. Comble d'ironie, Jack l'Éventreur était indirectement responsable de cette innovation, car c'est James Maybrick qui avait conduit Florie à sa perte.

A sa libération, Florie a passé quelque temps avec les religieuses de la Maison de l'Épiphanie, un couvent situé à Truro, en Cornouailles. Puis elle a rejoint sa mère en France avant de rentrer en Amérique sous un nom d'emprunt. Elle y a trouvé un nouveau monde, où l'électricité avait fait son apparition, mais victime de surpopulation et pollué par une industrialisation croissante. Le choc a été rude.

Florie désirait vivre en paix, mais le public voulait connaître son histoire. Comme elle avait besoin d'argent et désirait remercier ceux qui l'avaient soutenue sans relâche, elle a écrit un livre consacré à sa vie derrière les barreaux et a parcouru tout le pays en prônant la réforme du système judiciaire. Mais elle n'a jamais abordé les événements de 1888-1889, ceux qui avaient failli lui coûter la vie.

Au bout de deux ans, elle a dû abandonner la vie publique, car il lui était impossible d'échapper à la curiosité malsaine de ceux qui venaient l'écouter.

Après un long séjour chez sa fille, en 1910, la baronne est rentrée en France, où elle est morte quelques mois plus tard. Pendant neuf ans, jusqu'à sa mort, elle a lutté pour obtenir la réhabilitation de Florie.

Comme elle n'était pas parvenue à récupérer les terres familiales, Florie s'est vite retrouvée sans argent. Elle a travaillé pendant une courte période dans une maison d'édition, mais sa santé s'est détériorée. Elle est alors partie s'installer à Chicago, où l'Armée du Salut a pris soin d'elle. Ensuite, elle a disparu pendant trois ans. C'est en 1918 qu'elle a contacté son amie Cora Griffin, en quête d'un emploi. Mlle Griffin avait une amie à Gaylordsville, dans le Connecticut, qui cherchait une gouvernante. Florie a été engagée.

L'année suivante, elle a acquis un petit terrain à Gaylordsville, sur lequel elle a fait construire un cottage de trois pièces. Avant de partir pour le Connecticut, Florie avait décidé de reprendre son nom de jeune fille, Florence Elisabeth Chandler. Elle le conserverait jusqu'à la fin de ses jours.

Mme Maybrick avait cessé d'exister.

Mais tous les acteurs de cette tragédie n'ont pas eu cette chance. Pendant que Florie purgeait sa peine de prison, nombre de ceux qui avaient joué un rôle de premier plan dans sa vie ont cherché par tous les moyens à se débarrasser de la gangue du passé.

Dans la préface de son étude de l'affaire Maybrick, Alexander MacDougall s'est adressé en ces termes à Bobo et à Gladys : « Ce livre est dédié par l'auteur à James Chandler Maybrick, âgé de huit ans, et à Gladys Evelyn Maybrick, âgée de quatre ans, dans l'espoir sincère qu'il les aidera à comprendre que le mot " MÈRE " n'est pas " indigne d'être entendu ou prononcé " par eux ET [aussi dans l'espoir] que, lorsqu'ils seront en âge de comprendre ce compte rendu des faits [...] relatifs aux accusations portées contre Florence Elizabeth Maybrick, âgée de vingt-sept ans, et à son procès, les enfants de cette dernière pourront se consoler tout au long de leur vie en songeant qu'il n'a jamais été prouvé que leur mère était coupable du meurtre de leur père JAMES MAYBRICK. »

Ce souhait n'a pas été exaucé. Florie ne devait jamais revoir ses enfants.

James et Gladys sont allés vivre à Londres avec le Dr Fuller et son épouse, qui recevraient cent livres par an pour s'occuper d'eux.

Pendant quelques années, Thomas Maybrick a envoyé à Florie des photographies de ses enfants. Mais lorsque James a été suffisamment âgé pour qu'on lui raconte la tragédie familiale, il a mal réagi. Il a adopté le nom de Fuller et a ordonné à l'oncle Thomas de ne plus envoyer de photos à sa mère. Florie en a eu le cœur brisé; elle a eu le sentiment que ses enfants étaient morts.

« Les innocents – mes enfants –, un bébé de trois ans et un garçon de sept ans, je les avais laissés derrière moi, a-t-elle écrit dans son autobiographie. On leur avait appris à croire que leur mère était coupable, et qu'elle n'existait plus pour eux, tout comme leur père défunt. Ils ont grandi sous un autre nom. Je ne sais rien d'eux. Quand le pathétique de cette situation touchera le cœur du lecteur, il comprendra combien mon cas est tragique. »

En 1893, Michael Maybrick a décidé de tirer un trait sur le passé. Sa popularité avait décliné à la suite de l'affaire et il est donc allé s'installer sur l'île de Wight. C'est à ce moment-là qu'il a épousé, sans doute pour une question de bienséance, sa gouvernante de longue date, Laura Withers. Il ne s'agissait pas là d'un mariage d'amour. Tous deux n'avaient rien de commun et n'ont même jamais passé leurs vacances ensemble. Mais Laura éprouvait une certaine satisfaction à conduire une voiture de maître à son chiffre, et à donner aux commerçants locaux le plaisir d'avoir pour cliente l'épouse du maire.

Michael a persuadé son frère Edwin de mettre lui aussi un terme à sa vie de célibataire. En 1892, à l'âge de quarante et un ans, Edwin a donc épousé Amy Tyrer, dont il a eu une fille elle aussi prénommée Amy. Bien des années plus tard, Amy décrirait son père de cette façon : « Au fond, c'était un vrai célibataire. Tous ses amis étaient célibataires. Certains venaient d'Amérique, mais c'étaient tous des célibataires. Père les invitait à dîner, mais ils n'étaient jamais accompagnés de femmes. A Pâques, il allait se promener en auto avec ses amis, tous des hommes. Il me faisait sentir que j'étais une enfant non désirée. Il ne manifestait jamais aucune affection. Ce que j'ai pu recevoir comme gifles ! »

A ce moment-là, Gladys et James avaient quitté Londres pour venir vivre avec leur oncle sur l'île de Wight. Amy Maybrick venait parfois y passer l'été. Elle redoutait ces visites. « Tous les Maybrick étaient froids, très guindés. »

En 1911, James Fuller a fêté ses vingt-huit ans. Il travaillait comme ingénieur des mines en Colombie britannique. Il était fiancé à une jeune fille du cru, et en apparence libéré de la griffe du passé. Mais le 10 avril, alors qu'il travaillait seul dans son laboratoire, il a téléphoné à sa fiancée. C'est la dernière fois qu'elle devait lui parler. James a été retrouvé mort un peu plus tard dans son laboratoire. Il avait apparemment confondu un verre de cyanure avec un verre d'eau. On a conclu à une mort accidentelle.

Lorsque la nouvelle a été annoncée à Florie, cette dernière a répondu avec amertume : « Je n'ai pas de fils. Le passé est mort et enterré. A mes yeux, ce garçon est mort depuis plus de vingt ans. »

Pour sa part, Gladys Maybrick a épousé un officier de marine, le capitaine Frederick Corbyn, que sa famille a immédiatement déshérité parce qu'il avait épousé une Maybrick. Gladys et son mari ont choisi de ne pas avoir d'enfants. La honte attachée au passé était trop grande.

« Il n'y a pas de Maybrick, seulement des Fuller », a déclaré Gladys.

Les Corbyn se sont installés au pays de Galles, où personne, pas même ses amis et ses voisins les plus proches, n'a eu connaissance de la véritable identité de Gladys Corbyn jusqu'à sa mort, en 1971.

Plusieurs histoires circulent sur le compte d'Alfred Brierley. D'aucuns affirment qu'il a émigré en Afrique du Nord, d'autres qu'il est mort en Amérique du Sud. Des années après sa libération, Florie a accordé un entretien exclusif et douloureux au *Liverpool Post and Echo*, dans lequel elle a admis que le souvenir d'Alfred l'avait aidée à endurer la prison.

« J'ai été assez bête pour croire que je trouverais le bonheur avec l'homme qui m'offrait l'amour que mon mari me refusait [...]. Ma déception a été amère, très amère. L'homme auquel j'avais tout sacrifié m'avait oubliée, pendant que je m'efforçais de préserver pour lui la jeunesse de mon cœur. »

La vérité au sujet de Brierley ne rend que plus poignante la confession de Florie. L'ancien amant de

Mme Maybrick est bien allé en Amérique du Sud. Dans une lettre écrite à Charles Aunspaugh depuis le Venezuela, il commenterait avec regret : « Les femmes s'y entendent pour nous rendre la vie difficile et un joli minois peut conduire un homme en enfer, je vous le dis. »

De retour en Angleterre, Brierley s'est marié, a eu un fils, et s'est installé à Hove, tout à côté de Brighton. Il est enterré au cimetière de St. Mary, à Newick, un village des Downs. Voici ce qu'on peut lire sur sa tombe : « Et le semeur est sorti. » Mais la citation biblique qui lui sert d'épitaphe se poursuit ainsi : « ... et certaines graines n'ont rien donné. »

En mars 1893, George Davidson, le meilleur ami de Maybrick, a été retrouvé noyé à Silecroft, près de Whitehaven, en Cumbria. Un mois plus tôt, il était parti en promenade par un soir d'orage, et personne ne l'avait revu. Voici ce qu'on lisait dans un journal à propos de sa mort : « Il se plaignait de ne pas pouvoir dormir. Il lui arrivait souvent de se lever la nuit pour aller se promener. »

Comme dans le cas de James Fuller, on a conclu à une mort accidentelle. Mais on ne peut s'empêcher de se poser des questions : le fait d'avoir été associé au nom Maybrick était-il un fardeau trop lourd à porter ? Et George Davidson souffrait-il d'insomnie parce qu'il lui fallait vivre avec le secret terrible que lui avait révélé son meilleur ami juste avant de mourir ?

William, le cousin qui avait fourni sa drogue à James, est pour sa part décédé en octobre 1888, à l'hospice de Liverpool.

Edwin Maybrick est mort en 1927, sans argent. Et c'est aussi en 1927 que Sarah Ann Maybrick a succombé à la démence sénile au Tooting Bec Mental Hospital, dans le sud de Londres. C'est cette année-là, enfin, que Florie est revenue en Angleterre pour la dernière fois. Elle avait pris le bateau pour Liverpool et s'est rendue à Aintree afin d'assister au grand National. Elle s'est présentée au bureau d'Edwin, mais il était sorti et n'a pas cherché à la contacter. Amy, la fille d'Edwin, a rapporté le soulagement éprouvé par son père lorsqu'on lui a dit qu'il avait manqué de peu sa belle-sœur.

Florie a passé le restant de ses jours dans la petite ville du Connecticut où elle était allée travailler comme gouvernante. Elle n'a pas conservé cet emploi très longtemps, et lorsque le petit revenu qu'elle percevait régulièrement ne lui a plus suffi, elle a fini par trouver en elle la gentillesse dont elle n'avait pas su faire preuve auparavant. Aussi, ses voisins et les élèves de l'école de garçons toute proche ont-ils toujours veillé à ce qu'elle ne manque de rien.

Florie est peu à peu devenue une recluse, plutôt excentrique. Sur chaque côté de sa petite maison, elle avait ménagé une entrée pour les dizaines de chats qu'elle hébergeait. Et si elle avait parfois à peine de quoi se nourrir, elle veillait toujours à ce que ses compagnons ne manquent pas de lait.

La « Dame aux chats », comme on l'avait surnommée, est parvenue à terminer sa vie dans l'anonymat le plus complet. Personne ne savait qui elle était, bien qu'on pût deviner à son maintien qu'elle avait dû être une dame.

Et Florie n'a jamais rien dit à personne, tout du moins pas en paroles. Mais sur la robe de dentelle noire qu'elle avait offerte à sa voisine Genevieve Austin, elle avait laissé l'étiquette suivante : « Mme Florence E. Maybrick ». Par inadvertance ? Quoi qu'il en soit, Mme Austin a gardé le secret pendant près de vingt ans. C'est seulement à la mort de sa voisine qu'elle a alerté les journaux.

Florie a été retrouvée morte le 23 octobre 1941, à l'âge de soixante-dix-neuf ans. Bien qu'elle ait été libérée quelque quarante ans plus tôt, elle n'en a pas moins purgé une peine de prison à vie. En effet, pour échapper au scandale qui la poursuivait partout, il lui avait fallu se transformer en recluse, avec ses chats pour seuls compagnons. Mais à sa mort, le scandale a de nouveau éclaté. En effet, le décès de

Florence Elizabeth Chandler Maybrick a fait la une de bien des journaux – l'histoire de cette jeune femme accusée d'avoir assassiné son mari allait de nouveau faire recette.

Au début du mois de juillet 1881, deux semaines avant son mariage avec Florie, le College of Arms de Londres a octroyé des armoiries à James Maybrick. Il lui en avait coûté soixante-seize livres et dix shillings, l'équivalent de trois mille deux cents livres d'aujourd'hui. Ces armoiries représentent un épervier qui, en héraldique, symbolise le pouvoir. Il tient dans son bec un brin d'aubépine [1], référence au nom de Maybrick.

La devise inscrite sur ces armoiries est :

TEMPUS OMNIA REVELAT

Le temps révèle tout.

1. En anglais : *may*. (*N.d.T.*)

Post-scriptum

Aujourd'hui, un ancien professeur de l'université d'Oxford, Martin Fido, véritable encyclopédie vivante en ce qui concerne Jack l'Éventreur, guide des groupes de touristes dans les ruelles sombres et malodorantes de Whitechapel. Le nom de certaines rues et de certains pubs a changé. Mais la même atmosphère de violence règne toujours dans ce quartier désolé.

Buck's Row, où Polly Nichols a été assassinée, s'appelle maintenant Durward Street. Les résidents avaient en effet gagné leur bataille pour que soit effacé sur le plan de Londres le souvenir de cette nuit tragique. Mais personne n'y habite plus. Les maisons ont disparu.

Berner Street, où Elizabeth Stride a trouvé la mort, a elle aussi disparu de la carte. Enfin, pas tout à fait. La plaque de cette rue arbore l'inscription suivante, en grosses lettres rouges : « Henrique Street anciennement Berner Street ».

La chambre de Miller's Court où a succombé Mary Jane Kelly a disparu en 1929 lorsque le marché de Spitalfields a été agrandi.

De l'autre côté de Commercial Street, les « pèlerins » pressés remontent le *Wicked Quarter Mile*, le « kilomètre du vice », puis s'engagent dans Dorset Street, où la pension

Crossingham offrait un toit aux « infortunées », les prostituées de Whitechapel.

Le pub Princess Alice, où Tablier de cuir, dit-on, venait rôder, se trouvait au coin de Wentworth Street et de Commercial Street. Il a été remis à neuf en 1980 et s'appelle maintenant le City Darts.

Le dimanche, le célèbre marché de Petticoat Lane, dans Middlesex Street, est toujours aussi chaotique, aussi bruyant et aussi cosmopolite. Toutes les religions se côtoient à Whitechapel. Dans Fournier Street, l'ancienne Huguenot Church est devenue une chapelle méthodiste, puis une synagogue. C'est aujourd'hui une mosquée.

C'est justement dans Fournier Street, à l'intérieur du Ten Bells, que Mary Jane Kelly avait été aperçue vivante pour la dernière fois. Voilà sans doute la raison pour laquelle ce pub a ensuite été baptisé « Jack the Ripper ». Mais récemment, des groupes féministes ont protesté contre l'exploitation ainsi faite de leurs « sœurs du trottoir », et le pub a dû changer de nom en 1988.

Il y a un siècle, les « filles » avaient l'habitude de se réunir au Frying Pan, le pub de Brick Lane où Polly Nichols a bu ses derniers shillings la nuit de sa mort. Aujourd'hui, ce pub est devenu un restaurant indien, mais la rue est restée le territoire des prostituées.

La légende de Jack l'Éventreur survivra-t-elle encore pendant un siècle ?

LA CONTROVERSE

La troisième partie présente les pièces de la controverse telles qu'arrêtées au moment de la publication.

RAPPORT DE KENNETH W. RENDELL

RÉSUMÉ

Ce livre et le texte présenté comme le journal de Jack l'Éventreur reposent sur l'idée que James T. Maybrick était Jack l'Éventreur et qu'il a écrit le journal. Des comparaisons d'écritures réalisées par plusieurs experts de premier plan, y compris celui qui avait été sélectionné par l'éditeur anglais, montrent sans aucun doute possible que Maybrick n'est pas l'auteur de ce journal.

L'un des principaux facteurs qui, selon ce livre, permettent d'établir un lien entre le journal et Jack l'Éventreur, est le suivant : des termes et des expressions relativement inhabituels, apparus pour la première fois en 1888 dans une lettre signée Jack l'Éventreur, adressée à un journal londonien, et publiée depuis à de nombreuses reprises, sont utilisés tout au long du journal. Celui-ci est ainsi lié à cette lettre de façon inexorable. Mais toutes les comparaisons réalisées entre les deux écritures concluent qu'elles émanent de personnes différentes.

Le style de l'écriture n'est pas victorien. Le type d'écriture remonte à une période comprise entre le début et le milieu du XXe siècle – mais pas à la fin du XIXe siècle. La mise en page, la pression de la plume et la distribution de l'encre concourent à indiquer que plusieurs paragraphes censés avoir été écrits à des dates différentes ont en fait été rédigés le même jour. Ces éléments sont incompatibles avec un journal, mais sont compatibles avec une contrefaçon de journal.

L'analyse des déplacements ioniques exécutée par son inventeur, Rod McNeil, pour déterminer depuis combien de temps l'encre se trouvait sur le papier, a permis d'établir une date moyenne de 1921, à douze ans près. Dans le passé, M. McNeil a réalisé ce test, pour lequel il emploie un microscope électronique à balayage, pour les services secrets américains et le FBI.

Le journal n'est pas rédigé dans un cahier ou dans un carnet prévu à cet effet mais dans un album – ce qui est très inhabituel. Les vingt premières pages sont déchirées, ce qui est illogique à moins d'envisager que le faussaire ait acquis un album datant de l'époque victorienne ou edwardienne, en ait déchiré les pages déjà utilisées, puis écrit le journal.

Aucune indication crédible ne prouve que ce journal est authentique. Tous les types d'analyse effectués prouvent ou indiquent que le journal de Jack l'Éventreur est un faux.

RAPPORT SUR LE JOURNAL DE JACK L'ÉVENTREUR

La question de l'authenticité du journal de Jack l'Éventreur a déjà conduit d'aucuns à établir un parallèle avec les Carnets d'Hitler. Et de fait, en lisant *The Diary of Jack the Ripper : The Discovery, the Investigation and the Authentication*, j'ai été immédiatement frappé par bien des similitudes. A de nombreuses reprises, les conclusions ne reposent pas sur les faits présentés; l'histoire du journal est non seulement inconnue mais illogique (celui qui en a fait la découverte est mort, et il a fallu cent ans pour trouver le journal, bien que son auteur écrive : « Je place maintenant ceci dans un endroit où on le trouvera. »); on sent nettement que l'auteur a abordé la question de l'authenticité avec un scepticisme discret et une bonne dose d'optimisme.

Toutefois, la différence principale avec les Carnets d'Hitler, c'est qu'il a été possible de déterminer très vite si ces derniers étaient vrais ou faux : on disposait en effet d'un grand nombre d'échantillons de l'écriture authentique d'Hitler, et d'un nombre considérable de faits biographiques et historiques dont l'exactitude ne pouvait être mise en doute. Dans le cas de Jack l'Éventreur, la situation est beaucoup plus complexe, car on ne dispose pas d'échantillon absolument authentique de l'écriture du tueur. Quant à l'individu présenté ici comme Jack l'Éventreur, à savoir James Maybrick, le livre affirme qu'il n'existe de lui qu'une signature authentique, peut-être deux. Heureusement, ces derniers jours, il est apparu qu'il existe un document suffisamment long et entièrement rédigé de la main de l'auteur présumé du journal. La situation était donc la suivante : il fallait déterminer si l'écriture était celle de Maybrick et si Maybrick était Jack l'Éventreur.

J'ai abordé la question de l'authenticité du journal de Jack l'Éventreur en décidant de l'examiner de tous les points de vue possibles. Initialement, je ne disposais que du texte non corrigé pour travailler. (Dans ce rapport je fais référence au « texte ou livre publié » lorsque des épreuves m'ont été remises. Mais à mesure que je signalais les erreurs et les contradictions contenues dans le texte, nombre de corrections ont été effectuées, et il se peut donc que plusieurs références ne soient plus de mise dans certaines des versions publiées.) J'ai commencé par examiner les informations contenues dans le journal. Le livre de 235 pages dû à la plume de Shirley Harrison décrit la prétendue découverte du journal de Jack l'Éventreur par Tony Devereux, qui l'a donné à Mike Barrett en refusant d'en expliquer la provenance. Le livre raconte ensuite que Barrett a fait des recherches et déterminé que les indices inclus dans le texte prouvaient qu'il était l'œuvre d'un marchand de coton de

Liverpool, James T. Maybrick. Barrett a également établi que ce dernier était Jack l'Éventreur. Le livre donne ensuite le détail de la vie de Maybrick, vraisemblablement sur la base des ouvrages écrits sur Maybrick à la suite de son meurtre présumé. Maybrick consommait régulièrement de l'arsenic et de la strychnine, et sa jeune femme a été accusée de l'avoir assassiné au terme de plusieurs années gâtées par des problèmes conjugaux. Après avoir expliqué les raisons pour lesquelles il se pourrait que Maybrick soit Jack l'Éventreur, l'auteur, Shirley Harrison, publie le texte du journal et une analyse du Dr David Forshaw, consultant en psychiatrie spécialisé dans la dépendance. Ce dernier indique qu'il s'agit bien là de Jack l'Éventreur. Après la description de l'authentification du journal, le livre se termine par le texte intégral du journal.

Le premier expert indépendant que j'ai consulté était le Dr Joe Nickell, auteur d'un livre réputé sur le suaire de Turin et d'un excellent ouvrage de référence : *Pen, Ink & Evidence*. Le Dr Nickell et moi-même avons débattu longuement du texte du livre tel qu'il nous avait été remis, et nous sommes tombés d'accord pour dire que l'auteur avait abordé le journal avec trop peu de scepticisme, que plusieurs suppositions étaient présentées comme des faits sans fondement avéré, qu'un certain nombre de ces « faits » étaient incorrects, voire contredits ailleurs dans le livre, et que sur la base des preuves présentées dans le livre, on ne pouvait tirer qu'une seule conclusion, à savoir que le journal était un faux.

Un exemple de conclusion importante qui ne repose sur aucun fondement avéré concerne l'utilisation du terme « *one off* ». La première utilisation connue de cette expression en Amérique remonte à 1925, et à 1934 en Angleterre. L'éditeur de l'*Oxford English Dictionary* a déclaré qu'il serait « surpris, mais pas sidéré s'il s'avérait que la première apparition de ce terme avait précédé 1934 d'un demi-siècle. » L'un des éditeurs du *Webster's* a eu une réaction similaire. Pourtant, après avoir cité ces deux sources nommément, Shirley Harrison écrit : « J'ai moi-même découvert des utilisations orales de cette expression à la fin de l'ère victorienne, qui n'apparaissent pas dans les dictionnaires. » Aucune source n'est donnée à l'appui de cette affirmation, aucune explication non plus. Ainsi, l'un des facteurs qui font le plus douter de l'authenticité du journal est expédié sans autre forme de procès. Ce n'est qu'un des nombreux exemples de déclarations qui ne reposent sur aucun fondement apparent. Il est également très clair pour quiconque est familier de la prose victorienne que bien des expressions utilisées ne correspondent pas à cette période.

Certains « faits » sont contredits par le livre lui-même. Ainsi, l'auteur écrit : « Qui d'autre que l'Éventreur aurait pu savoir que Catharine Eddowes portait sur elle une boîte d'allumettes vide en fer-blanc ? Ce fait n'avait jamais été mentionné avant la découverte du journal. » Mais Harrison écrit également : « " Une boîte d'allumettes en fer-blanc, vide. " Cet objet en apparence sans intérêt est le plus important du lot. (...) il n'a été mentionné que dans la liste officielle établie par la police, qui n'a pas été publiée (...). La liste a été publiée pour la première fois en (...) 1987. » Cette information était bel et bien disponible dans la liste officielle établie par la police, mais Harrison n'en tient pas compte. Un faussaire compétent, me semble-t-il, aurait pu la trouver, tout comme l'auteur, en 1987.

L'un des éléments auxquels le livre attache le plus d'importance prouve, si l'on accepte les « faits » tels qu'ils sont présentés, qu'il s'agit bien d'un canular. Une lettre a été envoyée le 25 septembre 1888 au « Patron, Central News Office, Londres ». Cette lettre, qui date véritablement de 1888, était signée *Jack l'Éventreur.* A-t-elle vraiment été écrite par le meurtrier ? On l'ignore. Mais le journal reprend certaines des expressions qu'elle contient. Cette lettre est citée page 87 comme preuve de l'authenticité du journal. « (...) le langage utilisé dans la lettre rappelle celui qui prévaut dans le journal. “ J'en ai après les putains ”, “ la substance rouge ” et les “ drôles de petits jeux ” sont autant d'expressions qui semblent sorties tout droit de l'esprit torturé de Maybrick, de même que les interjections moqueuses – “ *ha ha* ”. » De fait, ces expressions qui apparaissent dans la lettre de 1888 sont utilisées à plusieurs reprises dans le journal. Mais bien plus loin, le livre rapporte que Sue Ironmonger, experte consultée par l'éditeur anglais à Londres, « ne voit pas de correspondance entre l'écriture du journal et celle de la lettre adressée au “ Cher Patron ” ». Si elle a raison, une seule conclusion s'impose : si la lettre a été écrite par Jack l'Éventreur, alors le journal, qui copie le langage de la lettre mais dont l'écriture n'est pas la même, ne peut être qu'un faux. Et si la lettre de 1888 est une contrefaçon de l'époque, alors le journal ne peut encore être qu'un faux, puisqu'il copie le langage mais que les deux écritures ne correspondent pas.

Ayant conclu que le texte du livre était contradictoire et manquait de sérieux, et qu'il serait donc extrêmement malavisé d'y voir la moindre preuve factuelle, je désirais vivement lire dans leur intégralité les rapports originellement remis à l'auteur par les experts engagés pour prouver son authenticité. J'ai pour habitude d'insister pour consulter les dossiers et les rapports complets, au cas où j'interpréterais différemment le rapport d'un expert : jamais je n'avais été autant fondé à le faire que dans le cas présent.

Le Dr Nicholas Eastaugh avait été engagé pour examiner le journal, et le test qu'il a effectué l'a été de façon très compétente. Sa conclusion – aucune des composantes de l'encre n'est en contradiction avec la date de 1888 – est correcte, mais le livre ne rapporte pas qu'il a signalé, dès le mois d'octobre 1992, que d'autres tests essentiels devaient être effectués. En août 1993, il a encore essayé de convaincre l'éditeur britannique d'autoriser les analyses complémentaires qui étaient nécessaires. Le livre déclare par ailleurs que le Dr Eastaugh a « déterminé que la poudre noire trouvée dans les petits-fonds du journal était (...) du charbon animal ». En vérité, voici ce qu'il a conclu : « Il est possible que la poudre noire soit à base de charbon animal. » (La présence de charbon animal est significative du fait que l'auteur présumé du journal consommait de l'arsenic et de la strychnine.)

Le livre s'appuie également sur les déclarations d'un autre expert, le Dr David Forshaw. Son rapport de cinquante-neuf pages est abondamment cité. C'est ce rapport qui porte à croire que d'un point de vue psychiatrique, il s'agit du journal d'un individu dont la personnalité est celle d'un auteur de crimes en série. (Lorsque je me suis renseigné au sujet de l'expérience et des qualifications du Dr Forshaw en tant que spécialiste des auteurs de crimes en série, on m'a répondu que son travail était confidentiel et qu'il ne pouvait en être débattu.) Mais le rapport qu'il a remis à l'auteur et à l'éditeur contient deux déclarations tout à fait inattendues, compte tenu de ses commentaires tout au long du livre. Au début de ce très long rapport, Forshaw écrit : « Si l'on part de l'hypothèse selon laquelle ce journal est authentique, le but de cette contribution est d'en venir à comprendre l'homme qu'était James Maybrick et l'état d'esprit de Jack l'Éventreur. » A l'évidence, aux yeux du Dr Forshaw, son rôle ne consistait pas à authentifier le texte comme l'œuvre d'un auteur de crimes en série dont la personnalité correspondrait à celle de Jack l'Éventreur telle qu'on la connaît. Son rôle était d'expliquer le texte en posant comme hypothèse qu'il était authentique.

Mais le dernier paragraphe du rapport du Dr Forshaw est encore plus surprenant. Il est biffé et n'a pas été publié : « Si le journal est authentique, il raconte une tragédie. Ce récit est vraisemblable, et en vérité il se tient. Toutefois, il existe d'autres possibilités : il pourrait s'agir d'un faux ancien ou moderne, ou le produit d'un cerveau contemporain des meurtres de Jack l'Éventreur, mais victime d'illusions. Si l'on considère le journal dans le détail, les connaissances relatives au profil psychopathogique des auteurs de crimes en série sembleraient indiquer, à mes yeux en tout cas, que les deux options les plus probables sont les suivantes : il s'agit d'un document authentique ou d'un faux moderne. Un examen légal approfondi du journal lui-même et de sa provenance serait une composante essentielle pour décider entre les deux. »

Quand j'eus terminé de lire le rapport du Dr Forshaw, sa pertinence dans le cadre de l'authentification du journal m'est apparue comme gravement entamée. J'ai décidé qu'il serait inutile de demander à deux psychiatres légaux spécialisés dans les auteurs de crimes en série d'examiner le texte et de me dire si, d'après eux, il était probable qu'il soit l'œuvre d'un tel tueur. Mieux valait d'abord faire expertiser l'écriture et le contenu du journal.

Les détails historiques contenus dans le texte d'un manuscrit sont toujours très importants lorsque l'on désire établir l'authenticité de ce texte. Or, le livre assure le lecteur que les faits historiques contenus dans le journal sont corrects. Toutefois, compte tenu de l'imprécision extraordinaire relevée dans les autres chapitres, je n'avais aucune raison de croire que les « faits » historiques décrits par Harrison échappaient à cette règle. La stratégie idéale consisterait à demander au Dr Nickell, historien exceptionnellement minutieux, de déterminer dans quelle mesure le texte du journal correspondait aux informations dont on dispose au sujet de Jack l'Éventreur, qu'elles aient été ou non publiées, et aux informations concernant la vie de James Maybrick. Bien que les responsables de Time-Warner n'aient jamais hésité à déclarer qu'ils retarderaient la publication jusqu'à ce que toutes les recherches nécessaires aient été effectuées, il m'est apparu qu'un examen minutieux de l'écriture et du texte permettrait sans doute de parvenir à un résultat concluant, et j'ai donc décidé de procéder à ces tests en premier lieu. S'ils se révélaient peu concluants ou positifs, la précision et la probabilité des faits historiques mentionnés dans le texte pourraient être mises à l'épreuve.

Quiconque n'a jamais examiné de contrefaçons littéraires ignore la ressource dont font preuve les auteurs de tels canulars. Dans le cas présent, d'aucuns ont affirmé que la complexité du journal excluait une contrefaçon. Ils ne savent pas que pratiquement tout le monde avait dit que personne ne pourrait fabriquer près de soixante carnets d'Hitler, créer de toutes pièces l'autobiographie d'Howard Hughes ou le journal de Benito Mussolini. De même, à les entendre, jamais un jeune homme de Salt Lake City n'aurait pu fabriquer des lettres et des manuscrits dont le contenu ébranlerait jusqu'aux fondations de l'Église mormonne. Mais si un enquêteur présume qu'un texte est trop complexe pour être un faux, il risque d'être dupé. Les faussaires ne sont pas toujours motivés par l'argent ou par la soif de célébrité – ils peuvent l'être par la simple satisfaction de tromper les experts. Le fait de connaître le profil psychologique des faussaires est presque aussi important que de savoir analyser l'écriture.

Le 20 août 1993, Robert Smith, l'éditeur anglais, a apporté le journal original à Chicago pour que l'écriture, l'encre et le papier y soient examinés. Je l'ai rencontré au laboratoire de Maureen Casey Owens, ancienne présidente de l'*American Society of Questioned Documents Examiners* et auteur de nombreux documents consacrés aux questions de graphologie légale. Elle a en outre travaillé pour le *Chicago Police Departement* pendant vingt-cinq ans, en qualité d'expert. Robert L. Kuranz, chimiste spécialisé dans les encres depuis trente ans, et le Dr Nickell se sont joints à nous.

Ma réaction immédiate, qui a également été celle de Mme Owens et du Dr Nickell – je l'ai appris par la suite – c'est que le journal avait été écrit beaucoup plus récemment que la fin des années 1880. J'ai aussi été frappé par l'uniformité de l'écriture et de l'encre – très inhabituelle dans un journal – uniformité qui m'a tout de suite rappelé ma réaction à la première lecture des Carnets d'Hitler.

J'ai également été surpris de constater que le journal avait été rédigé dans un album, et non dans un cahier ou dans un carnet prévu à cet effet. Les albums, d'un format beaucoup plus grand et dont le papier épais est très absorbant, étaient utilisés pour coller des cartes postales, des photographies, des cartes de Saint-Valentin et autres, et je n'en avais jamais vu qui ait été employé comme journal intime. C'était possible, mais très improbable.

Le fait qu'environ vingt pages avaient été déchirées au début a éveillé des soupçons en chacun de nous. Aucune explication logique ne peut justifier que l'auteur présumé, Maybrick, homme aisé, ait agi de la sorte. Pour commencer, il aurait acheté un journal victorien normal, mais si, pour une raison ou pour une autre, il désirait utiliser un album, il en aurait acheté un neuf. Il n'en aurait sans doute pas choisi un qu'il avait déjà pour en déchirer le contenu. D'un autre côté, il était très probable qu'une personne désirant fabriquer un faux journal, et ne connaissant pas la différence entre un album et un journal, ait acheté un journal dans un marché aux puces, ait déchiré les pages déjà utilisées, et se soit servie des pages restantes pour sa création.

Les trois premiers tests légaux ont été effectués dans le but d'écarter toute révélation inattendue : des analyses à base d'ultraviolets et d'infrarouges, et une analyse électronique pour détecter les moindres traces sur le papier. L'analyse à base d'ultraviolets a montré que des objets rectangulaires, probablement des cartes postales, avaient été collés sur la première page (aujourd'hui manquante) : en effet, leur contour apparaît sur la première page existante. Ces analyses ont également montré que l'encre du journal n'avait pas été affectée par l'âge. Bien souvent, l'encre d'une page laisse une empreinte sur la page voisine, surtout si ces pages sont restées en contact pendant plus de cent ans. Mais il est difficile de détecter ce phénomène sans le secours de rayons ultraviolets.

Le journal a ensuite été photographié à l'aide d'appareils perfectionnés pour que des épreuves très précises puissent être obtenues à partir des clichés. Elles seraient étudiées une fois le journal reparti pour Londres. Chacun d'entre nous a alors examiné le journal à l'aide d'un microscope stéréoscopique, en se concentrant sur l'encre et sur l'écriture.

Un certain nombre d'échantillons de l'encre ont ensuite été prélevés par Bob Kuranz grâce à un instrument similaire à une seringue hypodermique. Des échantillons microscopiques de l'encre et du papier ont ensuite été placés dans des capsules pour analyse.

Pendant que ces prélèvements avaient lieu, Maureen Owens, Joe Nickell et moi-même nous sommes retrouvés à l'extérieur du laboratoire. Nous avons tous conclu qu'à ce stade rien ne permettrait de croire qu'il s'agissait d'un journal victorien authentique. L'album lui-même, mais aussi l'uniformité de paragraphes soi-disant rédigés sur une période de plus d'un an, nous laissaient très sceptiques.

Nous avions également étudié une photographie en couleurs et grandeur nature de la lettre au « Cher patron » (mentionnée précédemment) et aucun d'entre nous ne pouvait distinguer la moindre ressemblance entre son écriture et celle du journal. Nous avons décidé d'effectuer une analyse et une comparaison très détaillées du journal et de la lettre, en gardant à l'esprit que l'auteur de la lettre au « Cher Patron » avait peut-être déguisé son écriture. Nous étudierons aussi l'uniformité de l'écriture, incompatible avec un journal. En effet, chaque fois que l'auteur d'un journal reprend la plume, son écriture est quelque peu différente, ce qui permet de déterminer si plusieurs paragraphes prétendument écrits à des dates différentes ont en fait été rédigés le même jour – ce qui est toujours une possibilité, sauf quand l'écriture change.

L'éditeur anglais avait également apporté une photocopie du certificat de mariage de Maybrick, sur lequel figure une signature authentique que personne ne conteste, et une autre du testament de l'auteur présumé du journal. Smith a précisé que ce testament était en général considéré comme un faux, sans doute l'œuvre du frère de Maybrick. Lors de cette réunion, toutefois, nous ne nous sommes pas intéressés au testament.

Durant la semaine qui a suivi, Bob Kuranz a utilisé des techniques chromatographiques pour analyser l'encre, en quête d'un élément qui ne correspondrait pas à la date. Mais il n'en a décelé aucun (il a en fait exécuté le même travail que le Dr Eastaugh). Nous ne nous attendions pas à trouver des composantes qui permettent d'affirmer que l'encre était de fabrication récente, mais nous ne pouvions pas écarter cette possibilité. (Il est relativement facile d'obtenir ou de fabriquer de l'encre à partir des composantes utilisées en Angleterre à l'époque victorienne.)

Entre-temps, certains des échantillons extraits par Bob Kuranz avaient été envoyés à Rod McNeil pour qu'il procède à une analyse des déplacements ioniques, qui déterminerait depuis combien de temps l'encre se trouvait sur le papier. Mais nous craignions que la nature du manuscrit, à savoir un album dont le papier était relativement plus absorbant, ne rende cette analyse plus difficile.

Maureen Owens et moi-même avons continué d'examiner l'écriture, et il est devenu de plus en plus évident que l'analyse de l'écriture serait concluante en elle-même. Nous avions conclu que la lettre adressée au « Cher patron » n'avait pas été écrite par l'auteur du journal (rappelons que la graphologue engagée par l'éditeur anglais, Sue Ironmonger, était parvenue à la même conclusion). La seule interrogation qui demeurait, au sujet de cette lettre, était donc la suivante : l'auteur du journal aurait-il pu la rédiger en déguisant son écriture ? Mme Owens dispose d'une expérience de vingt-cinq ans en la matière et elle peut identifier sans difficulté une écriture déguisée : selon elle, ce n'est pas le cas dans la lettre en question.

Notre dernière analyse de l'écriture du journal a

confirmé ce que le Dr Nickell, Mme Owens et moi-même avions soupçonné dès le départ : le style de l'écriture ne correspond pas à la manière dont on formait les lettres à la fin des années 1880. L'uniformité de l'encre et le même aspect couché de l'écriture lorsqu'on passe d'un paragraphe à un autre ne sont pas naturels et suggèrent que le faussaire en a rédigé plusieurs d'affilée. Le manque de variété dans la mise en page suggère la même conclusion.

Mais le plus surprenant, et aussi le plus important, c'est qu'un examen minutieux du testament de Maybrick indique que la signature qui figure sur ce dernier est identique à celle qui figure sur le certificat de mariage, et que ce testament a bel et bien été écrit par James Maybrick. Ce résultat m'a plutôt surpris, étant donné ce qu'on m'avait affirmé, à savoir qu'il était fort probable que Michael Maybrick en était l'auteur. (On ne m'a jamais montré les documents qui justifiaient cette assertion.)

L'analyse et la comparaison du testament de Maybrick et du journal de Jack l'Éventreur montrent de façon concluante que ces documents ont été écrits par deux personnes différentes. Ces deux textes auraient été rédigés à la même époque, et tous deux sont suffisamment longs pour qu'on puisse se faire une opinion. Il est donc possible de parvenir à une conclusion qui ne laisse aucune place au doute. Il n'y a pas d'autre possibilité : l'auteur du journal de Jack l'Éventreur n'est pas James Maybrick. Même si l'on ne tient pas compte de la lettre au « Cher Patron » ni des nombreuses contradictions dont cette histoire est truffée, les faits historiques contenus dans le journal identifient avec une telle clarté l'auteur comme James Maybrick que la preuve qu'il n'a pas écrit le journal ne permet d'atteindre qu'une seule conclusion : il s'agit d'un faux.

Lorsque j'ai eu terminé ce rapport, les résultats du test effectué par Rod McNeil pour déterminer depuis combien de temps l'encre se trouvait sur le papier ont été achevés. Son test, l'analyse des déplacements ioniques, mesure à l'aide d'un microscope électronique à balayage le déplacement des ions depuis l'encre sur le papier. Son analyse a déterminé une date moyenne de 1921, à douze ans près. McNeil, l'inventeur de cette analyse, a effectué des tests similaires pour les services secrets américains, le FBI, et il a correctement établi la date de fabrication des documents imprimés dans l'affaire du meurtre mormon.

RÉFUTATION DU RAPPORT RENDELL PAR ROBERT SMITH

Le rapport de Kenneth Rendell concernant le journal de Jack l'Éventreur est fondamentalement imparfait, erroné et sujet à caution. J'ai apporté le journal le 21 août 1993 à Chicago où Mr. Rendell, commerçant en documents, me rencontra et entreprit les tests avec son équipe. Ces tests effectués sur le journal et le rapport qui en résulte furent bouclés à la hâte en deux semaines en ne tenant pas compte, dans une large mesure, des quinze mois de recherches et de tests réalisés par notre auteur, mais aussi par nos chercheurs et nos experts. Cette rapidité témoigne de leur manque de compréhension envers le document à authentifier.

Rendell admet laconiquement la précision des tests effectués sur l'encre et le papier par le Dr Nicholas Eastaugh qui révèlent qu'aucun élément présent dans cette encre et ce papier ne sont en contradiction avec les années 1888-1889. Cette conclusion est essentielle, car elle écarte une fraude semblable à celle révélée par l'analyse de l'encre et du papier des prétendus journaux d'Hitler et de Mussolini. Cependant, Rendell suggère que l'encre a été apposée sur le papier à une date ultérieure.

Un test par émission ionique conduit par R.J. McNeil

lui a permis de conclure que le journal avait été rédigé entre 1909 et 1933, avec la proposition médiane de 1921. Cela veut dire, si je comprends bien, que McNeil peut, en utilisant un microscope à scanner, mesurer la distance que le fer contenu dans l'encre parcourt le long des fibres du papier. De cette façon, il obtient des données lui permettant d'indiquer combien d'années il faut au fer pour parvenir à son point le plus éloigné, c'est-à-dire à celui où il subit le test. Aucun détail sur ce test n'est indiqué pour prouver ce qui est, selon les déclarations écrites de McNeil, une manière de dater remarquablement précise. Dans son ouvrage consacré aux recherches chimiques en archéologie, publié en 1984, Mr. McNeil admet une variation de trente années, en plus ou en moins, par rapport à la datation indiquée par ses tests, mais ne fournit pas plus d'explication quant à la façon dont ils sont menés. Il n'apparaît pas non plus, à ma connaissance, qu'il ait publié des commentaires sur ce sujet en particulier, ou sur d'autres.

Nous croyons, pour notre part, que McNeil et Rendell ne sont pas en mesure d'expliquer eux-mêmes ou de fournir une explication scientifique satisfaisante sur leur technique de datation, ou même de prouver qu'un test totalement satisfaisant sur le journal est possible. Notre propre expert en encre et en papier, le Dr. Nicholas Eastaugh, a confié le journal à Robert Wild, de l'Université de Bristol, hautement qualifié en examen par microcospe électronique et qui a effectué plusieurs tests sur le document. Aucun résultat probant n'a pu être obtenu.

En effet, lorsque l'instrument bombarde le papier avec des électrons, cela provoque une charge statique qui altère les signaux. Même si McNeil avait été capable de montrer qu'il avait trouvé une technique pour franchir la charge statique, il lui resterait à expliquer de quelle façon il utilise le microscope pour dater les manuscrits avec un degré qui soit d'une exactitude satisfaisante. Les Dr Wild et Eastaugh restent sceptiques quant à cette éventualité. De plus, il apparaît que les tests en question n'ont pas été vérifiés, de façon indépendante, par la communauté scientifique.

Nous défions McNeil de produire son rapport détaillé sur le journal afin qu'il soit étudié par d'autres chercheurs et de permettre à un autre spécialiste en microscopie électronique de vérifier son test et sa technique de datation.

Cependant, même si nous admettions les résultats de McNeil, une datation avec une marge de plus au moins douze ans est invalidée par l'évidence historique. Martin Fido, historien reconnu et spécialiste de Jack l'Éventreur – qui, de plus, ne croit pas au journal –, déclare cependant que la date suggérée de 1921 est « l'éventualité la plus insensée et que la science donne au document une date historiquement réfutable ».

Il est fâcheux que Rendell passe à côté de presque toutes les évidences historiques à l'exception d'une seule : la référence dans le journal à « une boîte vide en fer-blanc trouvée par la police sur le lieu de l'assassinat de Catharine Eddowes ». La présence de cette boîte ne fut pas mentionnée à l'époque et fut seulement révélée dans un communiqué de la police publié pour la première fois en 1987. Rendell dit : « Le fait que cette information était disponible dans les rapports officiels de police est ignoré. Autant que nous pouvons en savoir, un faussaire compétent aurait pu trouver une telle information. » Mais pas en 1921. En effet, les archives de la police n'ont pas été ouvertes au public avant 1984.

Rendell n'envisage pas d'avantage les références évidentes dans le journal au fait que l'Éventreur retire le cœur de Mary Kelly. Cet élément fut consigné uniquement dans les registres secrets de l'enquête menée par le Coroner. Ces registres ne furent jamais ouverts à la presse ou au public, puis disparurent en 1888 et furent envoyés anonymement en 1987 à Scotland Yard. Les références à la boîte vide en fer-blanc et au cœur de Mary Kelly sont suffisants à eux-mêmes pour invalider les tests de McNeil et le rapport de Rendell.

De toute façon, il fut impossible pour quiconque d'obtenir de telles informations avant 1980.

Rendell a également pris le parti de ne pas inclure une autre évidence historique dont Shirley Harrison fait mention dans son ouvrage et qui aide à établir l'authenticité du journal. Depuis les meurtres de 1888 jusqu'à 1950, la police, la presse et tous les autres spécialistes de l'Éventreur lui attribuèrent les assassinats d'Emma Smith et de Martha Trabam. Maintenant, il est communément accepté que ces deux femmes n'ont aucun lien avec l'Éventreur. Si le journal avait été écrit par un faussaire (en 1888 ou autour de 1921), il aurait certainement inclu ces deux meurtres faussement attribués.

Dans l'ouvrage, nous reproduisons une photographie datant de 1888 du corps de Mary Jane Kelly, au-dessus duquel figurent les initials FM, qui correspondent à celles de Florence Maybrick. Le journal mentionne explicitement ces initiales quand il décrit le meurtre. Cette photographie fut publiée seulement en 1975 et la présence des initiales n'a jamais été remarquée ni écrite avant la publication de notre ouvrage. Qui d'autre, à part l'Éventreur, aurait pu connaître ces initiales et les écrire dans son journal.

Les exemples ci-dessus sont quelques extraits des évidences historiques dont Rendell aurait dû tenir compte s'il avait été soucieux de présenter un rapport plus objectif. D'ailleurs, il le dit lui-même : « Le contexte historique du texte d'un manuscrit est d'une grande importance pour déterminer, son authenticité. » Pourquoi, alors, n'a-t-il pas d'avantage poussé l'analyse historique et n'a-t-il pas fait appel à des spécialistes du cas de Jack l'Éventreur ?

La négligence apportée au rapport est évidente en plusieurs cas : Rendell fait allusion à l'auteur du journal comme étant James T. Maybrick (voir rapport). Ce « T » est un produit de son imagination. En effet, Maybrick n'a pas de nom intermédiaire. Un autre exemple de ces insinuations est que l'examen aux ultraviolets révèle « des traces rectangulaires, probablement celles de cartes postales ». La taille des cartes postales depuis le début du siècle jusqu'à maintenant est à peu près de 5 pouces et demi sur 3 pouces et demi alors que ces rectangles, qui sont visibles à l'œil nu, ont 3 pouces et demi sur 2 pouces et demi. Cette erreur n'est pas encourageante venant d'un expert en manuscrits et en imprimés divers.

Rendell a beaucoup à dire sur les analyses graphologiques et fait du testament de Maybrick un point majeur de son rapport. Il conclut son examen de ce document en disant : « Il y a une évidence suffisante pour atteindre à une conclusion définitive. Il n'existe pas d'autres possibilités : l'auteur du journal de Jack l'Éventreur n'est pas James Maybrick. » Si son rapport prétend être si objectif, pourquoi n'envisage-t-il pas la possibilité que le testament soit un faux ?

Avant Rendell, trois ou quatre pages dans l'ouvrage expliquent pourquoi le testament n'est probablement pas écrit par James Maybrick. Un témoignage recueilli pour le procès de Florence Maybrick accusée du meurtre de son mari est très explicite. Il révèle que les frères sans scrupules de James Maybrick l'ont forcé à rédiger un nouveau testament, quand il devint évident qu'il était sur le point de mourir. Un témoin a vu deux des frères pénétrer dans sa chambre avec des papiers la nuit qui a précédé sa mort et entendu James Maybrick se plaignant d'une contrainte. Pouvons-nous croire que cet homme mourant, partiellement paralysé par les effets d'un empoisonnement chronique à l'arsenic et à la strychnine, ait pu, pendant les derniers moments de sa vie, écrire un testament d'une main aussi ferme ? Qu'il aurait pu, par deux fois, mal orthographier le nom de sa fille, en écrivant Eveleyn au lieu d'Evelyne ? Qu'il ait pu déshériter ses deux enfants pour lesquels il avait une passion, afin de transmettre tous ses biens à ses frères ? Il y a également de nombreuses différences dans les mots du testament tel qu'il apparaît dans une transcription publiée en 1891 dans l'ouvrage de l'avocat Alexander MacDougall, peu de temps après la mort de Maybrick, et le testament qui existe aujourd'hui à Sommerset House. Par exemple, le testament actuel comporte les termes légaux très importants : « léguer » et « en sa présence » mystérieusement ajoutés. Une main, peut-être deux, ont agi, mais pas celle, nous le pensons, de James Maybrick. Est-ce même la signature de James Maybrick qui se trouve sur le testament ? Maureen Casey Owens, spécialiste en documents de l'équipe de Rendell, l'identifie comme étant la même que celle qui figure sur son certificat de mariage. Cependant, un rapport que nous avons commandé de notre côté à Reed Hayes, un expert certifié, stipule qu'il a découvert plus de dissemblances que de ressemblances entre les deux signatures. Un troisième expert, Ana Koren, spécialiste en documents pour le ministère de la Justice israélien, dit ceci : « Le testament a été écrit avec une plume très épaisse, ce qui rend très difficile les comparaisons avec d'autres documents. » Par conséquent, la crédibilité du journal ne peut être mise en cause sur la base de l'écriture du testament.

Un autre point dans le rapport Rendell concerne la lettre commençant par « Cher patron » dans laquelle l'Éventreur se vante de ses méfaits et emploie les expressions « substance rouge » et « Ha, Ha » qui apparaissent également dans le journal. Nous suggérons que la lettre a été presque sûrement écrite par l'Éventreur. Dans mon souci de faire examiner à Rendell le meilleur matériel possible, j'ai apporté à Chicago une photographie professionnelle de la lettre originale, qui a été montrée au public seulement en juin 1993. Nous n'avons pas eu besoin de Rendell et d'Owens pour nous dire que l'écriture ne correspondait pas avec celle du journal. En effet, nous le disons dans notre ouvrage.

La graphologie n'est pas une science et son exactitude

est sujette à de nombreux débats (le désaccord entre Hayes, Owens et Koren sur la comparaison des signatures de Maybrick en est un excellent exemple). Nous soutenons que l'auteur du journal aurait pu déguiser son écriture dans la lettre commençant par « Cher patron » et qui fut envoyée anonymement à l'Office Central de Presse. Il avait les meilleures raisons possibles pour cacher son identité.

Les commentaires de Koren sur la lettre sont les suivants : l'écriture n'est ni spontanée ni naturelle. Chaque lettre est tracée lentement pour former une écriture de façade. Elle déguise ainsi la personnalité de l'auteur et cela rend très difficile la comparaison avec l'écriture spontanée du journal.

Il est donc très osé de la part de Rendell de déclarer que « l'examen de l'écriture porte une conclusion en elle-même ». L'analyse graphologique est beaucoup moins sûre que les méthodes scientifiques ou historiques pour vérifier un document. Nos deux principaux experts, Sue Iremonger et Anna Koren, après plusieurs mois de recherches, ont trouvé très peu de points sur lesquels s'accorder.

J'attire maintenant l'attention sur la conclusion de Rendell : « Il est également presque évident à quiconque est familier avec la prose victorienne que de nombreuses expressions et mots ne coïncident pas avec l'époque. » De son propre avis, le journal pourrait, au plus tôt, dater de 1909; vingt ans (période écoulée entre 1889 et 1909) est un laps de temps très court dans le développement du langage. Nous défions Rendell de produire un seul mot ou une seule phrase qu'il considère comme n'étant pas usités à l'époque victorienne et nous répondrons formellement et immédiatement. Rendell se réfère particulièrement à l'expression « one off » qui apparaît pour la première fois dans le dictionnaire (Webster's) en 1925. Dans l'ouvrage, Shirley Harrison relate l'opinion des éditeurs du Webster's et du Oxford English Dictionnary, à savoir qu'il peut s'écouler plusieurs décades avant que des mots et des expressions passent de la forme orale ou d'une zone d'utilisation purement technique, à leur inscription dans un dictionnaire. « One off », justement, était une expression utilisée dans le commerce du bâtiment pour les commandes de matériaux et apparaît par la première fois dans les archives de l'entreprise Trayner's dans le Kent en 1860.

Un des plus importants rapports que nous avons commandés est celui du Dr David Forshaw, expert psychiatre et professeur d'internat à la clinique Maudsley de Londres, établissement internationalement respecté.

Le Dr Forshaw a une parfaite connaissance des dépendances et des comportements des tueurs en série. Rendell relève seulement le premier et le dernier paragraphe de son rapport et ignore le reste de son expertise de 15 000 mots, dans laquelle le Dr Forshaw établit un lien étroit entre les actes et les réactions de l'auteur du journal et ceux que l'on reconnaît aux tueurs en série. Il considère que les symptômes physiques et psychiques de la dépendance à l'arsenic tels que décrits dans le journal correspondent à ceux qu'il a observés en qualité d'expert. Le Dr Forshaw admet tout à fait l'hypothèse que le journal ait été rédigé par un tueur en série sous dépendance. Rendell a décidé qu'il n'était pas nécessaire de faire examiner le journal par un autre expert psychiatre, spécialisé dans les tueurs en série. Étant donné le haut niveau des expertises sur ce sujet aux États-Unis, je considère cette lacune comme très préjudiciable à l'indépendance de son rapport.

Pour résumer, en écartant l'hypothèse d'un faux récent, Rendell contribue à établir l'authenticité du journal. De plus, son opinion est plus subjective que scientifique. Il fait des suppositions à la légère et des conclusions de même. Et, détail primordial, tous les sujets de désaccord qu'il soulève sont clairement débattus dans notre ouvrage.

Je suis très heureux d'avoir ainsi encouragé à un débat sur l'authenticité du journal. Tout ce que je demande aux lecteurs de notre ouvrage est de considérer un témoignage et de juger par eux-mêmes.

Robert SMITH
Directeur Général
Éditions SMITH GRYPHON
Septembre 1993

COMMUNIQUÉ DE ROBERT SMITH,

directeur général de Smith Gryphon, et de son auteur, Shirley Harrison, en réponse aux critiques du *Sunday Times* du 19 septembre 1993.

L'article publié par le *Sunday Times* est à maintes reprises inexact, trompeur et malveillant. Les opinions de ceux qui ont été consultés ne font rien d'autre que d'ajouter au débat et n'établissent aucune sorte de preuve. Nous nous interrogeons pour notre part sur les motifs réels du *Sunday Times*, et d'autres encore plus virulents, qui les poussent à critiquer le journal.

Le *Sunday Times* prétend qu'il existe « six raisons qui prouvent que c'est un faux ». Trois d'entre elles sont basées sur un rapport fondamentalement imparfait rédigé par un spécialiste en expertise de documents, David Baxendale. Lorsque nous avons mis en lumière la gravité de ses erreurs, il a offert de renoncer à tous ses honoraires à condition « que nous n'utilisions aucun élément de son rapport pour quelque raison que ce soit ». Nous avons accepté et sommes liés par un accord de confidentialité.

La plus grande insistance est mise sur un test conduit par le Dr Baxendale sur la solubilité de l'encre. Notre expert, le Dr Nicholas Eastaugh, avait prévenu : « Un tel test peut être subjectif et donc douteux. En effet, il doit être mené en comparant d'autres exemples. Ceci pour la raison que de très nombreux facteurs interviennent dans la façon qu'à une encre de vieillir et de se solubiliser. »

Dans notre esprit, il n'y a aucun doute que Baxendale

n'a pas écarté une certaine subjectivité pour rédiger son rapport. En effectuant également des tests de solubilité, le Dr Eastaugh a trouvé que l'encre du journal se comportait conformément à d'autres encres appliquées sur des papiers connus et datés de l'époque victorienne. Il a également confirmé qu'il n'y avait aucun élément ni dans le papier ni dans l'encre du journal qui soient en contradiction avec la date de 1888-89.

Le *Sunday Times* déclare que le journal est « un faux moderne ». Cependant, il déclare également que Kenneth Rendell confirme la plupart des découvertes du *Sunday Times*. Or la conclusion de Rendell est que le journal a été écrit « en 1921 avec une marge de douze ans en plus ou en moins ». Au moins une des deux équipes de chercheurs se trompe. A notre point de vue, les deux sont dans l'erreur.

Nous acceptons que l'album victorien ait pu être utilisé pour des photographies parmi d'autres souvenirs. Nous rejetons cependant l'affirmation de Baxendale qu'il date de l'après Première Guerre. La taille des photographies est parfaitement en concordance avec celles de l'époque victorienne et nous pouvons produire des exemples.

Le *Sunday Times* et ses experts attire l'attention sur le fait que l'expression « one off » n'était pas utilisée à l'époque victorienne. Mais elle l'était et figure dans les archives de l'entreprise de bâtiment Trayner, située dans le Kent, en 1860.

A notre avis toutes les soi-disant « contradictions entre le journal et les faits connus concernant James Maybrick et Jack l'Éventreur » ou bien n'existent pas ou bien sont expliquées par Shirley Harrison. D'autre part, il existe un très grand nombre de faits qui coïncident avec James Maybrick et Jack l'Éventreur. L'historien spécialiste des affaires criminelles et expert du cas de l'Éventreur dit : « Le journal ne manifeste aucune contradiction avec les faits connus et il a attiré notre attention sur des incongruités et des évidences de toute sorte qui avaient échappé à l'attention lors des précédentes recherches. »

Le *Sunday Times* déclare que l'écriture du journal ne correspond pas à celle qui se trouve sur le certificat de mariage de Maybrick et sur son testament. Il néglige cependant de préciser à ses lecteurs que quatre pages de notre ouvrage relatent les évidences historiques qui indiquent la probabilité que le testament ne soit pas écrit de la main de Maybrick. Nous avons également le rapport de l'expert américain, Reed Hayes, qui conclut que les signatures du testament et du certificat de mariage présentent plus de différences que de ressemblances.

Le Dr David Forshaw, professeur de psychiatrie à l'hôpital Maudsley, spécialisé dans la pathologie des personnes dépendantes et des tueurs en série, a écrit un rapport de 15 000 mots sur le journal et confirme « que le contenu du journal est parfaitement en accord avec le comportement d'un tueur en série souffrant d'un empoisonnement chronique à l'arsenic ». Le *Sunday Times* néglige de faire mention à ce rapport.

Shirley Harrison et moi-même croyons que ses recherches sur le journal soutiennent solidement notre sentiment que le journal est authentique. Le public décidera par lui-même lors de la parution de l'ouvrage, le 7 octobre 1993.

REMERCIEMENTS

La possibilité de travailler sur un projet aussi extraordinaire ne se présente qu'une fois dans le cours d'une existence. Voilà un an, ce journal a été remis à l'agence littéraire Rupert Crew Ltd, de Londres. Pour lui faire passer tous les tests nécessaires avant de le révéler en toute confiance aux lecteurs du monde entier, nous nous en sommes remis à la bonne volonté d'un grand nombre de personnes, qui nous ont généreusement offert leur temps et leurs efforts.

A mesure que les documents nous parvenaient, Sally Evemy, ma collaboratrice de Word Team, a rassemblé et vérifié les informations reproduites dans ce livre.

Nous tenons tout particulièrement à remercier :

Doreen Montgomery, de Rupert Crew Ltd, notre agent. Sans elle, ce projet n'aurait pas vu le jour.

Robert Smith. Je connais peu d'éditeurs qui auraient consacré tant d'enthousiasme à ce projet.

Keith Skinner, Martin Fido et Paul Begg, qui nous ont conseillés et guidés à travers les arcanes du monde de Jack l'Éventreur.

Paul Feldman, dont l'insatiable appétit de recherche nous a tous contraints à rester constamment vigilants.

Les éditeurs Rick Levine, de New York, et Richard Dawes, de Londres.

Roger Wilkes, qui nous a généreusement prêté sa collection personnelle de notes sur Maybrick.

Naomi Everett, de la bibliothèque de Liverpool, dont la patience s'est révélée précieuse.

Dr Nicholas Eastaugh; Dr David Forshaw, Sue Ironmonger; Anna Koren; Melvyn Fairclough; Martin Howells; Dr A. Morton; Sidney Sabin; Nicholas Campion; John Astrop; Lawrence Warner; Dr Glyn

Volans; Juge Richard Hamilton, de Liverpool; Bill Waddell : Tony Miall; Richard et Mollie Whittington Egan; Paul Dodd, de Battlecrease House; Brian Maybrick; Gerard Brierley; Mme Berkeley Chappelle-Gill; Derek Jarman et John Matthews, de l'île de Wight; Dr W. Taylor, de l'hôpital Fazakerley; Pompes funèbres Seddons, de Southport; David Fletcher Rogers; Walkleys Clogs; Le *Special Hospitals Service*; Andrew Brown, des archives de la *Metropolitan Police*, New Scotland Yard; Colin Inma, du *Financial Times*; Nick Pinto, du *Public Record Office*; R. H. Leighton & Cie, Southport; Colin Wilson; Donald Rumbelow; le personnel des bibliothèques et des archives régionales consultées dans tout le pays.

Nous remercions aussi l'*American Heritage Center* de l'université du Wyoming, qui nous a autorisés à publier des extraits des conversations de Florence Aunspaugh avec Trevor Christie, ainsi que les éditions Harper & Collins, qui nous ont autorisés à publier un extrait de *Hunting the Devil*, de Richard Lourie.

SOURCES PRINCIPALES

Public Record Office, Kew; Public Record Office, Chancery Lane; General Register Office, St. Catherine's House; Principal Registry of the Family Division, Somerset House; Patent Office; Companies House; British Library; Newspaper Library; American State Archives, Washington, D.C.; Bibliothèque Nationale, Paris; Victoria State Library, Australie; H.M. Land Registry; New Scotland Yard : Black Museum; Merseyside Police; Lancashire Constabulary; Ministère de la Défense; Université de Liverpool; Université du Wyoming; Collection Christie; Royal Liverpool University Hospital; Département d'Histopathologie du Fazakerley Hospital; Historic Manuscripts Commission; College of Heralds; Freemasons; Post Office Archives; Postal Museum; Post Mark Society; Shoe Museum; Liverpool Maritime Museum; Whitworth Museum, Manchester; Cotton Association; Chambre de commerce de Liverpool; Cimetière de Coldestone Park; Cimetière de Lewisham; Cimetière de Southwark; Pompes funèbres Seddons; Stylos Parker; Archives du John Lewis Partnership; Boddingtons.

Archives locales de Liverpool, Lambeth, Lewisham, Tower Hamlets, Manchester, Southwark.

Bibliothèques : Tunbridge Wells, Morden, Carshalton, Sutton, Sunderland, Camden, Westminster, Liverpool, Chester, Manchester, Rochdale, Royal College of Surgeons, Royal College of Psychiatrists, Royal Society of Medicine, British Toxicological Safety, Wellcome Research Unit, Science Library, Patent Office.

Bureaux des archives : West Sussex, Lancashire, Chester, Newport, île de Wight.

Bureaux de l'état civil : Liverpool, Caenarfon.

Cet ouvrage a été réalisé par la
SOCIÉTÉ NOUVELLE FIRMIN-DIDOT
Mesnil-sur-l'Estrée
pour le compte des Éditions Lattès
en octobre 1993

Imprimé en France
Dépôt légal : octobre 1993
N° d'édition : 93227 – N° d'impression : 25074